A MATTER OF DISCOURSE

A Matter of Discourse

Community and Communication in Contemporary Philosophies

Edited by
AMÓS NASCIMENTO

Routledge
Taylor & Francis Group
LONDON AND NEW YORK

First published 1998 by Ashgate Publishing

Reissued 2018 by Routledge
2 Park Square, Milton Park, Abingdon, Oxon, OX14 4RN
711 Third Avenue, New York, NY 10017, USA

Routledge is an imprint of the Taylor & Francis Group, an informa business

Publisher's Note
The publisher has gone to great lengths to ensure the quality of this reprint but points out that some imperfections in the original copies may be apparent.

Disclaimer
The publisher has made every effort to trace copyright holders and welcomes correspondence from those they have been unable to contact.

A Library of Congress record exists under LC control number: 97077554

ISBN 13: 978-1-138-60883-2 (hbk)
ISBN 13: 978-1-138-60886-3 (pbk)
ISBN 13: 978-0-429-46468-3 (ebk)

Contents

List of Contributors

Rainer Forst (Goethe-Universität Frankfurt, Germany) has taught in Germany and in the United States and written on various topics in moral and political philosophy, as well as on critical theory. He is co-editor of *Ethos der Moderne. Foucaults Kritik der Aufklärung* and author of *Kontexte der Gerechtigkeit*, where he analyzes the debate between liberalism and communitarianism and proposes a theory of justice beyond this controversy.

Dietmar Köveker (Université Paris, France), has taught in Germany and France, and published on epistemology and discourse theory. In *Grenzverhältnisse: Kant und das 'regulatve Prinzip' in Wissenschaft und Philosophie*, he interprets and criticizes Kant's regulative ideas in light of the contemporary philosophy of science. He has researched and written also on the concept of 'discourse' in postmodern philosophy.

Cristina Lafont (Northwestern University, Evanston, United States), has taught in Spain, Germany and in the United States, and works on theories of truth in the tradition of German and Anglo American pragmatic theories of meaning and reference. She published *La razón como lenguaje*, *Sprache und Welterschließung* and a series of texts on discourse theory.

Eduardo Mendieta (San Francisco University, United States), has published on discourse theory, Latin American philosophy and post-modernism, developing a project on the impact of these ideas in Europe and in the Americas. He is the editor of Karl-Otto Apel's *Selected Essays* (two volumes) and *From Pragmatism to Pragmaticism*, as well as of Enrique Dussel's *The Underside of Modernity*.

Wilson P. Mendonça (Universidade Federal do Rio de Janeiro, Brazil), has taught and lectured in Brazil, the United States and Germany. He has written widely on Frege and Wittgenstein and published a series of articles on Kantian and contemporary moral philosophy for collections and journals such as *European Journal of Philosophy*, *Kant-Studien* and *Dialectica*.

Amós Nascimento (Frankfurt Universität, Germany), has worked and researched at universities in Brazil, the United States and Germany. He has written on rationality, aesthetics and cultural criticism for journals and books in these countries and is co-editor of *Grenzen der Moderne*.

Marianna Papastephanou (University of Cyprus, Cyprus) has taught in Wales and researched in Germany. She has written on ethics, feminism and epistemology after the linguistic turn, and is the editor of *From a Transcendental-Semiotic Point of View*, a collection of Karl-Otto Apel's essays on pragmatics and language.

Max Pensky (State University of New York at Binghamtom, United States), has researched in Germany and France, and published on critical theory and ethics. He is the translator of J. Habermas' *The Past as Future*, and has written for journals and books such as the *Cambridge Companion to Habermas*.

Hans Schelkshorn (Universität Wien, Vienna, Austria) has published and lectured on discourse ethics and Enrique Dussel's liberation ethics in Austria, Germany, Brazil and Mexico. He published *Ethik der Befreiung* and *Diskurs und Befreiung*, and works on the question of an intercultural ethics as the basis for a critical theory in times of globalization.

Allison Weir (Wilfried Laurier University, Kitchewer, Canada) has taught and lectured on feminism and discourse theory in North America and Europe, and written extensively on the question of rationality and subjectivity for journals and collections such as *Feminists read Habermas*. In her book, *Sacrificial Logics: Feminist Theory and the Critique of Identity*, she presents a detailed account of these themes in contemporary theories.

Acknowledgements

I owe an intellectual debt to Karl-Otto Apel and Jürgen Habermas for having the opportunity to study with them at the Frankfurt University and to develop my interest and knowledge of the themes presented in this collection. The contributors of this collection will surely endorse my words. Many of us had the same experience as we met at colloquia, seminars and conferences held in Frankfurt . It goes without saying that I also owe thanks to the authors. They have helped a great deal in the elaboration of this book, not only with their contributions, but especially in the process of discussing the theme, writing the chapters, making suggestions, improving the texts, and correcting the proofs. The essays collected here show that scholars interested in discourse theory continue the work of Habermas and Apel in many directions, but also criticize their insights, develop distinct forms of argumentation, consider other contexts and themes which were left out until now. They bring about something new and important that is now shared with others.

I am also very thankful to many other persons, and I want to make sure that I list all their names. Margaret Griesse and Russell Thomasson have done a wonderful work proof-reading different parts of the whole manuscript, and Margaret spent hours discussing the ideas in this book. Many thanks also to Eduardo Mendieta and Rainer Forst for their help with the translations. Manuel Franzmann and Geniovan Carlin were very helpful in the process of editing the manuscript. I am also grateful to the editorial staff at Ashgate, Anne Keirby, Pauline Beavers, Ann Newell and especially Sarah Markhan and John Irwin for their support and attention.

I am obliged to mention the academic and institutional support I received for this project. Axel Honneth welcomed the idea and gave valuable suggestions to improve the scope of the book, and I express my gratitude for his support. Enrique Dussel and Nancy Fraser were also very receptive to the idea and I am pleased to acknowledge their words of encouragement. Many ideas guiding the conception of this collection were presented and discussed at different conferences, but they were developed especially during a tutorial seminar on the idea of community in Europe and Latin America which I gave with Kirsten Witte at the Department of Philosophy in Frankfurt. Thanks to her, to Matthias Lutz-Bachmann and to the students for the contributions to discussion and the support they offered. Most of the research, contacts and part of the work for this book were done while I was a Researcher sponsored by the Conselho Nacional de Desenvolvimento e Pesquisa, CNPQ (Proc. 202666/91.3).

Finally, I would like to thank Petra Hardt, Claudia Brandes and Beth Mullen for their prompt answers to my questions on matters of copyright and acknowledge the following publishing houses for permission to reprint, translate and quote previously published material:

Preface

The concepts of community, communication and discourse are repeated today in different contexts and related primarily to the criticism of claims to universality, impartiality, general validity or certainty. This criticism is expressed in a plurality of forms: in the critique of liberalism, in the charges against epistemic foundations, in the proposal for cultural relativism, in the affirmation of the death of the subject, in the uncovering of gender and ethnic biases, in the disclosure of negative aspects of globalization. The amount of information and plethora of theories that have arisen in order to interpret this variety of claims is overwhelming, and any attempt at making sense of such a plurality seems to be doomed to fail. We have plural theories about a plurality of facts. How, then, can we make sense of plurality? Despite the pressing need to answer this question, few people are willing to put themselves at risk and consider how different positions deal with the above concepts and issues. There are few who would struggle with the idea of uncovering the underlying connections and similar assumptions in distinct theories and affirm that they have a general common purpose. Notwithstanding, the general common purpose of the essays presented here is to introduce distinct approaches to the issues above and reveal some points that are common to different theoretical positions in philosophy, discussing their implications, and opening the way to further initiatives.

The very title indicates that the concepts of community, communication and discourse will be considered in the *plural*, and therefore we can now concentrate on some preliminary clarifications concerning the *unity* of the book. I want to be clear about the perspective guiding the selection and organization of the essays. All of them develop a direct or indirect consideration of the discourse theory and discourse ethics developed jointly by Jürgen Habermas and Karl-Otto Apel, which is a model of critical theory.

Critique or critical theory is, it might be said for the sake of a definition, the philosophical inquiry and reflection upon human thinking and agency, which requires not only clearly established and publicly available standards that can be accepted generally, but also a commitment to live up to these same standards and to ensure that they are applied consistently by others. Leaving aside the specific questions that may arise in relation to this definition, it is important to see that distinct theoretical positions such as discourse theory, pragmatism, liberalism, communitarianism, liberation ethics, feminism and postmodernism would agree with the characterization of their projects as 'critical'. Despite the differences that exist between the concepts of discourse of Jürgen Habermas and Judith Butler, between the understanding of community by Enrique Dussel and Michael Walzer, or the conception of communication by Iris Young and Karl-Otto Apel, they all represent varieties of the most interesting and sophisticated positions that have contributed to our understanding of critical theory. Therefore, critical theory is understood here in a broad sense that includes these distinct perspectives. But the authors in this collection have discourse theory as point of departure, because it is one of the most relevant attempts to establish reliable grounds for a critical theory.

The program of a discourse theory and discourse ethics developed by Habermas and Apel has a cognitive and deontological approach to critical theory that is inspired by Immanuel Kant and tries to incorporate insights of contemporary philosophical conceptions such as pragmatism, speech-act linguistics, political liberalism, developmental psychology, deontological ethics and others. Drawing on these positions, discourse theory develops a conception of universalizability that stresses the necessary conditions for personal autonomy, interpersonal solidarity, collective responsibility and universal justice. Guiding all these levels is a conception of procedural discourse which establishes that those ideal norms which are affirmed without a pragmatic or performative self-contradiction and accepted by those affected as intersubjectively valid can be taken as universally justified.

The basic objection that has been raised against such a theory, is that it works with ideal or transcendental presuppositions that may have a critical intention, but end up losing sight of the concrete and specific situation or motivation of humans as cognitive, moral, as well as emotionally and aesthetically motivated agents embedded in different contexts. Moreover, discourse theory is affected also by objections raised against those formal approaches upon which it relies. Critics of formalism and rigorism have shown that serious problems arise when one assumes an ahistorical and contextless perspective; communitarian critics of liberalism point out the problem of impartiality as a form of indifference; postmodernists affirm that claims to universality in discourse may lead to a totalitarian assimilation of differences; feminists affirm that an abstract developmental approach does not allow for the consideration of persons as concrete subjects with specific needs and traits; new approaches to ethics insist on the need of a reflection about the material conditions to a formal philosophical discourse. These challenges have provided enough material for a set of debates, in which Habermas and Apel try to specify their position. In general, discourse theory insists on a formal universality with the argument that precisely this universality is the condition that allows for differences, but the explicit recognition of pluralism and multiculturalism have become so imperative today that discourse theory is now forced to clarify its formal and universal position in relation to a variety of topics.

Before we proceed, it is important to clarify that there are also differences between Apel and Habermas. In his transcendental-pragmatic version of discourse theory, Apel insists on the uncircumventionability [*Unhintergehbarkeit*] of the transcendental presuppositions of argumentation. For Apel, these presuppositions provide the basis for both a transcendental-semiotic theory based on Peirce and a macro-*ethics of co-responsibility* for collective actions at a global level. Habermas defends a theoretical approach based on a formal-pragmatics which is more concerned with discursive procedures to be applied at the social level. In his practical philosophy, he differentiates between *ethical* questions related to personal and collective perspectives of the good life, *pragmatic* questions concerning the means for the realization of social, political or economic goals, and *moral* questions which address issues of justice, human rights and global peace in a universal perspective. Even with this differentiation, both versions of discourse ethics maintain universality as their core and at the same time attempt at being more sensitive to pluralism and contextual differences. It remains to be seen if these internal differentiations are tenable and, if they are, how these distinct aspects can be made compatible within a consistent theory.

In this horizon we can introduce the essays collected here. All the essays have a broad view of discourse theory as point of departure, and consider if the universal and transcendental basis of this theory can be maintained in view of many challenges. A new generation of scholars from Europe and the Americas present, analyze and criticize discourse theory in its relation to pragmatism, communitarianism and postmodernism, to feminism and liberation ethics. By going in and out of these different theoretical projects and contexts, they emphasize the issue of pluralism and construct a web that indicates new directions for critical theory. This process is demarcated by five general parts with specific thematic divisions that present distinct perspectives on a similar topic.

The first part, 'Communities, contexts and challenges to discourse theory' introduces the general theme in a more social-political tone and tries to outline a framework that orients the discussion and allows for the recognition of different approaches and contexts. In his introductory essay, 'The fact of pluralism and the multicultural quest for community', Amós Nascimento presents the appeal to 'community' and emphasis upon communication in relation to distinct cultural backgrounds, and shows how this appeal corresponds to different forms of critique to liberalism. Although liberalism is connected to democracy and the appeal to a 'community' has been connected to a conservative heritage, the positions discussed in the essay are both opposed to liberalism and representative of a critical theory. Nevertheless, these theoretical positions are still prey to some ambiguous assumptions which can be regressive instead of critical. Therefore, a wider understanding of discourse and communication must come as a correction to an ambiguous view of 'community'. In 'Which person? Whose community?' Rainer Forst establishes a bridge between the more formal approach to ethics and the necessary attention to a variety of contexts. In a critical review of the critique of John Rawls' liberalism by communitarian authors such as Michael Sandel, Charles Taylor and Michael Walzer, Forst shows that the debate implicitly refers to a variety of contexts. On this basis he argues for the need of a differentiation of the idea of person in relation to the contexts of ethics, law, politics and morality, and makes a plea for a more general framework that accounts for such variety. In this way, issues concerning individuality and the distinct forms of belonging to a community can be addressed with appropriate concepts on the levels of ethical, legal, political and moral theories.

The second part, 'Plurality and cognitivism in light of Anglo American pragmatism' deals with the tension between pluralism and universalism in Habermas' discourse ethics, with specific attention to the problem of contextualism in a pragmatic perspective. Cristina Lafont and Wilson Mendonça address this topic concentrating on the issue of cognitivism. In 'Pluralism and universalism in discourse ethics', Lafont is concerned with the problem of affirming the possibility of one right answer in moral matters, while holding to the idea of a plurality of the good. Based on the parallel between questions about truth and questions about moral rightness, and in dialogue with Hilary Putnam's contribution to the debate on realism and anti-realism, and its implications in ethics, she argues that once one distinguishes between a plurality of 'interpretations' and the necessary reference to the 'same' needs and interests at issue, we can hold on to plurality in ethics without giving up the universalist core of discourse ethics. In 'Are moral concerns irreducible to ethical concerns?' Wilson Mendonça takes a different path, arguing that the strict separation between the local and somewhat culturally biased values of a particular ethics and the universal norm based on a cognitive approach that presumably escapes this bias is untenable on rational grounds. He develops this point as he turns to the semantic and cognitive approach in moral philosophy, and counterpoints Habermas' position with John Mackie and John Dewey. Out of this pragmatic base, Mendonça underscores the naturalistic implications in morals and concludes that the universalist core of discourse ethics itself is contextually and historically bound.

The third part, 'The postmodern discourse on the Other in the French context', establishes a bridge to a different setting, presenting Jean-François Lyotard's postmodern critique of discourse and Emmanuel Levinas' ethics of alterity. Having Kant as his point of departure, Dietmar Köveker's essay, 'Lyotard's conception of conflicting claims to validity', considers the postmodern understanding of discourse as conflict. While discourse theory stresses the argumentative aspect and the search for consensus as conditions for the validity of claims, the postmodern perspective insists much more on dissension as something more basic to any argument. According to Lyotard, it is the emphasis upon conflicts or 'differends' that allows us to criticize universalist pretensions and affirm the irreducibility of the other. By means of a detailed analysis and comparison of Lyotard's 'differend' with the idea of a 'conflict of reason with itself' in Kant's transcendental dialectics, Köveker considers the tension between validity and infinity that is inherent to a discursive approach and reveals the Kantian assumptions lying behind the logic of Lyotard's conception of conflict in discourse. In 'The limits of solidarity', Max Pensky amplifies the scope presented thus far as he deals with the problem of the 'other' in discourse. He starts by affirming that although solidarity has had a prominent place in moral theories, it is still obscure, especially because a basic question concerning spontaneity, symmetry and responsibility in a situation of communication or in the construction of community is not always considered. Pensky discusses some aspects of discourse ethics and arrives to the position defended by Levinas, namely that ethics presupposes the putting of our spontaneity into question in the presence of the other person we face. Accordingly, he affirms that the 'Other' presents an alternative position within discourse which questions the priority given to oneself. Despite some problematic aspects in Levinas' ontological views, Pensky concludes, this approach helps us at least to acknowledge the limits of traditional conceptions of solidarity.

The fourth part, 'The concrete other as subject in feminist perspective', goes from a generalized view of the 'Other' to a 'concrete other' and 'situated self', and articulates different ways of talking about the self as other in a feminist perspective. Going deep into the question concerning subjectivity, Allison Weir and Marianna Papastephanou take the path opened up by Kristeva and the feminist critique of discourse theory by authors such as Nancy Fraser, Iris Young and Judith Butler. In 'Toward a model of self-identity', Weir concentrates on Habermas' views and compares them with Kristeva in order to show the convergence in both approaches and propose a dialogue between discourse theory and the feminist theory developed out of Kristeva's psychoanalytical approach. After criticizing relational and postmodern approaches in feminism and reviewing Habermas' interpretation of the self in George Mead, she points out that Kristeva's discussion of the child's identity development is both compatible and complementary with the intersubjective model proposed by Habermas. She concludes that this approach is necessary for a discourse theory that recognizes the feminist perspective as well as for a feminist position that reflects on the conditions for social critique. In 'Subjectivity in process', Papastephanou agrees with Weir about the compatibility between Kristeva's idea of subjectivity and discourse theory, but at the same time she presents some questions concerning deficits in Kristeva's phenomenological and psychoanalytic approach to subjectivity and rationality. Working with a hermeneutic framework, Papastephanou discusses both the critique of the subjectivistic philosophy by Habermas and Apel, including the recent interpretation of Kristeva's work by feminist philosophers. She concludes that although Kristeva is clear in rejecting irrationality and in criticizing subjectivism, she still maintains a dualist view of rationality that clashes with the conception of intersubjectivity based on communicative reason.

The fifth part, 'Liberation, globalization and the Latin American context', amplifies the scope without losing sight of the issues discussed in the other parts. The Latin American perspective of liberation ethics is introduced, bringing more concrete global issues into the discussion. Taking up the debate between Karl-Otto Apel and Enrique Dussel in 'Liberation and discourse', Hans Schelkshorn reveals the background that lies behind many of the assumptions of these two positions and their implications. By showing how two proposals for a universal ethics touch the ground of specific contexts, he argues for a necessary complementarity between discourse ethics and liberation ethics when global questions are at issue. He shows which aspects are irreducible to another in each theory, which points become problematic in light of their mutual criticism, what is specific to their cultural situation and has more limited application, and, finally, what are the convergent and complementary aspects which become relevant for a global ethics. In his conclusion Schelkshorn shows that while discourse ethics aims at a strong deontological justification, liberation ethics insists on the need of a material core for the sake of the realization of such a project. In 'Modernity, postmodernity and challenges to discourse ethics' Eduardo Mendieta sets the debate between Karl-Otto Apel and Enrique Dussel in the wider framework of the contemporary critique of modernity, adding Lyotard's views on justice to this context. He places Apel's ethics in a field of tension, showing how he addresses the challenges to discourse ethics put forward by Lyotard and Dussel. After presenting, comparing and contrasting them, Mendieta rejects the many paradoxes in Lyotard's approach and the externalist ontology implicit by Dussel, but concludes that discourse ethics has to take the criticisms of these positions seriously, so that a formal deontological ethics be able to respond to the effects of globalization.

Each of these parts represents a block centered around a specific topic that sheds light over the general theme. In each block there is also an internal dialogue, for each author addresses the specific topic and the general theme from a particular perspective, reacting to or complementing what the other says. But the debate is not closed in itself. It is important to note the progression and the cross-references of the discussion. It starts with a social political tone, with distinct understandings of community. There is a move to a formal epistemic consideration of the general theme, but then the distinction between ethics and morality is reassessed. Moreover, the discussion advances from epistemology to ontology, gaining even more abstraction in the talk about the 'other', but at the same time this 'other' becomes concrete, for now issues of subjectivity and intersubjectivity in relation to the 'other gender' arise, before we arrive at issues of collective identity and global ethics. Now the 'other' is a general class of poor and oppressed, understood in a broader material sense of political economy. We start with the fact of pluralism, we learn about contextuality, heterogeneity and differences, and we finally come to the undeniable fact of globalization. There is, therefore, a constant tension. Globalization presents us with problems that call for a universal approach, but it is also important to keep an eye on the autonomy of the person and the question of diversity and plurality, avoiding that one perspective disappears or be subsumed into the other. Since we can neither project subjectivity in order to account for universality nor deduce personality from universal categories, the possible alternative seems to be elsewhere, perhaps in a balance or cooperation among distinct approaches.

The process shown in this collection indicates the necessity of considering discourse in reference to specific agents embedded in a context, but the essays collected here indicate also the possibility of going beyond one's own context by means of communication. That is why I spoke of a web. The conjunction of these texts reveals a connection between critical philosophical programs in Europe, the Anglo American context and Latin America; it shows some basic theoretical and practical problems in contemporary theories; and points to new fields that are already being established and need to be considered in terms of a critical theory. Moreover, this collection introduces the ongoing discussion by a group of scholars in interaction, who are able to come in and out of the different contexts and theories, presenting a first-hand and in-depth analysis of the issues at stake. In the course of the very construction of such a web, the basic concepts of discourse, community and communication cannot be forgotten as instruments which make us aware of this interaction. It is in this light that we can affirm that these issues become a matter of discourse.

Amós Nascimento

Communities, contexts and challenges to discourse theory

1 The fact of pluralism and the multicultural quest for community

Amós Nascimento

My primary aim and first challenge in this essay is to outline a general frame that enables us to see the interaction and tension among the several positions that will be discussed by different authors in this book. But I also want to take this opportunity to advance some theses. It is obvious that projects such as discourse theory in Germany, communitarianism in the United States, liberation ethics in Latin American countries such as Argentina and Brazil, postmodern poststructuralism in France and feminism in these different contexts are culturally and theoretically distinct, and there is no need to stress the differences now. Therefore, I will take a different path and deal with a second challenge, namely to show that the above positions share some basic critical convictions which need to be brought to the surface. I want to underline that they refer to the idea of community and emphasize different forms of discourse as means to a critique of liberalism. Here the third challenge is to show this without reductionism, generalization or appeal to an externalist perspective. Thus we have to recognize pluralism as we deal with this triple task, which I want to discuss in light of three general theses:

1 There is a traditional and even conservative sense of 'community' which is taken up by progressive positions that develop a critique of different forms of liberalism;

2 This critical 'turn to community' is not limited to one particularistic setting, but arises simultaneously in distinct contexts and is expressed through different forms of discourse, but questions remain concerning the reach, limits, and interaction between these positions;

3 The common concern with community and communication reveals a larger critical background shared by these positions, but this cannot be seen as universal, for it still mirrors a specific cultural bias.

These three points could lead us to the conclusion that contextualism is unavoidable and the affirmation of particularities without assuming a universalist point of view is the only antidote that remains for a critical position that questions the projection of biases unto others. Nevertheless, in my conclusion I will suggest that a strict particularistic assumption is untenable, and alternatives are necessary in order to avoid the problematic consequences of particularism. I will first develop the three general theses in detail, before I come to this point.

Back to community? Conservative and metaphysical assumptions of the traditional critique of liberalism

Community is an old and ambiguous term that has distinct applications, from the Greek notion of *koinonía*, through the idea of *communis* in the Latin tradition, up to the concepts of *communauté* and *Gemeinschaft* in the context of the European Enlightenment. But it has regained popularity, especially in the United States, first with pragmatism at the beginning of the twentieth century, and then again with the recent communitarian critique of liberalism. For these reasons community is one of the most repeated concepts today in philosophical programs, political speeches and social initiatives. The term is used above all to indicate particular collective identities within the now fragmentary image of the nation-state. Much has been gained with these turns to community, especially regarding our sensibility to cultural and contextual differences, but we need to remember that community is old and ambiguous concept with conservative connotations.

Edmund Burke, the patron-saint of conservatism, was one of the first to attack liberalism and democracy. In his critique of the Enlightenment, he appealed precisely to the ideas of community, plurality and even to anti-colonialism, vehemently condemning the control exercised by the colonial forces over the Americas, criticizing the use of violence in the French Revolution, and denouncing the 'arbitrary power' of the British Empire in East India (see Nisbet 1976). A passage from his *Reflections on the Revolution in France* suffices to show his point, as he affirms that governments are 'not morally at liberty at their pleasure, and on their speculations of a contingent improvement, wholly to separate and tear asunder the bands of their subordinate community, and dissolve it into an unsocial, uncivil, unconnected chaos of elementary principles' (quoted in Nisbet 1976:413). This is nothing but a claim for the priority of contingent values over abstract rights, which brings us then to the contemporary critique of liberalism. In the United States, communitarians opposed liberal individualism and questioned precisely the priority of abstract universal rights over goods, i.e. the primacy of impartial norms instead of shared forms of solidarity embedded in a specific culture (cf. Rasmussen 1988).

The link between community and conservatism explains why John Rawls reacts to communitarianism and defends a *political liberalism* while rejecting 'metaphysics' (1985, 1993:xix-xx). He insists that a 'well-ordered democratic society is neither a community nor, more generally, an association', since in his view the notion of community applies either to a church or medieval society, which was 'more or less united in affirming the catholic faith' and was guaranteed by the Inquisition (Rawls 1993:36-43, 146). Because, he continues, rights are not dispensations from god or particular clan conventions, the idea of community in these terms must be given up. Rawls wants to avoid two issues. If the *consensus* of Catholic universalism was despotic, the sectarian relativism after the Protestant Reformation with clashing interpretations that led to civil wars and intolerance was no less problematic (1993:xxif.). Nevertheless, he acknowledges the 'fact of pluralism' and presents a *political* conception of justice that could be accepted by different religious, cultural and philosophical views and guarantee diversity – provided that these views are 'reasonable'. His hope is that a political view of 'justice as fairness' could lead to the alternative of an *overlapping consensus* (1993:36-37).

Many points can be drawn from these ideas which have motivated a great number of detailed studies (Sandel 1982; Kymlicka 1989; Moon 1993; Forst 1994), but two basic concerns mentioned by Rawls take us to the heart of the question I want to emphasize: the metaphysical appeal to religion to bring society together and the cultural or anthropological particularism which is instrumentalized by political conservatism remain in modern societies. It is not surprising, therefore, that this issue has become the subject of many recent texts by Rawls (Rawls 1993, 1995a, 1995b) and his commentators (cf. Macedo 1995; Quinn 1995). The uneasiness with this theme comes to the surface also in Rawls' recent debate with Habermas (Rawls 1995b:133, 134, 136, 137; Habermas 1995, 1996:95f.).

Concerning the religious interference on political matters, I would like to establish some differentiations in relation to these controversial issues. Let me give some examples, which will also serve as a presentation of the four contexts which I will be dealing with later. To a certain extent, the 'turn to community' motivated by religious-metaphysical worldviews shows a frustration regarding the fulfillment of old dreams such as 'the American way of life', the idea of a 'Brazilian Miracle', the promises of 'French Socialism' and the 'German Reconstruction'. These ideas express an optimism of some years ago that is now being questioned on ecological, social and economic grounds. This frustration and consequent turn to conventional values can be indeed related to intolerant forms of religion: to a fundamentalist longing for a common Christian tradition in the United States, which has been at the center of cultural and political debates since the election of Jimmy Carter and cynically supported by some intellectuals; to populist views that express a nostalgia for conservatism and the military dictatorship in Brazil and constitute a large fraction in the Parliament; to the xenophobia of the Front Nationale that gains wider acceptation in France; to belligerent movements in Germany proposing a turn back to the times of the national socialist dictatorship and using Luther's slogans – '*von den Juden und ihre Lügen*' – to justify anti-semitism.

The avoidance of religion *in general* would appear, therefore, as the best strategy for a critical position, thus confirming the separation of church and state, secularism, and the Enlightenment. Nevertheless, there are also critical views which run parallel to the above movements and express a religious longing for community as well, but with an emphasis on progressive political values such as democracy and social justice: in the United States, liberal groups and African American churches have been associated since the beginning of the twentieth century in the civil rights movement; in Brazil and in other Latin American countries, the base communities follow liberation theology and raise their claim for social transformation in the public sphere, having an impact on the whole continent; in France, the association between existentialism, marxism and catholicism led to the Christian socialist movement *Communauté*; a church movement against political authoritarianism in East Germany, *Demokratie jetzt*, served as prelude to the unification of east and west, and its leaders are now leading politicians in the German Parliament. These examples show that secularism alone does not seem to be a sufficient criterion for a critical philosophy or political theory, so we need a better account of the issues depicted above.

This picture shows that everything is possible in a turn to community: from a metaphysical claim to justify critical politics to a reactionary critique of liberal individualism and democracy. Going back to the controversy around liberalism, my simple claim is that the problem is not with religious values backing communitarian attitudes, but rather that these values and attitudes can be related to *political conservatism* or to *political liberalism*. Therefore, the problem is not necessarily with religion as a matter of individual choice or collective belief, but with the underlying political assumptions related to it. I do not want to dwell so much on this point, but see how these issues are at play in the philosophical quest for community.

Now we can go back to Rawls' and to our point of departure. A critique of liberalism that applies the concept of community without clarifying it would be more akin to the metaphysical grounding of a regressive theocracy in the Middle Ages, thus coming closer to Burke's conservatism and to the *ancien régime*, and trivializing the separation between church and state. Nevertheless, I want to show that there are critical positions that appeal to the concept of community in their critique of liberalism, but they are to be distinguished from both religious metaphysics and political conservatism. This thesis has to stand out: these critical positions perform an *overlapping critique of liberalism* by turning to the concept of community. These positions are at work in the same contexts we saw above. In the context of the United States, communitarians argue that collectivity is forgotten in the bureaucratic state and in liberal individualism. In Brazil and Latin America a strong critique of capitalism is articulated in different versions of liberation ethics – in education, theology, economy and philosophy. In France, the anthropological critique of foundational myths and the analysis of cultural and artistic movements leads to an aesthetic ideal for politics beyond the *bourgeoisie*. In Germany the issue is raised by discourse theory, for which the critique of society and of the anti-democratic experiences in the twentieth century demand the establishment of norms for rational argumentation among members of a community of communication. In each of these contexts there is also a constant feminist critique that points out the limits of liberalism and its critics.

The simple topography developed above confirms at least that the turn to 'community' and the critique of liberalism represent a *general* phenomenon. It is a case of *overlapping consensus* that shows a critical impetus and cross-references among different positions. The attempt at describing these various forms of discourses at once is risky and the risk in comparing them is even greater, but this can also be rewarding. Interesting questions arise: can one community be defined by excluding others? Who are these others? Is there a transcendental standpoint in relation to a community capable of including all? In the end the most important question is: where are the limits of communities and who establishes such limits? In what follows, I want prepare the ground for a possible answer to these questions, as I show the 'turn to community' in these different theoretical proposals.

Critical perspectives on community

Having shown the wide context and the ambiguity of the concept of community, we now turn to the critical discourses already mentioned, considering them from within and recognizing their *locus*. The point of emphasis now is: these views on community represent different and complementary critiques of forms of liberalism that bump against religious issues and stress distinct aspects of discourse and communication.

Community and life: liberation ethics in Brazil and Latin America

If we take the practical role and the theoretical mediation of liberation ethics in its many versions in Latin America, we can observe a clear religious background and a concrete political point of departure. Out of this there is not only a program that follows Marx's critique of *economic liberalism* – or, more precisely, *neoliberalism* – and simultaneously dismantles his critique of religion, but also a political reading of religion as means to this end – i.e. a reinterpretation of the history of religions as a history of the struggles of the poor, whereas the biblical *exodus* becomes a paradigm that can be applied to Mexicans crossing over the border to the United States or to asylum seekers in Europe. I will first stress the sociological and political influence of this discourse on civil society and then relate it to philosophical issues.

The 'base church communities' [CEBs, *Comunidades eclesiais de base*] are a Latin American phenomenon whose social relevance is evident not only in the term 'base', that refers to a social pyramid in which the majority at the bottom are poor who are opposed to and oppressed by the rich (C. Boff, 1978; L. Boff, 1981), but also in the name 'community' [*comunidade*] (Guimaraes, 1978:75-98). It should not be forgotten that it is connected to the word 'church', which points to an institutional dimension of religion (CELAM 1969; Guimaraes 1978:51-50), that is also a *liaison dangereuse*.

One element in the practices of these communities, however, is not always acknowledged. What their members call *conscientização* and 'communication of consciousness' – following Paulo Freire's 'pedagogy of liberation' (1974, who follows Karl Jaspers' views on communication) –, is an effective method of going from individual to individual and constituting a group that works together on weekends on a common grassroots project [*mutirão*], developing an analysis of the problem of *dependência* (cf. Cardoso & Falleto 1974; Hinkelammert 1970) by means of an argumentation process that can reach the sophistication of the finest philosophical analysis. This emphasis upon 'interpersonal communication' led to an intellectual guerrilla that had the sympathies of liberals and activists worldwide and almost elected the socialist candidate of the Worker's Party in Brazil. For this reason, one of the criticisms raised against these communities was that they were not religious at all, but political groups edged in the ecclesiastic structure. This critique is exaggerated, since with the Latin American Conference of Catholic Bishops (CELAM) in Medellín there was an official recognition of the CEBs: 'a local or ambiental community, which corresponds to the reality of an homogeneous group, which should have such a dimension that would enable the personal and fraternal contact among its members' (CELAM 1969: § 243). This definition is not free of problems: it mirrors a solipsistic idea of a 'communication of consciousness', is limited to a brotherhood, and has a problematic view of homogenization.

A different approach is reflected in the concept of 'community of life' in a philosophical version of liberation ethics which has been advanced mainly by Enrique Dussel in Argentina and Mexico, and has had an impact in Latin America at large. Together with a theological, moral and political 'option for the poor', liberation ethics raises a call for 'life in face of death' in the southern hemisphere, and Dussel is able to bring these claims together in a philosophical program (see Dussel 1994). His works dealt first with a hermeneutic project that goes from Las Casas' defense of the 'Indios' in the sixteenth century to the present struggle of the base communities (1993a), showing Latin America as the 'underside of modernity' (Dussel 1996). By analyzing this history in light of Emmanuel Levinas' ontology and Marx's critique of *economic liberalism* (in the ideas of life in a 'community of producers' [*Produzentengemeinschaft*] and human life's value as living surplus labor [*lebendige Mehrarbeit*]) Dussel rescues the concept of a 'community of life' that points to the 'realm of freedom' (1988; see also Kymlicka 1989). Note how the theological idea of 'life' now has an economic and moral sense! Freedom here is not the neoliberal *laissez faire* but 'liberation' from economic oppression and from dependence based on a 'developmentalist fallacy' (1993b; 1996:56f).

Important now is to observe this concept of 'community of life' as the keystone of an ethics that radicalizes Levinas' ontological emphasis upon 'interpersonal communication', interaction, 'proximity' and the 'encounter with the totally other' (1995), thus being also compatible with the practice of the base communities. It is also important to note that this view is very far from a feminist perspective of the 'other' – as Ofelia Schulte has noted. Dussel takes the ontological category of 'totality' to show that this applies not only to persons but also to social and economic systems. A given society is a system in itself that can be criticized analogically, i.e. by opposing what is to what is not. Since capitalism is a globalized totality, there is a need for a universal ethics that shows the 'other' of capitalism, the poor. This is expressed in philosophical, political, economic and theological terms as a 'communitarian ethics' [*ética comunitaria*] (1986), thus representing a common point with communitarianism, discourse ethics and neopragmatism (see Dussel 1993b; 1995; 1996: 19f., 129f.).

This position deserves a more detailed account, but within the limits of this essay, I just want to note that although it is important to demystify the economic categories underlying economic liberalism – such as that of an 'invisible hand' that abstracts from agents and is used to justify capitalist market economy –, the point of arrival here is not necessarily the same community at the point of departure. What has happened to the *base* community? It seems to be now lost in the global machinery. This does not invalidate Dussel's point in favor of the poor, but shows the difficulty in working out the hermeneutics of a given community and claiming universal validity through ontological categories, without loosing the ground. The community with which we started in Brazil was concerned with specific contextual problems and generalized its principles by communicating it from case to case, recognizing differences and, thus, privileging a dialogue that is constructed without abstracting from the situation. Dussel's critique of eurocentrism and exploitation of a community of producers by a community of consumers emphasizes totality and proximity to arrive at a 'generalized other' that gains the status of universal. Although he is right in claiming that a universal ethics is necessary to cope with problems of economic globalization, the question that remains is what kind of mediation allows us to go from the local to the global without abstracting from persons and cultures. This is a basic question of the communitarian debate.

Cultural community and the critique of liberalism in the United States

In the Anglo American context, communitarians affirm that the recognition of diversity of persons and communities is necessary as a basis to affirm the identity, language, culture and moral of individuals. This demand is made by Robert Bellah, Michael Walzer and Alasdair MacIntyre, and has gained wider reception in the public sphere and in social policy, representing what I want to call the critique of *constitutional liberalism*.

Robert Bellah is known for his sociology of civil religion and his plea for communitarianism (1975, 1980, 1985, 1987). Following Durkheim, he observed how ontological individualism eroded morality, and as alternative he proposed a social realism with emphasis on values 'common to the biblical and republic nations'. He stresses this religious element in the civil rights movement (1980), and although he follows Rousseau's notion that 'civil religion' is a guarantee for civil society, he is less cautious than Rousseau, who was conscious of the risk of dogmatism and intolerance in civil religion. Later Bellah partially recognized this problem – for even among Christians there are conflicts (1987:17f.) –, but in the end he still holds that the religious values of Western nations would be sufficient to bind society together (1985). If we turn to our previous considerations on religion, it becomes obvious that this Dukheimian conception of a religious basis to morality is not related to a clear political condition, thus remaining ambiguous and falling prey to misinterpretation. Bellah has given us a description of the situation, but did not provide enough tools to cope with it.

A similar appeal to community was expressed by Walzer as he observed the need for communal solidarity, but he went a step further, as he demanded attention to different 'shared meanings'. At the social level he saw high indexes of social disintegration and a clash between values, gods and goods of different communities, and denounced the mistake in reducing them all to a single standard (1983:10). Relating this to the example of Medicaid, he showed the failure of liberal distributive justice and advocated that the members of different communities (political, liberal etc.) should decide about their own good (1983:89). Religion and communication are also at play here, as it was also in Walzer's previous works (e.g. 1966, 1975). In the chapter 'Divine Grace' of *Spheres of Justice* (1983:243ff.) he criticized the Protestant emphasis on the individual's affair with god because such an individual grace does not play any role in communion or communication with others. Now, it is important to see how Walzer is able to work with the internal categories of a religious community to make his point. For instance, he came closer to liberation ethics (see Walzer 1985, referring to Croatto and Gutiérez), especially its interpretation of the *exodus* and of the role of prophetic leaders in the liberation of the Hebrews from captivity in Egypt.

From these premises Walzer deducts that the prophet is the one who reminds the community of its moral sources and criticizes those who break the covenant and forget the poor. But now the question is: who is the prophet and how do we distinguish a well intentioned charismatic person from a charismatic political leader that instrumentalizes this power. We need principles to judge, but Walzer does not provide them, since he affirms that philosophy has no primacy over democratic values 'connected' to a given context. Even when he later defends a 'reiterative universalism' akin to a marxist view of social criticism (1987:40), he goes all too fast to an affirmation of universalism out of a contextual basis, thus projecting particularities as universal. In any case, the important point to rescue is the emphasis upon a 'community of interpretation' in its internal structure, expressed in 'civil society'. In a more political reading, this community is the stage where there are different claims to justice on the basis of specific communal 'shared values' that shall be respected in their particularities (1983:314; 1991). What remains open and unclear is the basis for the mediation between the particular and universal understanding of community.

A more sophisticated and controversial position is surely that of MacIntyre, who has been labeled a conservative due to his turn to Thomism and his emphasis on specific liturgical traditions. Needless to say, here we find religious issues again. In fact, MacIntyre started his career with a concern with morality, marxism and theology (1966, 1968) and with an interest on the question concerning secularism (1967). He began by criticizing Engels for his view that secularization would prevail in England, and then asked which authority could challenge the power of the Church in providing morality for a community (1967:21, 51). Echoes of this same idea are present in two of his most provocative books, considered a manifesto of communitarianism. In *After Virtue* (1981) he questioned the very concept of morals to defend the heterogeneity of morals and claim that morality 'presupposes a sociology' (1981:22) that relates values to concrete communitarian contexts which are forgotten in modern liberal democracies (1981:23ff.). He points out, moreover, that in both the more individualistic view of Rawls' liberalism (1981:232f.) and in the universal collectivism of marxism there are no rational grounds for the universal foundation of morality. To avoid both extremes, he suggests an Aristotelian middle term, namely the particular collectivity – i.e. a particular generality (1981:175f.).

In *Whose Justice? Which Rationality?* (1988) MacIntyre reaffirmed that a particular community is determined by a cultural tradition that provides identity for its members, and connected this issue more clearly with the 'epistemological crisis' of modernity. Rationality and justice are thus contingent to a specific tradition, they are not universal, and therefore the project of Enlightenment is doomed to fail (see also 1981:53). Following this position he identified himself within three traditions (Aristotelianism, the christian theology of Augustine and Thomas Aquinas, and the Scottish Enlightenment – to which we must add, according to some authors, a Celtic humor) and argued for the transformation of liberalism into just another tradition that should give up its universal pretensions. This led to the accusation of a self-refuting relativism, but to contradict this he envisioned the possibility of learning from others by means of communication. Before he summed up the narratives to transform liberalism (having Rawls as his main target) he affirmed the impossibility of talking about justice without taking the linguistic community into account (1988:369, 370ff.). Nevertheless, although MacIntyre refers to the process of intercultural learning by means of communication among different traditions, he does not explore, for example, that the variety of meanings can be a result of immigration or that differences can be assessed by means of communication.

The feminist critique of the ambiguous idea of community in communitarianism touches precisely this point. Iris Young questions the ideal of community in neoconservatism, romantic feminism and communitarianism, and proposes the normative ideal of 'city life' as a public stage for social and political action and exchange (1990:227). She also requires that we account for group difference and heterogeneity in order to avoid an 'assimilationist ideal', insisting on the role of rhetoric in communication (1990:118f., 182). This alternative to communitarianism transforms the classic idea of *polis*, criticizes the utopia of isolated communities, and brings a strong argument for multiculturalism, pointing to groups and places that have been forgotten by dominant discourses. However, the idea of a 'city life' alone makes it difficult to account for the action of groups such ecological, tribal and peripheral movements whose specificity lies on their situatedness beyond the urban context. Moreover, we can also recognize that communitarians have critical intentions that are compatible with the feminist claim for attention to particularities. But here we still do not know how to circumscribe these different issues.

With the above remarks we can move to some conclusive points. In general, we have seen that communitarians would try to answer at liberation ethics by insisting on the local, but sooner or later they bump against the global and tackle metaphysics. This, however, does not mean that we have to give up particularities. Communitarians raise a cultural criticism against liberalism and are closer to critical positions, as they reject the idea of culture as commodity that could be chosen and changed as one changes clothes. However, as the feminist critique shows, communitarians pay less attention to differences internal to a community and can be diagnosed as suffering from a nostalgic view of the good old days, when groups could be seen as isolated and immune to external influences. For instance, they have the context of the United States as point of departure and reject the idea of universalism, but they raise their claims to a wider public in different contexts, although they do not seem to admit it. One could still say that this is an argument for 'generality', not 'universality', but this does not answer the basic question: how do you go beyond the limits of your community?

Other points could be brought up – for instance, concerning the autonomy of the individual within a community –, but I want to note that with the projection of bias beyond their contingencies and without reflecting upon it, communitarians could be easily accused of ethnocentrism, thus contradicting the claim for cultural pluralism. The idea of a 'cultural preservation and identity' is indeed important, but we still need a norm that would avoid something like forgiving our trespasses and avoiding those who trespass against us. As the feminist critique shows, it is possible and necessary to develop an account of the 'other' as persons within and beyond one's own community. This leads us then to postmodern poststructuralism.

Aesthetic community: the postmodern critique of cultural liberalism

The label postmodern poststructuralism is applied to a whole generation of French thinkers such as Michel Foucault, Jacques Derrida, Jean-François Lyotard, Julia Kristeva and others who inherit and criticize Saussure's linguistic structuralism, Heidegger's phenomenological hermeneutics, Lacan's psychoanalysis and the critique of capitalist society and culture by Marx and Nietzsche. In these cases, emphasis is give to the 'other' as an element of resistance and pleasure, which leads to an aesthetics that criticizes *cultural liberalism*, i.e. a bourgeois culture of consumption.

Bataille could be a first example of an aesthetic turn to community, since he wanted to create a new surrealist and 'acephalic' community around the Collége de sociologie in Paris and proposed a 'negative community' as the community of those who do not have a community (Jay 1993:228). Other references are Phillipe Lacoue-Labarthe and Jean-Luc Nancy (1978). They develop a critique of the conservative and mythological appeal to community in German romanticism and national socialism (Nancy & Lacoue-Labarthe 1980:58-65). Nancy's conceptions have become the prototype of a 'French communitarianism', especially after his book on the 'inoperative community', *La communauté désoeuvrée* (1986; cf. Ingram 1995:151-175; Vogl 1994:19f.) and his turn to Kant's idea of aesthetic judgment (Nancy 1991:48; cf. Ingram 1995:166). This points to an aesthetic dimension that needs to be surveyed in different authors, but the emphasis here will be upon Lyotard, who explicitly relates community, politics and aesthetics.

Already in his first book, *La phénoménologie* (1954), Lyotard appeals to community in order to criticize the solipsism of Descartes and Husserl. He notes that even Husserl's concept of 'intersubjectivity' is contradictory, for it affirms an 'intersubjectivity for me', so he proposes a 'community of persons' [*communauté de personnes*] (1954:32-34), which is later radicalized, in political and ethical terms. Politically, he applies the idea of community to criticize French imperialism and colonialism in Algeria, going from the anthropological view of *commune* to expressions such as *communauté tribale*, *communauté religieuse*, *communauté effectivement algérienne* and arriving at a *communauté européenne* (1989:181) that is later relativized in terms of *communautés de langue et de culture* (1989:42, 56, 143f., 215f., 247). It is important to note that already here he matches 'cultural liberalism', bourgeoisie and consumption (1989:55, 58f., 89, 107, 156), thus establishing the connection between economy, culture and aesthetics.

In view of this background, it is not surprising that after developing his philosophical views on art and psychoanalysis Lyotard comes back to his critique of liberalism in light of a 'libidinal aesthetics' that has ethical, economic and political connotations. So, for instance, in *L'économie libidinale* (1974) the emphasis lies upon the body [*corps*] in its generatives – corporation, incarnation, etc. – as the medium for *symbolic exchange*, which is explained by Lyotard in his interpretation of Marx' analysis of the communitarian character of pre-capitalistic societies (Lyotard 1974:155-165). In this way Lyotard plays with the words common, commune, community commutative, and communism, but in the end he rescues the idea of a 'community of persons', which now reappears in light of Levinas' ethics. I will not dwell so much on this background, also because a series of new turns led to a specific conception of 'aesthetic community' and to a polemic encounter with the discourse theory of Jürgen Habermas and Karl-Otto Apel.

The book *La condition postmoderne* (1979) can be seen as provoking a turn in philosophy and is known enough to dispense further commentaries. For example, Lyotard gives up basic elements of his libidinal aesthetics because they do not lead to a *political* conception of justice, and instead of Marx and Freud he takes up Kant and Wittgenstein. Nevertheless, it is important to note Lyotard's argument against Habermas in this book, as he affirms that the German philosopher just projects a community of experts [*communauté des experts*] (1979:40, 72, 98) searching for consensus, which abstract from other discursive forms (1979:104-106). For the sake of heterogeneity, Lyotard concludes that one has to reject this formal view of consensus in discourse and community in order to make room for informal communitarian forms of communication (1979:105-108). At this point we find a synthetical knot in which Lyotard's previous ideas on community and discursive dissension come together.

In *Le différend* (1983), which he considered his 'book of philosophy' [*mon livre de philosophie*], Lyotard relates Wittgenstein's concept of 'language games' to Kant's ethics and philosophy of history to describe a constant 'conflict of discourses', concluding that justice can only be a commitment to reveal these hidden conflicts (Lyotard 1983:9). Conflicts occur not only between two or more phrases, but also between two genres of discourse or two cultures. This has been analyzed in detail (cf. Readings 1991:107f.), but what goes unnoticed is that Lyotard now reconsiders the idea of a 'community of persons' [*communauté de personnes*] (1983:183-186), and interprets this as an aesthetic 'community of senses' [*communauté de sentiments*]. This is nothing but the conception of *sensus communis* from Kant's *Kritik der Urteilskraft*, which is now interpreted in light of a libidinal aesthetics and theory of communication and seen as the community of senders and receivers of phrases about beauty [*la communauté des destinateurs et des destinataires de la phrase sur le beau*]. The same is valid in relation to the sublime. On this basis, Lyotard now turns to Apel to criticize his conception of a 'community of communication', for in his view this is another formalization (Lyotard 1986). As we can see, Lyotard rejects both Habermas' views on discourse and Apel's conception of community to propose aesthetics as an informal discourse that is intrinsically conflictive and as an enlarged form of community (see 1988a), because aesthetics is not reduced to linguistics, but includes bodily expressions in communication and sensibility to others.

But now we may ask: what is political about it? First of all, the critique of liberalism remains. Coming close to Burke, Lyotard criticizes the French Revolution for being an imposed 'community representative of another community' (1983:210-217). He also rescues Burke's views on the sublime. Moreover, Lyotard rejects a universal cosmopolitan community as the idea of a universal history, a universal 'we' – *la fraternité republicaine* –, because in his view this is nothing but a narrative that imposes one view of community upon others. His alternative then is a contingent aesthetic community that has a political function as well. Conceived in aesthetic terms, discourse is the 'shock of the new'. There is *always* something, a possible new link or a possible encounter with the 'other' (1983:§ 40-41) which reveals what was hidden until then. Thus, in aesthetics any claim to totality remains indeterminate. Here, again, we find Kant. As he dealt with the sublime in his aesthetics, Kant spoke of unavoidable conflicts, of incommensurability and heterogeneity, and affirmed that aesthetic claims do not require conceptual mediation but the immediacy of experience. All this is interpreted by Lyotard in a political way. In the same way art does not represent but only presents something that is 'irrepresentable' in conceptual terms (1983:243f.; 1991), in politics heterogeneity cannot be 'represented' by something else. People must present themselves.

All this is fascinating, but there are some problems. There is a theological twist in Lyotard's talk about a 'totally other' being revealed as sublime (cf. 1988b:13f.; 1993) which is also inherited from Kant: the view of the Jewish taboo on graven images as something sublime that presents itself. But Lyotard assumes a privileged position to tell us what is presentable or re-presentable, and demands that we be open to the 'other', since conflicts may be pleasurable. But who knows? On the other hand, he has different views of universality which are not distinguished: search for consensus in discourse is the same as a violent clash and assimilation of cultures. While his critique of cultural universalism applies, Lyotard does not provide enough principles for judging and differentiating these cases. We can understand the motivation of his critique of liberalism as a bourgeois culture and his search for a concept of justice based on aesthetic considerations, but we can also see a hidden universal claim – there is something that is 'always' the case – that is not clarified. In the end, the critical point is obvious. Due to generalizations and the lack of justification of a general principle, the aesthetic community as substitute for politics remains prey to its own trap: it remains indeterminate.

Community of communication as critique of solipsism in discourse ethics

The turn to community can be observed also in Germany. With a mere genealogical interest in the history of the word community [*Gemeinschaft*] in German social thought, the most appropriate reference would be Luther, who connected community, communion and communication. Since that time the term reappears in Kant, Hegel and Marx (cf. Riedel 1974), having a sociological tone in Tönnies (1887) and Weber (1920). But this tradition was appropriated by the national-socialist dictatorship in ideas such as '*die Gemeinschaft*', '*das Volk*' and '*Blut und Boden*', and due to this anti-democratic appropriation, the term 'community' acquired a negative status in Germany (Joas 1993; Honneth 1992, 1994). Notwithstanding, the idea reappears in discourse theory, as Apel and Habermas develop an ethical conception of linguistic community which is confronted with this history and with the new problems of justification of principles without relying on the maxims of a Hobbesian *methodical solipsism*.

Apel's lengthy historical study *Die Idee der Sprache in der Tradition des Humanismus von Dante bis Vico* (1963), followed the hermeneutical method and showed the importance of language in Europe's nation-building after the Renaissance, i.e. how the idea of a national language as being presupposed in the construction of community. Influenced by Heidegger at first, he stressed the *a priori* of anthropological and linguistic community, which is explained in the conception that language or communication is the medium through which a person interacts with nature as well as with other humans (1973 2:132ff.). This claim is then related to a theory of rationality that dialogues with analytical philosophy. With Wittgenstein, he affirms the linguistic community as means for a critique of methodical solipsism (1973 1:365f.). With Peirce's pragmatism – i.e., the view of a community of interpretation (Royce 1913) and a community of investigation (Peirce 1938) –, he went beyond the mere assumption of a cultural community and defined the *a priori* of an intersubjective interaction of real human beings in an unlimited 'community of communication' [*Kommunikationsgemeinschaft*] (1973 2:376f.), that provides the key for a transformation of Kant's universalism (1973 2:164f.). Thus he arrived to his program of a transcendental hermeneutics, pragmatics and semiotics, which has practical application in discourse ethics [*Diskursethik*] (1973 2:358-435, 1988).

The central point should be clear: Apel criticizes solipsism by means of a conception of community. This implies also a critique of liberalism, insofar as methodical individualism is a corollary of methodical solipsism. In fact, Apel makes a point similar to MacIntyre, as he says that there is a complementarity between the idea of privacy in liberalism, existentialism and the marxist ideology, but in his version of discourse ethics Apel goes further to say that a mere reduction to a particular community does not solve the problem. Neither an individual's soliloquy nor a particular community but a dialogue among members of a 'real community of communication' is necessary, which anticipates an all-inclusive 'ideal community' as regulative idea (1973 2:423f., 1988:9-13, 110-122). The reflection on the difference between both real and ideal enables the critique of society for not having accomplished the universalization of democratic ideals. Questions may be asked, for instance, on how Apel can tell us that the ideal of a community of argumentation is not a projection of a specific value among others, thus being biased; or from which perspective can we talk of ideas as regulative. On the other hand, we must acknowledge, with Apel, that without a formal and deontological position that guarantees for a formal universality in ethics, no self-consistent alternative to the solipsistic Hobbesian model would be possible. How does this apply to politics? This question is answered more directly by Habermas.

Already in *Erkenntnis und Interesse*, Habermas agreed explicitly with Peirce, Mead and Apel on the social primacy of a community, and equally emphasized the universal character of the Peircean notion of 'community of all beings' (1968:139). From this insight he proposed that communication was the 'ideal regulator' of human emancipation, in opposition to the functionalistic systemic theory. Taking Mead's views of linguistic community and role-taking, Habermas was able to criticize functionalism for its neglect of the person, and to propose social interaction not on instrumental grounds, but based on the sharing of a common ground, 'being member of the same linguistic community' (1971). These Meadean motives reappear in *Theorie des kommunikativen Handelns* (1981 2:42,77-88), when the idea of a communication community is consistently applied to criticize Durkheim's appropriation of the juridical motive of *volonté generale* and its articulation in terms of a sacred force of a community of faith [*Glaubensgemeinschaft*]. For Habermas, this should be secularized by a rational and consensual 'unity of a communication community' (1981, 2:126, 139), as proposed by Apel.

Apel and Habermas share many of these ideas. But when the theory of communicative action was applied as practical philosophy, the Peircean conception of community started to play different roles (1991a:147; 1991b: 155-159). With Mead, Habermas affirms the 'appeal to a larger community' as the rational ground for a formal pragmatic discourse ethics (1981, 2:119, 141f.; 1983:45; 1991a:25, 142). With Rawls and Dworkin, he develops new insights on legal theory, explicitly stressing the binding force of a 'constitutional community' or 'legal community' [*Rechtsgemeinschaft*] as equiprimordial [*gleichursprünglich*] to the moral community emphasized by Apel (1992: 181-187). So Habermas proposes a 'detranscendentalization' of community in order to disconnect this concept from religious ideas and foundationalist claims (see 1996:11f.). This brings us back to Rawls' initial point, since the main issue of this detranscendentalization is to avoid a 'god's eye view'.

We are dealing with a dialectical concept of community. Looking back, we can identify two corresponding types of liberalism at play in discourse ethics. First, Apel and Habermas presuppose a critique of religion and metaphysics as that of Rawls – associated with a claim for postmetaphysical and postconventional morality (Apel 1988, 1993; and Habermas 1991b:49f., 119f.). Second, they also propose a critique of individualistic society, thus keeping the impetus of social and democratic ideas and coming closer to the positions described above. But the problem concerns a view of culture that recognizes some aspects of the communitarian and postmodern critique, while avoiding the problems denounced and criticized by liberation ethics. Once again, feminists show where the limits are (see Neehan 1995). Nancy Fraser shows that a discourse-ethical formalism overlooks the subordination of women hidden in spheres that are considered private and particular (Fraser 1989). Seyla Benhabib proposes the turn to a 'concrete other' and suggests the necessity of a 'community of needs and solidarity' (1992). Iris

Young proposes that we go beyond the assumptions of a relation of 'copresence of subjects' to value other forms of communication that are excluded in the discourse theoretical model (1990).

Although discourse ethics has developed a radical critique of methodical solipsism, which lies at the basis of what may be called a *formal liberalism* that is constitutive to the other forms, they address just one of the two horns introduced at the beginning. With Rawls, the liberalism defended is political, associated to secularism and opposed to metaphysical views, but concrete economic or cultural forms of liberalism and specific aspects such as those indicated in the feminist critique are less considered, thus representing a deficit in the very definition of the political. Habermas has attempted to deal with the feminist critique (1992:380f., 502f.) and recognizes some motivations of the communitarians' critique of society; Apel agrees with the critique of liberation ethics to the economic exclusion of the south by the northern hemisphere and with the hermeneutic aspect of communitarianism (Apel 1993:150ff.). They emphasize the points of differentiation, but the disagreement lies neither on the turn to a community nor in the critique of forms of liberalism. Therefore, we can see that discourse theory converges with the other positions on an *overlapping critique of liberalism*.

Liberalism, plurality of communities and intercultural communication

There are convergences, divergences and complementarities between the theories seen above, and in my view the most important issue is the division of labor within a critical theory. I have developed a description of these positions and at the same time I have drawn a line of argumentation that shows a convergence of critical theories in an 'overlapping critique of liberalism' that does not fall into conservatism. What is the importance of such a convergence? Is this 'overlapping critique of liberalism', in the end, particular or universal? I hope to have made it sufficiently clear that the circumscription of criticism to a solipsistic individual, to specific traditions, to a bourgeois culture or to economic values that can be used as forms of oppression are criticized by the positions seen above. But on the other hand, I also emphasized the problem of a metaphysical view that is many times seen as universalist and forgets particularities and pluralism. Thus, despite my internal reconstruction, the double tension with which we started seems to remain, albeit in a different way. To conclude with this overview, I will shortly address this issue, coming to my proposal for a way of coping with the difficulties we have seen.

Multiculturalism and the overlapping critique of liberalism

After disclosing some characteristic elements in the above positions, a retrospective view is needed to evaluate the tension between particularistic and universalistic accounts as well as some forms of dualism that seem to remain today. The outcome can be summarized in a few points.

1 They all take the concept of community in order to criticize society, but are distinct from the religious-metaphysical or conservative positions seen at the beginning. But since the concept remains ambiguous, they add different correctives to it: life, culture, aesthetics and communication.

2 The distinct adjectives attached to the concepts of community show the correspondent political critique of different aspects of liberalism. Liberation ethics attacks economic liberalism, communitarians attack legal and political liberalism, postmoderns reject the liberal view of a bourgeois culture, discourse theory attacks the principle behind liberal individualism, namely methodical solipsism. In this critique they go beyond the political dualism between liberalism and conservatism and it becomes difficult to define their position as a *juste milieu*. On the other hand, they acknowledge liberal democratic principles, while holding to a view of liberal secularism that still needs a clear definition.

3 Out of their specific criticisms they all propose specific understandings of community, but they do not define very clear the inner and outer limits of their communities and their relation to internal and external forms of critique. In liberation ethics, one does not know if the *community of life* based on the 'option for the poor' is limited to a *favela*, to Latin America, or to the Catholic Church in many continents. Communitarians are not clear about the notion of a *cultural community,* whether 'shared values' correspond to a tribe, university or nation. Postmodern poststructuralism proposes an *aesthetic community* and points out the need of going beyond bourgeois values in our commitment to justice and heterogeneity, but it does not provide consistent principles to meet this goal. Discourse theory defines a context-transcendent *community of communication* with the intention of going beyond the limits of cultural conventions and national boundaries, but here the question about the geographical limits of this discourse and the possibility of accepting other forms of discourse remains open. In all cases, it becomes obvious that they all refer to the macro-social level, to wide contexts beyond their own.

4 They point to different levels of communication. It is assumed normally that communication is the basic element of interpersonal relations and this is the level emphasized by the base community inspired by liberation ethics. But since we are dealing here with the macro-social level, there is the need to make room for this wider dimension, and communitarians jump from the personal case to 'our' group or culture. Postmodernism acknowledges the primacy of a communicative process and stresses the need to recognize the 'other', but its views on alterity and discursive conflict are self-refuting, due to the lack of more general principle of judgment. As discourse theory makes a strong case for the *a priori* of communication and works out the application of this principle at the institutional level, there is a further move in terms of a procedural universalism. As a matter of fact, Habermas and Apel try to generalize this approach in their defense of a world instance for justice such as the United Nations, in light of Kant's project for eternal peace. But here the formal universalism suddenly becomes material, and new problems arise.

Thus far we have seen that 'community' is a *general* idea and not internally contingent or particular to the specific positions described above. Comparing these positions we were able to see the wider background of the 'turn to community' in different contexts and theories. Their agendas are clear when it refers to the internal motivations of their initiatives, which is a critique of their respective societies and of specific aspects of liberalism. They try to avoid the problems of regressive religious-metaphysics and political conservatism. Moreover, they are also aware of other issues: pluralism and multiculturalism, the problematic of relativism, the ambiguity of communal values and the move between contexts. But now certain limits become blurry. Comparing these positions, we were able to see the wider background they share as they go beyond their own contexts, and we can conclude that there seems to be something underlying these different discourses, which allows for such a convergence.

From intercultural communication to multicultural communities

The above critical projects turn to the concept of community in order to address practical problems in specific contexts and to criticize liberalism. This shows that while liberalism may be tenable as a political project, other issues arise in the arena of interpersonal and intercultural relations which are forgotten. Now a question remains: where are the limits of the distinct views of community described above, and how can we be in and out of their reach?

I would like to answer this question by pointing out to something that seems trivial and refers to the religious-metaphysical and conservative meaning of community mentioned at the outset. The idea of a community has definitely a Judeo-Christian bias that brings together many parts of the world (Europe, Anglo America and Latin America), but not necessarily other parts of the world – nor even certain cultures in Europe and the Americas. This notion of community has different forms that are not limited to a territory, ever since people began to immigrate and to communicate with others, but the 'shared community' implied in these discourses reveals a danger of eurocentrism that is not explicitly taken into account. The move beyond our context, without reflection, becomes dangerous because a naive emphasis on 'community' can be a way of affirming the internal 'we' in opposition to the external 'they', or a way of assimilating or appropriating others.

Nevertheless, there is also something else which is common in these different contexts and allows us to say that this problem could be avoided. These theories indeed stress different levels of communication and are in communication with each other as they move beyond strict particularistic conventions. Trivial as it may be, this affirmation entails some claims that add fire to the discussions on *universalism.* This is a 'trans-contextual or cross-cultural turn to community by means of communication' and we are entitled to explore this venue. Liberation ethics stresses interpersonal relations amidst the contingencies of poverty and denounces the structural aspects of poverty in world economy; communitarians criticize individualism and are more sensitive to multiculturalism; postmoderns develop our sensitivity to 'others' and to other forms of communication; discourse theory presents a secular principle upon which these varieties could be articulated.

With a change of emphasis we see that the turn to community is neither particular nor universal. This does not mean that philosophical discourses are to be tied only to 'shared values' which lead to enlarged communities that are immune to consensus. I hope to have shown that in conceptual and in practical terms there is 'communication'. Words for dialogue are provided as part of a 'shared lexicon' resulting from dialogue, not always without conflict. If this dialogue does not work, it is not a failure in the principle of communication. We have to use other words that are more appropriate (ethnocentrism, dogmatism and the like), instead of reducing the issues to undefined 'community' interests, without seeing that they have cause, effect and relevance on a larger scale. To maintain a coherent critical position that is socially and politically relevant *we should try to deduce community from communication, instead of trying to derive everything from an ambiguous concept of community.*

References

Apel, K.-O. (1963), *Die Idee der Sprache in der Tradition des Humanismus von Dante bis Vico*, Bouvier: Bonn.

— (1973), *Transformation der Philosophie*, 2 Vols., Suhrkamp: Frankfurt.

— (1988), *Diskurs und Verantwortung. Das Problem des Übergangs zur postkonventionellen Moral*, Suhrkamp: Frankfurt.

— (1993), 'Das Anliegen des anglo-amerikanischen "Kommunitarismus" in der Sicht der Diskursethik', in Brumlik, M. & Brunkhorst, H. (Hg.) *Gemeinschaft und Gerechtigkeit*, Fischer: Frankfurt.

Bellah, R. (1975), *The Broken Covenant. American Civil Religion in Time of Trial*. New York: Seabury.

— & P. Hammond [eds.] (1980), *Varieties of Civil Religion*, Harper & Row: San Francisco.

—, R. Madsen, W. Sullivan, A. Swidler, and S. Tipton. (1985), *Habits of the Hearth. Individualism and Commitment in American Life*. Berkeley:Univ. of California Press: Berkeley.

— & Frederick Greenspahn [eds.] (1987), *Uncivil Religion: Interreligious Hostility in America*. New York: Crossroad: New York.

Benhabib, S. (1992), *Situating the Self. Gender, community and postmodernism in contemporary ethics*, Routledge: New York.

Boff, C. (1981), *Comunidade Eclesial. Comunidade Política*, Vozes: Petrópolis.

Boff, L. (1981), *Igreja, Carisma e Poder*, Vozes: Petrópolis.

Cardoso, F.H. & Falleto, E. (1974), *Dependencia y Desarrollo en América Latina*, Siglo XXI: Mexico (DF).

CELAM (1969), *Conferencia de Medellín*, Vozes: Petrópolis.

Dussel, E. (1986), *Ética Comunitaria. Liberta o Pobre!*, Vozes: Petrópolis.

— (1988), *Hacia un Marx Desconocido. Un Comentario a los Manuscritos del 61-63*, Siglo XXI & UAM: Tztapalapa.

— (1993a); *El Encubrimiento del Otro*. Nueva Utopía: Madrid.

— (1993b), 'Auf dem Weg zu einem philosophischen Nord-Süd Dialogue. Einige Diskussionspunkte zwischen der "Diskursethik" und der "Philosophie der Befreiung"' in A. Dorschel et. al. (Hg.) *Transzendentalpragmatik*, Frankfurt: Suhrkamp.

— (1994), *Historia de la Filosofía y Filosofía de la Liberación*, N. América: Bogotá.

— (1995), 'Die Priorität der Ethik der Befreiung gegenüber der Diskursethik', in E. Arens (Hg.) *Anerkennung der Anderen*. Freiburg: Herder: Freiburg.

— (1996), *The Underside of Modernity*, Humanities: Atlantic Highlands (NJ).

Forst, R. (1994), *Kontexte der Gerechtigkeit. Politische Philosophie jenseits von Liberalismus und Kommunitarismus*, Suhrkamp: Frankfurt.

Fraser, N. (1989), *Unruly Practices. Discourse and Gender in Contemporary Social Theory*, University of Minnesota Press: Minneapolis.

Freire, P. (1974), *Pedagogia do Oprimido*, Paz e Terra, Rio de Janeiro.

Guimarães, A. (1978), *Comunidades de Base no Brasil*, Vozes: Petrópolis.

Habermas, J. (1968), *Erkenntnis und Interesse*, Suhrkamp: Frankfurt.

Habermas, J. (1971), *Theorie der Gesellschaft oder Sozialtechnologie: Was leistet die Systemforschung?*, Suhrkamp: Frankfurt.
— (1981), *Theorie des kommunikativen Handelns*. 2 Vols., Suhrkamp: Frankfurt.
— (1983), *Moralbewußtsein und kommunikatives Handeln*. Suhrkamp: Frankfurt.
— (1991a), *Texte und Kontexte*. Suhrkamp: Frankfurt.
— (1991b), *Erläuterung zur Diskursethik*. Suhrkamp: Frankfurt.
— (1992) *Faktizität und Geltung. Beiträge zur Theorie des Rechts und des demokratischen Rechstaates*, Suhrkamp: Frankfurt.
— (1996), *Die Einbeziehung des Anderen*, Suhrkamp: Frankfurt.
Hinkelammert, F. (1970), *Dialectica del Desarrollo Desigual*, CEREM: Santiago.
Honneth, A. (Hg.) 1992. *Kommunitarismus. Eine Debatte über die moralischen Grundlagen moderner Gesellschaften*, Campus: Frankfurt.
— (1994), *Desintegration. Bruchstücke einer soziologischen Zeitdiagnose*, Fischer: Frankfurt.
Ingram, D. (1995), *Reason, History and Politics. The Communitarian Grounds of Legitimation in the Modern Age*, SUNY Press: Albany (NY).
Jay, M. (1993), *Downcast Eyes*, University of California Press: Berkeley.
Joas, H. (1993), 'Gemeinschaft und Demokratie in den USA. Die vergessene Vorgeschichte der Kommunitarismus-Diskussion', in Brumlik & Brunkhorst (Hg.) *Gemeinschaft und Gerechtigkeit*, Suhrkamp: Frankfurt.
Kymlicka, W. (1989), *Liberalism, Community and Culture*, Clarendon: Oxford.
Lyotard, J.-F. (1954), *La phénoménologie*, Presses universitaires de France: Paris.
— (1974), *Économie libidinale*, Minuit: Paris.
— (1979), *La condition postmoderne*, Minuit: Paris.
— (1983), *Le differend*, Minuit: Paris.
— (1986), 'Grundlagenkrise', *Neue Hefte für Philosophie* 26, 1-33.
— (1988a), *L'Inhumain*, Galilée: Paris.
— (1988b), *Heidegger et les 'juifs'*, Galilée: Paris.
— (1989), *La guerre des Algériens: Écrits (1956-1963)*, Galilée: Paris.
— (1991), *Leçons sur l'Analytique du sublime: Kant, Critique de la faculté de juger (§ 23-29)*, Galilée: Paris.
— (1993), *Un trait d'union*, Les éditions Le Griffon: Québec.
Macedo, St. (1995), 'Liberal Civic Education and Religious Fundamentalism: The Case of God vs. John Rawls', *Ethics* 105/3, April 1995, 468-496.
McIntyre, A. 1966. *A Short History of Ethics*, MacMillan: New York.
— (1967), *Secularization and Moral Change*, Oxford University Press: Oxford.
— (1968), *Marxism and Christianity*, Schocken Books: New York.
— (1981), *After Virtue*, University of Notre Dame Press: Notre Dame.
— (1988), *Whose Justice? Which Rationality?*, University of Notre Dame Press: Notre Dame.
Moon, D. (1993), *Constructing Community*, Princeton Univerty Press: Princeton.
Nancy, J.-L. (1986), *La communauté désoeuvrée*, Ch. Borgois: Paris.
— (1991), *La comparution. Politique à venir*, Bourgois: Paris.
— & Lacoue-Labarthe, Ph. (1978), *L'Absolu litteraire*, Ed. Du Seuil: Paris.

Nisbet, R. (1976), *The Social Philosophers*, Paladin: Forgmore (UK).
Neehan, J. [ed.] (1995), *Feminists read Habermas*, Routledge: New York.
Peirce, C. (1938), *Collected Papers*, Harvard University Press: Cambridge (MA).
Quinn, Ph. (1995), 'Political Liberalisms and their Exclusions of the Religious' (Presidential Address at the 93th Meeting of the APA Central Division). In *American Philosophical Association. Proceedings and Addresses*, 69/2, 35-56.
Rasmussen, D. [ed.] (1988), *Philosophy and Social Criticism* [Special Issue on Universalism and Communitarianism], 14/3-4.
Rawls, J. (1971), *A Theory of Justice*, Harvard University Press: Cambridge (MA).
— (1985), 'Justice as Fairness: Political Not Metaphysical', *Philosophy and Public Affairs* 14/3,223-251.
— (1987), 'The Idea of an Overlapping Consensus', *Oxford Journal of Legal Studies* 7/1, 1-25.
— (1993), *Political Liberalism*. New York:Columbia University Press: New York.
— (1995a), 'Reply to Habermas', *The Journal of Philosophy* Vol. XCII, No. 3, March 1995, 132-180.
— (1995b), 'Political Liberalism, Religion and Public Reason (Rawls Symposion)', *Religion & Values* in *Public Value* 3/4, Summer 1995, 1-11.
Reading, B. (1991), *Introducing Lyotard*, Routledge: New York.
Riedel, M. (1974), 'Gesellschaft - Gemeinschaft', in Brunner, O., W. Conze, R. Koselleck (Hg.), *Geschichtliche Grundbegriffe. Historisches Lexikon zur politisch-sozialen Sprache in Deutschland.* Klett-Cotta: Stuttgart.
Royce, J. (1913), *The Problem of Christianity*, 2 Vols., MacMillan: New York.
Sandel, M. (1982), *Liberalism and the Limits of Justice*, Cambridge University Press: Cambridge.
Tönnies, F. (1887) [1979],*Gemeinschaft und Gesellschaft*, Wissenschaftliche Buchgesellschaft: Darmstadt.
Vogl, J. [Hrsg.] (1994), *Gemeinschaften. Positionen zu einer Philosophie des Politischen*, Suhrkamp: Frankfurt.
Walzer, M. (1965), *The Revolution of the Saints. A Study in the Origins of Radical Politics* [1966], Weidenfeld & Nicolson: London.
— (1975), 'Civility and Civic Virtue in Contemporary America', *Social Research* 41/4, 593-611.
— (1983), *Spheres of Justice. A Defence of Pluralism and Equality*, Basic Books: New York.
— (1985), *Exodus and Revolution*, Basic Books: New York.
— (1987), *Interpretation and Social Criticism*, Harvard University Press: Cambridge (MA).
— (1991), 'The idea of civil society', *Dissent*, Spring1991, 293-304.
Weber, M. (1920) [1964], *Wirtschaft und Gesellschaft*, JCB Mohr: Tübingen.
Young, I. (1990), *Justice and the Politics of Difference*, Princeton University Press: Princeton.

2 Which person? Whose community?

On the controversy between liberalism and communitarianism

Rainer Forst

Contemporary discussions of the concept of justice are still bound to a discourse that oscillates between Plato's conception of justice as part of the eternal and divine idea of the good (*Rep.* 517) and Aristotle's view that justice must be seen as 'something human' that has to be determined in an appropriate and balanced way within changing social relations (*Nich. Eth.* 1137a30). The problem of a theory of justice seems to lie, therefore, in the necessity of a mediation between these two dimensions – the 'earthly' and the 'divine', a historical *ethos* and a universal morality. Justice is a notion situated simultaneously *within* and *beyond* communities, traditions, and forms of self-understanding; it has to be valid for a specific political community, but at the same time be critical of such a community and point out its limits; its perspective is that of both those inside and those outside the 'cave'.

The controversy between liberalism and communitarianism can be seen as a footnote to this traditional discourse. According to communitarian critics, liberalism is, particularly in the form presented by John Rawls in *A Theory of Justice* (1971), an example of a theory that has a 'thin' and atomistic instead of a 'constitutive' and intersubjective conception of the person as its point of departure. In this way, this theory gives priority to abstract principles of the right over individual and communal conceptions of the good, deprives the political community of its ethical content, and replaces a concrete hermeneutics of social self-understanding with a universalism of Kantian inspiration. In short, it is a contextless theory. It is important to see, however, that although all these issues are intertwined, they refer to different philosophical problems which concern different theoretical perspectives on the person, on law, politics, and morality.[1] A positive aspect of the debate between liberalism and communitarianism is that it highlights these complex dimensions of a theory of justice, but a disadvantage is that these levels are not always sufficiently differentiated. For instance, once one shows the importance of ethical values and communal ties with respect to the constitution of personal identity, one cannot one-dimensionally deduce that the 'priority of the good over the right' applies to the other levels of theoretical issues.

In fact, the very concepts 'communitarianism' and 'liberalism' are problematic, insofar as they give the impression that any possible position on one level implies a certain position on each of the other levels. But this is not the case, as Charles Taylor (1989b) and Michael Walzer (1990a) have emphasized. Internal developments of the debate have shown that mediating positions are both necessary and possible. Communitarian theories recognize certain individual rights and egalitarian principles in order to be able to differentiate the communities they defend from those which deserve moral criticism. And liberal theories present their principles as a formal enabling condition rather than primarily as a limitation to the good and communal life. There is a search for ways to combine individual rights with the integrity of communities, political unity with social difference, as well as universalism with contextualism.

In what follows, I will attempt to indicate how such a combination is possible and, more importantly, to show how it arises out of a reconstruction of the debate. To that end, it is necessary to start with a critical analysis of the communitarian thesis that a theory of justice which is not based on specific and particular conceptions of the good within a community is doomed to fail, because it involves a claim to impartiality with respect to the justification and the observance of general principles that relies on 'non-persons' who exist without communities, traditions, and ethical bonds. According to this communitarian thesis, principles of justice can be valid only for persons *within* a community, for these principles are nourished by communal conceptions of the good and right, being thus an expression of concrete relationships. The point of conflict between communitarians and liberals is not, therefore, that a theory of justice has the task of justifying principles that correspond to a 'reasonable' (as Rawls defines it) conception of the person (and also of the community) – the conflict lies in the different conceptions of person and community to be found in communitarian and liberal theories.

However, if one asks communitarians and liberals *which person* and *whose community* they consider as central, one realizes that they not only have different conceptions of person and community as points of departure, but also that these notions belong to different normative conceptual levels and refer to distinct though *not* necessarily incompatible forms of recognition: recognition as an *ethical person* with an individual life history, as an abstract *legal person*, as an equal *citizen*, or as a *moral person* who deserves moral respect. These conceptions of the person correspond to four different conceptions of an ethical, legal, political or moral community, respectively. These distinctions can be gained from the debate, positively, by analyzing the arguments of both sides and, negatively, by observing also that they often are at 'cross-purposes' (Taylor). The differentiation of these normative dimensions allows one to see that the communitarian thesis according to which persons are to be conceived only as members of communities does not yet answer the questions concerning which person and whose community are being referred to and which norms or values can have a claim to validity within these distinct *contexts of justice*.

Ethical identity and legal neutrality

Michael Sandel's critique of Rawls is instructive for an analysis of the debate between liberalism and communitarianism not only because this critique started the whole controversy, but also because the discussion between Rawls and Sandel shows clearly the necessity of distinguishing between ethical and legal forms of recognition.

Sandel tries to show that Rawls' theory is based upon an atomistic conception of the person as an 'unencumbered self' which is mirrored in the idea of an 'original position'. According to Sandel, the instrumental rationality and the mutual disinterest of the parties in this original situation are symptomatic of a liberal theory which aims at grounding principles of justice ('right') that establish a formal framework within which subjects who are basically without an identity are free to choose their conceptions of the good: 'As the right is prior to the good, so the subject is prior to its ends' (1982:7). From his critique of Kant and Rawls, Sandel concludes that all deontological theories are based on a conception of the self as an atomistic and possessive individual to whom the liberty of choice is the highest freedom, who sees norms only as external limitations, and who has a purely superficial relation to values, to conceptions of the good and to communal obligations.

Against this view of the person, Sandel (following Taylor) proposes his theory of the self constituted in communities, which basically affirms that the identity of the self is internally interwoven with the collective identity of a 'larger life' and comprehended [*aufgehoben*] in a 'wider subject' (1982:172).[2] The 'limits of justice' lie, therefore, in the moral limits of these communities: within them there can be norms only in the form of social self-understandings that provide an identity to a collective. Principles external to this life context would just have a destructive impact. Hence, since there is no 'deontological person', there can be no deontological morality (1982:14).

Three objections to Sandel's critique of liberal deontological theories are especially important here: first, arguments against his interpretation of Rawls' theory; second, against his conception of a political community; third, against his own conception of the self.

Rawls questions the very first of Sandel's assumptions, namely that an atomistic anthropology underlies his theory. Even though he still emphasizes an 'ideal of the person' as guiding his theory (1971:584),[3] this ideal of a 'moral person' neither explains the constitution of personal identity nor can it be found in the 'original position' in the way Sandel thinks it can. Rawls' conception of the person, which in his later work becomes central to his theory, is, according to him, a 'political' conception, inasmuch as it is neither metaphysically nor anthropologically grounded but follows from a reconstruction of the basic moral powers which must be expected from the citizens of a democratic society of fair cooperation (Rawls 1985:232ff.). These moral powers consist, on the one hand, in the capacity of forming a conception of the good and being able to revise it and pursue it rationally; and on the other, in the capacity for a sense of justice, i.e. the capacity to accept and observe principles of justice in a system of social cooperation.

The 'moral person' is not primarily represented in the description of the rational parties, but in the whole depiction of the original situation. Both of the moral powers of being rational (having a personal conception of the good) and being reasonable (having a cooperative sense of justice) constitute the 'original position', insofar as the idea of the rational leads to the description of the parties, while the reasonable leads to the restrictions imposed on their considerations by the 'veil of ignorance' (Rawls 1980: 524ff.). Finally, the rational and the reasonable are reflected also in the list of basic goods as 'general all-purpose means' for the pursuit of the 'highest-order interests' to realize the two basic moral powers. Therefore, Rawls' conception of the person cannot be derived from the description of the parties but from the description of the 'original position' as a whole, since it is the 'device of representation' of rational *and* reasonable persons who possess both a capacity for realizing the good and an effective sense of justice.

This conception of the person is not located on the level of the qualitative identity and the constitution of the self as discussed by Sandel. Rather, Rawls' minimal conception of the 'moral person' corresponds to the 'public identity' of persons 'as a matter of basic law'; it does not prejudge the 'nonpublic identity' of persons, their 'affections, devotions and loyalties', nor their 'religious, philosophical or moral convictions' and conceptions of the good (1985:241 and 1993:30f., where instead of 'nonpublic' he uses the less misleading term 'noninstitutional'). As a person of basic legal relations Saul is the same person, even if he becomes Paul and his ethically constituted identity drastically changes.

The differentiation between legal-political and ethical-personal identity makes it obvious not only that Rawls' conception of the person and its representation in the 'original position' contradict Sandel's interpretation, but also that the distinction between ethical and legal conceptions of the person implies different notions of community as well. Rawls distinguishes between 'state' and 'community' in the sense that a differentiated, legally constituted political community is characterized by the 'fact of pluralism': within this political community there is a plurality of communities which are integrated by particular conceptions of the good. The political-legal community is a 'social union of social unions', so to speak, a political community of ethical communities (Rawls 1987:10; 1988:268ff.). Sandel, in turn, does not sufficiently distinguish these forms of community, since for him 'family or tribe or city or class or nation or people' are all 'constitutive communities' (Sandel 1982:172). He assumes then that the political community shapes personal identity in the same way as a family, i.e. that the structure of reciprocal relations of recognition and duties are structurally similar in both cases. Such a view, however, does not do justice to the ethical pluralism of modern political societies and misses the point of the distinction between the recognition of a person as a legal person with equal rights and the recognition of a person in his or her biographical individuality with a particular conception of the good and an individual as well as a community-based identity. The interpretation of legal forms of recognition as 'thick' ethical ones does not allow for a conceptual space for the recognition of a person as an autonomous legal subject with rights to freedom of action.

In a third respect, Rawls' reply questions Sandel's theory on the very level of personal-ethical identity. For even though Rawls' conception of the person does not determine the specific modes of the constitution of the self, it includes the moral power of rational reflection on one's own conception of the good. To be sure, Sandel takes this possibility of self-reflection and revision of values and life goals into account as well, but he does not explain how a subject whose identity is inextricably interwoven with the identity of a community as a 'wider subject' can have a reflective and critical power in relation to this community (Sandel 1982:179f.). Thus he does not do justice to the possibility of having an 'I' that determines himself or herself amidst the tension of different projects, values and community obligations. At this point both liberal and feminist critics agree: Sandel establishes an all too strict connection between the values and traditions that constitute a self and the duty to affirm these values and traditions in a normative sense (see Okin 1989:chs. 2 and 3; Friedman 1990; Kymlicka 1990:207f.). His alternative to the 'unencumbered' self is too much encumbered by its communal ties.

Both Sandel and Alasdair MacIntyre infer from the communal constitution of the self a one-dimensional communal constitution of all intersubjective norms and obligations within a political community. In this way, they not only employ a problematic conception of the person with respect to individual reflexivity (cf. MacIntyre 1981:218ff.), but they also fail to distinguish between 'ethical' and 'legal' person, between ethical and legal community, as well as between ethical values and obligations and legal norms and duties. In this context, 'legal person' refers to the person as having subjective rights and being the subject of positive law – as a person with equal rights without regard to his or her particular ethical identity. On the other hand, the term 'ethical person' designates a person in his or her qualitative identity, special character, values, life history, individuality, commonality and 'personality'. This identity is developed in 'webs of interlocution' (Taylor 1989a:36), in communally constituted space and time – in ethical communities such as the family, among friends and, *mutatis mutandis*, in communities integrated through 'strong evaluations', such as religious or cultural communities.

In this respect, ethics and law are not in a relation of competition, they rather presuppose one another in the following way: to recognize a person as a legal person means to respect his or her right to his or her own identity and integrity. This requires a reciprocal granting of rights that is no more 'atomistic' than the conceptions of the good and of communal life which are protected by these rights.[4] It is one thing to recognize (and respect) a person as a bearer of rights, and another to recognize (and esteem) a person through his or her personal characteristics.[5] To argue for individual rights does not mean to argue for individualistic life plans of 'unencumbered' persons. Legal-'negative' autonomy (personal freedom of action) and ethical-'positive' autonomy (self-realization) are related in a variety of ways, but they should not be falsely put in opposition to one another. Rights protect ethical identities.[6]

In normative terms, both realms are different with respect to the action-guiding principles or values that dominate within them. In ethical contexts, values, self-understandings and 'comprehensive doctrines' (to use Rawls' term) rule which answer the question concerning the good life 'for me'; their ethical validity depends on whether a person can identify himself or herself with these values in the light of his or her own identity, biography and communal bonds. With regard to questions concerning the coexistence of 'all', however, there is a need for norms that are generally justifiable, so that all persons concerned can agree upon them. General norms have to be 'not reasonable to reject', as Thomas Scanlon puts it (Scanlon 1982:110). Rawls explicates this notion of 'reasonable' by identifying the 'reasonable' conceptions of the person (with two moral powers) and of society as a system of fair cooperation. To him, these notions are 'ideas of practical reason' (Rawls 1993:90, 110; on this see Forst 1997a), which are fundamental to the formulation of the 'original position' and to the construction of principles of justice. These principles in turn form the center of an 'overlapping consensus' which is sustained by all citizens and secures the stability of a just society. According to Rawls, the most basic assumptions about the moral powers of the person are not reasonably rejectable, given our capacity for practical reason. In this way, the principles of justice that are constructed on their basis are generally acceptable to free and equal citizens without presupposing that they give up their ethical identity. What is indeed required, however, is the recognition of each person's equal right to an ethical identity: 'Justice draws the limit, the good shows the point' (1988:252). The priority of justice indicates the priority of general principles that equally protect and obligate all persons.

Thomas Nagel has formulated the basic idea of a theory that calls for a general and impartial justification of general principles of justice without starting from a specific conception of the person as the basis for a construction of normative principles. According to him, general norms must satisfy a criterion of validity which is different from that of ethical values: general norms must be able to claim a 'higher order impartiality' (Nagel 1987:216). Nagel explains this impartiality and 'truth' of principles within the framework of a theory of 'public justification' that provides two arguments for the possibility of an 'epistemological division between the private and the public domains'. First, an argument of reciprocity: in the procedure of public justification no person can claim a right for himself or herself which he or she denies to others (e.g. the right to practice a religion one believes in); and secondly, an argument of generality: a person must be able to justify his or her reasons for certain norms in a general and rational, objective way. Those suggestions or positions that do not satisfy this test are considered to be mere ethical 'beliefs', whereas justifiable norms may raise a claim to truth and objectivity (Nagel 1987:226ff.).

Nevertheless, Nagel does not sufficiently take into account that the claim to the objectivity of moral norms can only be a discursively redeemable claim to their intersubjective validity and that ethical values and moral norms present valid answers to *different* types of questions. Thus they do not compete in such a way that the impartial moral standpoint implies that one looks at ethical values 'from outside' and calls their ethical validity into question.[7] The moral point of view must be a common *interpersonal* and not an *impersonal* point of view, as Nagel assumes. Ethical values are not objectified, generalized and validated from a neutral perspective, but must be justified reciprocally and generally whenever they raise claims to general moral validity. Rather than a differentiation between the 'good' and the 'just' in a primarily epistemological way, one needs, following Habermas, to distinguish between the normative questions 'what is good for me as the person I am?' on the one hand and 'what can be justified in the general interest?' on the other (Habermas 1983:53-125; 1991:100-118). But more important than the specific terminological formulation of these questions are the different *criteria of validity* necessary to answer them intersubjectively. Only those norms that can be justified reciprocally and generally can raise a claim to generally binding validity. Therein lies the very core of a procedural and deontological theory.

The talk about norms of 'justice', however, covers up the distinction between moral and legal norms. Indeed, the mode of general justification applies to both. But while moral norms are universally valid for all moral persons and must be justifiable to each individual, legal norms are valid for 'all' within a given legal community and demand not moral but 'legal' action that obeys positive law (cf. Habermas 1992:135ff.). The most fundamental legal norms – especially basic rights – have a moral core, but the form of general justification that grants legitimacy to them is the acceptance by the citizens of a given political community. Both dimensions are central for the claim of legal norms to be 'just'. The much discussed claim to the 'neutrality' of these norms is, therefore, to be understood as a claim to reciprocal and general justification that avoids declaring certain ethical values as binding without having passed that procedure (cf. Rawls 1988:260ff.; Marneffe 1990). Between ethical values and legal norms there is, so to speak, a *border of generality and reciprocity* which separates both sides but at the same time leaves them their own space. Ethical values can only raise the claim of being generally binding when they correspond to these criteria, while general norms may enter into the ethical realm only insofar as they are able to show that they represent generally justifiable interests.[8]

These considerations contradict the conception of an *ethical* liberalism that regards the principle of reciprocal and general justification as well as fundamental liberal legal norms (e.g. religious freedom) as based upon a liberal theory of the good, i.e. a theory of the autonomous life as a 'liberal self' (cf. Raz 1986; Dworkin 1990; Macedo 1990; Galston 1991; Kymlicka 1992). If the principle of justification were to be founded on the 'good' or on the 'value' of liberal autonomy (whatever this may exactly entail), then it could only be binding under the condition that a person recognizes this good for himself or herself and equally accepts as right – according to grounds important to his or her own self-understanding – that this good has to be granted to others who are then to be seen as addressees of moral justification. This ethical reading of the principle of justification leaves no room for the concept of a categorical *right* or *duty* of justification – i.e. of the moral duty to provide good, *reciprocally non-rejectable reasons* for the validity of norms all are subject to. Hence this reading violates the basic demand inherent in the claim to legitimacy of modern law; namely, that mutually enforceable norms have to be generally justifiable. These norms – insofar as they are basic norms – must be able to vindicate a normative (and not a merely factual) validity and authority before each person, independent of his or her identity; they must be based on 'shared reasons' (Korsgaard 1993) without generalizing particular values in the attempt to maintain a specific form of life. This does not mean that these norms must be equally compatible with any ethical value – for all that it implies is that, where the right claims priority over the good, this priority must be reciprocally and generally justifiable. Ethical liberalism cannot solve the dilemma as to how an ethical good of 'justice' or 'autonomy' can claim such a priority over other goods (cf. Forst 1997b).

The demand that general norms be generally acceptable has to be understood as a demand of practical reason – of practical reason *in* contexts of intersubjective justification (see the third section below). What counts as a good reason is therefore not to be defined in an ethical way (by taking recourse to subjective or objective values) but has to be established through mutual argumentation. It is this normative precaution that leads to a granting of 'abstract' rights to legal persons, which in turn provide a form of general recognition and protection of their concrete identities. Only in this way can the legal person constitute a 'protective cover' for the ethical person. The fact that the law makes ethical autonomy possible – i.e., that it enables and at the same time limits individual self-determination – does precisely *not* imply that the law is justified on the basis of an idea of the good – even if this were only a 'formal' idea. The law protects ethical persons as legal persons from non-justified claims by others because it draws the necessary *moral* border of generality and reciprocity. The recognition of this border, however, is not without consequences with respect to individual ethical life; rather, it implies specific cognitive and moral requirements that persons are seeking to reach mutual justification, i.e., that they be 'reasonable' in a practical sense.

This theory of law sketches an ideal connection of particular ethical identities and the legal form of recognition. In opposition to this, however, it is obviously the case that those norms that constitute historical as well as present forms of the legal person are everything but 'neutral'. These norms bear the mark of a multiplicity of exclusions of social groups. Even a legal system that tries to be 'color blind' and, *mutatis mutandis*, 'gender blind', in order to promote formal equality, perpetuates practices of exclusion in a society characterized by pervasive inequality, for it treats as formally equal those who are substantially unequal – especially those who have been made unequal and are now stigmatized as 'different' (cf. MacKinnon 1989; Fraser 1989; Minow 1990; Rössler 1992). The claim to protect ethical identities often only covers up the marginalization of identities which do not correspond to a projected ideal that guides the definition of a socially autonomous person. Especially the traditional liberal (or republican) understanding of the limits between 'public' and 'private' questions leads to a concealment of power relationships in social spheres which must not be ignored by a theory of justice.

Nevertheless, from this criticism of general law one should not conclude that the language of law must be converted into an ethical language based on the 'values' of specific communal practices (as Sandel 1989:520f. suggests). Rather, it is important to realize that in a procedural understanding of law which implies its claim to general justifiability, Law has to take into account the claims to recognition which are brought forth by specific groups with general arguments. The distinction between ethical and general types of questions does not mean that ethical issues should be regarded as 'private', but it means that ethically based claims can be a legitimate basis for demands on others if they can be justified in relation to general principles of equality. This, in turn, does not presuppose that the groups raising these claims need to take up the existent general language and its concepts of public and private without any criticism. In fact, these groups reveal the 'false universality' of such general language when they criticize dominant notions of the 'private' and one-sided communal 'values'. Only in this way the law can become a protective cover for individual identities.

These conflicts surrounding the recognition of identities indicate the necessity of the forum of political discourse in which claims to justice have to be brought forward and recognized, so that they can be institutionally implemented. The principle of 'public justification' has to be put into practice. This implies a conception of the political community which, however, leads to another controversial point between liberals and communitarians: should we define 'citizens' primarily as legal or as ethical persons? Is the political community integrated by means of subjective rights or ethical values?

The ethos of democracy

In political communities persons are not only recognized as members of ethical communities or as persons with subjective rights, but also as co-citizens. This means that they are not only *addressees* but also *authors* of the law. To be a 'citizen' in the full sense implies having not only subjective-liberal rights but political and social rights as well – to be personally and politically autonomous. And the political community is precisely the place where these rights have to be fought for, have to be grounded, interpreted, as well as realized. Because of these various functions, liberal, communitarian, and feminist theories provide different answers to the question of the right conception of the political community and of political discourse.

As it has already been pointed out, Rawls' conception of the moral person corresponds to an ideal of the citizen in a fair and cooperative society. The 'social union of social unions', as Rawls conceives the political community, is not constituted by atomistic and self-interested individuals who are primarily concerned with the defense of their subjective rights. Citizens are not mere private legal persons, they also have the moral power of acting in a cooperative and just way. Since they understand themselves as members of a comprehensive system of cooperation, they agree on a distribution of social goods which contributes to social equality and to the 'fair value' of equal liberties. Moreover, citizens are capable of taking part in democratic discourses: they observe the 'limits of public reason' and base their arguments concerning fundamental political questions only upon those grounds that correspond to the 'political values' of the principles of justice. Only then can there be a 'public' reason (Rawls 1993:ch. VI). For these citizens, however, the political life is not necessarily the good life (compared to a republican view), and the primary goal of political discourse is to interpret principles of justice and to put them into practice in terms of social cooperation. The political autonomy of citizens, their democratic self-ruling, is subordinated to this goal.

This conception of political community and political life is too thin for communitarian critics. According to Taylor, this conception underestimates the necessity of a 'strong' identification of the citizen with his or her community and overlooks the fact that a democratic society can be held together only by a common *ethos* based on the ethical consciousness of a common past and future. This 'republican thesis' leads Taylor to question whether an 'overlapping consensus' or even more so a '*modus vivendi*' (cf. Larmore 1987:ch. 3; Ackerman 1989) between ethical communities is strong enough to guarantee the kind of identification that is necessary for a participatory democratic society. According to Taylor and MacIntyre (1984), patriotism is a healthy sign of the connection between individual and collective identity. Of course, this patriotism is more than a 'constitutional patriotism': '[W]e have to remember that patriotism involves more than converging moral principles; it is a common allegiance to a particular historical community. Cherishing and sustaining this has to be a common goal, and this is more than just consensus on the rule of right. Put differently, patriotism involves beyond convergent values a love of the particular' (Taylor 1989b:176). Because a political community is much more than a 'heap' of legal persons, it must be based on a stronger ethical-political unity, i.e., on a 'substantial moral practice' (*substantielle Sittlichkeit*) in Hegel's sense.[9]

In this way Taylor (as well as MacIntyre and Sandel) questions the liberal separation between 'state' and 'community': not only the ethical communities that arise in plural forms are constitutive for the formation of identities, but also and especially the political community. In fact, this very community is normatively integrated through conceptions of the good, from which specific virtues like patriotism are derived. To be sure, Taylor does not doubt that the notion of a free subjectivity, secured also in terms of rights, is among the values central to the self-understanding of modern societies. He only doubts whether this is sufficient to integrate a political community in normative terms. The language of a political community cannot be only universalistic, it must also be a particular and idiomatic one. Political unity is then thought of not as a 'social union of social unions', but as a unity based on cultural – and therefore, on pre-political – commonalities.

While this emphasis upon a substantial ethos of democracy criticizes the lack of identification among citizens in liberal theory, Benjamin Barber's theory of a 'strong democracy' stresses the necessity of participatory forms of exercising political autonomy (Barber 1984). His proposal is not based on a strong ethical view of the political community, but rather on an ethical understanding of citizenship and of the 'transformative' power of democratic discourse. In discourses, the private *bourgeois* turns into a community-oriented *citoyen* whose individual will is fused with the general will. By means of participation in the democratic process the identity of a citizen changes, in the same way as the identity of a bachelor is changed by the experience of marital life (Barber 1989:63f.).

In his reflections on citizenship and civil society, Michael Walzer has criticized both of these communitarian positions: the Hegelian substantialist thesis of an ethically integrated political community as well as the Rousseauian participatory view of democracy as the self-rule of a political body with one comprehensive will that unites all the virtuous citizens. The substantialist communitarianism overlooks the fact that a pluralistic society is not integrated anymore on the basis of a conception of the good common to all, but consists of a plurality of cultural and ethnic communities that form a political community in which membership can be defined only in terms of belonging to a political and not to an ethical collective (Walzer 1990b). Rousseauian communitarianism, on the other hand, does not realize that political life cannot raise a claim to be the good life. Given the fact that personal life develops in a variety of activities and associations which have taken up the political function of shaping opinions and the will, one can see that the view of a 'body of the people' with one will and opinion has to be given up (Walzer 1991). Ethical and political life are no longer unified, and the common tie that binds the citizens has worn thin.

According to the feminist critique, however, this bond is still too 'strong' and exclusivist, even in its liberal form. In their attempt to keep the public language of a political community safe from the ethical 'struggle of gods and demons', liberal theories perpetuate the separation between private and public issues which renders relations of power within the family, at the workplace, or in other social institutions inviolable (Benhabib 1989). On the other hand, communitarian theories of Hegelian and Rousseauian provenance exclude those identities which neither correspond to the supposedly general and collective identity nor want to be integrated into a (traditionally male) 'national body' (see the critique of Barber by Young 1990). Against the false affirmation of identities, feminist theorists propose an open model of political discourse that avoids both liberal and communitarian forms of exclusion. In this model, the public language among citizens consists above all in the very act of questioning this language (see Fraser 1990).

Is there a theory of a 'civil society' or a 'deliberative democracy' which brings together the valid concerns of liberal, communitarian and feminist theories? These concerns are: the emphasis on social pluralism and on personal liberties, the emphasis on the necessity of a solidary identification of citizens and of democratic self-rule, and finally the emphasis on the struggles and conflicts within a society. Recent theories of 'civil society' are differentiated according to these perspectives: they either emphasize the discursive constitution and affirmation of a collective identity (Cohen & Arato 1992:ch. 8) or the virtues of citizens (Shils 1991 and Taylor 1991) or the integration through conflict (Rödel, Frankenberg & Dubiel 1989). Also the theories of 'deliberative democracy' can be found in a more republican (Sunstein 1988 and Michelman 1988) or more proceduralist version (Habermas 1992:ch. VII and 600ff.; Manin 1987; Joshua Cohen 1989; Baynes 1992). While the former is focused on the process of the 'purification' of the citizens themselves in communal political practice, the latter is concerned with the 'laundering' of arguments in discourses of public justification, implying weaker assumptions regarding the political unity and virtues of citizens.

The conception of a form of political community that mediates between political identity and social difference as well as between consensus and conflict presupposes, therefore, a complex theory of recognition among citizens. Citizens must recognize each other not only as 'different' ethical persons with equal claims to rights as legal persons, but also as fully equal co-citizens – in a double sense.

On the one hand, they are equal in relation to their chances to participate in democratic processes in which all citizens can have a voice and must be willing to express their arguments and defend them with reciprocal and general reasons. This implies certain 'dialogical virtues' of equal respect, of openness to argumentation (taking the perspective of others into account), and of the possibility of accepting convincing grounds or of finding fair compromises. Moreover, it also requires that citizens be willing not only to take responsibility for one another in the sense that they 'respond' to each other, but also that they take responsibility for the actions of their political community in relation to third parties. In this case, the necessary form of political-collective identification with respect to those affected by political actions in the past and future is morally called for.[10]

On the other hand, citizens must not only accept all justified claims to recognition, but also *realize* them in practice in a solidary way. They must grant to one another the rights and means that are necessary for a fully equal membership in social life. This not only calls for political rights, but also for social rights that make it possible for citizens to live in a political community 'without shame' (Sen 1987:17). Concerning this point Rawls and Walzer agree: the aim of distributive justice is to allow for a life of self-respect and social recognition (Rawls 1971:§ 67; Walzer 1983:278). This reveals that even though the conditions for becoming a member of a pluralistic political community are not ethically demanding in the sense of a specific cultural or ethnic background, political membership is quite demanding with respect to the necessary solidary forms of the realization of the rights of this membership.

Out of these dimensions of recognition, implied in a complex theory of political and social justice, we can determine the functions of political discourses: they provide *fora* in which claims to recognition (to certain rights and resources) are raised and in which given structures of power are criticized; at the same time they provide *fora* in which these claims can be discussed and criticized in order to come to political decisions; and they also provide *fora* in which citizens grant one another the necessary means for the realization of this recognition, and take responsibility to apply their decisions into practice. A political community must be capable of integrating these functions of conflict, consensus, compromise, and solidarity, finding appropriate institutions for these purposes.[11]

The recognition that citizens owe to one another on grounds of justice is to be conceived, therefore, neither in ethical terms, as suggested by communitarians, nor according to the model of the mutual recognition of legal persons, as liberal theories emphasize. The specific form of mutual recognition as citizens implies:

1 the respect and tolerance of 'different' forms of life, as a reflection upon the pluralism of ethical communities which implies the mutual guarantee of subjective rights to freedom;[12]

2 the mutual recognition as a person to whom one has the duty to provide reasons for political arguments and claims (as author and as addressee of such claims) and with whom one has to take common responsibility for political decisions and their consequences for co-citizens as well as other affected persons.

3 It further implies that no citizen should be excluded from complete membership in a political community on ethical, social or political grounds, and that specific social goods are necessary in order to be an equal member of such a community. Which goods these are and what kind of distribution is justifiable cannot, however, be determined with the help of the notions of 'self-respect' or 'full membership' alone; rather, this has to be determined in political discourses in which the socially 'worst off' should have a veto right. In this sense, Rawls' 'difference principle' is the most adequate principle for determining social justice in a democratic society.

It is important to stress that the claims to recognition by citizens and the claims to the realization of their subjective rights to freedom as well as of their political and social rights are not based upon an ethical system of values that is shared by all citizens or on an anthropological ideal of recognition. Rather, they have to be understood within a recursive and discursive conception of justified political and social relations between citizens.[13] A 'civil society' deserves such a name according to the measure of the realization of these dimensions of recognition, in which communitarian and liberal concerns are taken up.

Universalism and contextualism

In ethical and legal-political relations of recognition, persons are integrated as members of communities according to different values or norms – on the basis of ethical self-understandings, mutual rights, and common belonging to a state. Persons are, then, esteemed as ethical persons, respected as legal persons, and regarded as co-citizens in each of these dimensions.

These three dimensions can be found in Kant's analysis of the 'civil state' [*bürgerlicher Zustand*], which is still a helpful starting point for the conceptualization of a political community. Kant first mentions the '*freedom* of every member of society as a human being', i.e., the ethical person in his or her striving after 'happiness' [*Glückseligkeit*]; second, the '*equality* of each member with every other as a *subject*', i.e., the equal rights of legal persons to be ruled according to general laws; and finally, the '*independence* of every member of the commonwealth as a citizen', i.e., the citizen as 'co-legislator' [*Mitgesetzgeber*], as co-author of the law (Kant 1793:72). But, for Kant, with these three aspects the question concerning the rights and duties of persons is not yet exhaustively answered. For him it is necessary to differentiate between ethical and legal-political values, norms, rights and duties (in relation to persons as members of ethical or political communities), and *moral* norms, rights, and duties of moral persons in general. Differently from being an ethical or legal-political person, a moral person is primarily a member of the all-encompassing community of humans: he or she represents 'bare' humanity in his or her person. The unconditional universality of the moral law transcends, according to Kant, the limits of ethical and political communities; the principle of moral justification is a principle of the recognition of each person as an autonomous author and addressee of moral claims. This form of recognition is the most basic: the recognition of persons as representatives of a community of human beings who deserve respect as moral persons, whatever their concrete (ethical or legal) identity may be.

'Autonomy' can, therefore, be understood differently in each practical context: in the ethical sense (as self-realization), or in the legal sense (as personal freedom of action within the framework of law), in the sense of political autonomy (as democratic self-legislation), or as moral autonomy (as action according to universally justifiable norms) (cf, Forst 1996). Translated into the terms of a theory of recognition and of the principle of general and reciprocal justification of valid norms, moral autonomy means that persons, as moral agents, have the duty of respecting other persons affected by their actions and of giving appropriate reasons for their moral legitimacy. Put differently, moral persons have the right to be recognized in their person as representing humanity and to demand the normative justification of those actions that affect them. Kant's central principle of always treating moral persons as ends in themselves means, therefore, that every human being has a basic moral right to reciprocal and general justification. The legitimate and non-abstract core of the idea of an 'ideal community of communication' consists precisely in the 'duty to present a justification' of moral claims to everyone affected (cf. Apel 1973:425), i.e., to *each* individual and *concrete* moral person (cf. O'Neill 1989:ch. 11). The word 'each' has the double sense of an encompassing universality and at the same time of individual concreteness. Without this form of 'universal' and at the same time concrete recognition of others the concept of 'human rights', for example, becomes empty. In this sense, moral rights which are not reasonable to reject constitute the normative core of the 'legal person'; however, these rights must be concretely defined and put into practice through positive law in a politically autonomous manner.

In the work of Hannah Arendt, whose republican theory of public freedom can be taken as a forerunner of communitarianism, one finds a very strong argument for the necessity of a basic human form of recognition as well as the emphasis on the necessity of legally securing this moral recognition in the form of membership in a political community. The fate of stateless persons deprived of their citizenship has shown, according to Arendt, that human rights represent an unconditional moral demand. Nevertheless, they must be translated into the basic 'right to have rights', into the security of being a member of a political community that institutionalizes these rights. Only then, she believed, is it possible to prevent 'crimes against humanity', in which those deprived of their rights and citizenship were not even counted anymore as members of the moral human community. The concept of 'crimes against humanity' is then meaningful, only if humanity itself be seen as a community before which actions must be justified, and only if the members of such a community be respected in their dignity, i.e., in their 'abstract nakedness of being human' (Arendt 1949:762).

This form of recognition escapes the communitarian perspective which places normative obligations only within an ethical community. In this regard MacIntyre is most explicit. For him the concept of human rights is meaningless, since it locates moral norms in an abstract realm of humanity which is, according to him, empty. There are no moral, but only ethical persons; there are no moral judgments that transcend the values of a community in which subjects learn what is good or right in the first place. Universalist conceptions of morality imply the notion of contextless moral persons who would not even be in the condition to know what it means to be a member of a community and to know about moral problems (MacIntyre 1981:69f. and 1988). There is, however, a fallacy in believing that persons cannot have moral duties (or, in epistemological terms, that they cannot know of such duties) which transcend the particular contexts in which individuals first learn and for the most part follow the standards of morality in a 'thick' form connected to a way of life – i.e., that humans *qua* members of a 'context of humanity' cannot have moral duties towards each other person. Moral norms are always embedded in specific ethical and political communities, but they do not end at the limits of these communities.[14]

Walzer's theory is an example of an attempt to connect moral universalism with the particularity and historicity of social conceptions of the good. He distinguishes between moral-general and particular-social, especially distributive, justice, because 'distributive justice is not the whole of morality, it does not even cover the spectrum of justice' (Walzer 1992:291 [transl. R.F.]; see also 1983:XV and 1994). Leaving aside the problem that Walzer's reconstruction of the 'spheres' of distributive justice does not (against his own claim) follow a particularistic form of argumentation, but is dependent upon a certain ideal of full membership in a democratic community (cf. now Walzer 1993a), he leaves no doubt that each 'maximalist' morality within a concrete community must also contain a 'minimal' core of mutual respect, i.e. a 'minimal and universalistic moral code'. This consists in a morality with respect to persons in general, for whom a shelter in a 'Hilton Hotel' would have to be guaranteed in order to protect their basic moral rights (Cf. Walzer 1987:15f., 24f.; 1994:1ff.). While the minimal moral standard does not substitute the maximalist morality of houses arranged and furnished in a particular way, the latter must not fall below this standard either. Although moral norms do not fully absorb the values and self-understandings of the local 'inhabitants', they do demand that the local morality respects foreigners (and, of course, the members of its own community) as autonomous moral persons in the sense explained above.

Insofar as Walzer considers individual *and* collective self-determination as universal values that are 'reiterated' in a variety of ways (cf. Walzer 1990c:518f.), the question about possible conflicts between individual and collective autonomy arises. He answers unambiguously with a theory of the primacy of individual rights: all rights of communities and states to secure their integrity and sovereignty 'derive ultimately from the rights of individuals' which are 'entailed by our sense of what it means to be a human being' (1977:53f.). Collective self-determination based on individual self-determination means the common establishment and arrangement of a particular moral home following truly and generally 'shared' (and not imposed) understandings. No 'social construction' of communally accepted values and practices can bypass the normative status of moral persons:

'We might say [...] that the construction of social-construction-with-human-agents has certain moral entailments. Among these is the right of subjective nullification, the right of the agents to refuse any given object status – as commodities, "hands", slaves, or whatever' (1993b:173).

As Walzer tries to ground a (minimal) universalistic morality on the basis of general human experiences in a *quasi* empirical and 'inductive' way, he implicitly presupposes, as much as Taylor does, the basic moral principle of respect for the autonomy of moral persons. According to Taylor, this principle is one of the 'strong' ethical values constitutive of the modern identity (1989a:6ff.; 1986). But, whereas Walzer needs to provide a criterion that explains in which way (subjective) morally relevant experiences lead to justified (intersubjective) moral claims, Taylor has to explain why the value of human dignity should have a special status amidst the variety of goods to be found in modern identity and why it has normative obligatory power also for those persons who do not have a 'modern' identity. To show this, it is insufficient to say that this is a strong value 'for us'. Moreover, even within the 'spirit' of modernity one could not claim the categorical authority of the principle of moral respect if this authority were dependent on the possibility that a person ethically identifies herself with the good of autonomy. For, normatively speaking, a person *must* respect the moral integrity of others independent of whether this demand is anchored in his or her horizon of values. Moral *rights* cannot be reduced to ethical *values*, since the former *must* be recognized by all moral persons while the latter *can* be accepted by persons according to their individual self-understanding (and their validity is dependent on this acceptance). The fact that a 'minimal' morality is mostly part of a 'maximalist' ethics of 'local people' or of a 'vision of the good' does not mean that it applies only to those locals who share this vision. The right of a moral person to demand that others justify those actions which affect his or her integrity is a right to be claimed *in* contexts of mutual recognition, but which at the same time *transcends* concrete contexts in its universal validity. As such, this right is based on the principle of practical reason, according to which general norms are to be justified generally and reciprocally. This notion of practical and justificational reason does not have 'ultimate' reasons at its disposal, rather, it reacts to the lack of such fundamental grounds. Reason does not speak for or represent concrete persons but only gives them the right to demand reasons. The moral point of view is not sufficiently explained by finding an answer to the question as to what *I* can identify with, but by answering the question concerning what can be justified *reciprocally* and *generally*.

With this conception of moral recognition a fourth dimension of personhood that plays an important role in the debate between liberals and communitarians is revealed. The conceptions of person and of community that are at the center of each specific level of this debate – ethical and legal person, citizen, and moral person, and the corresponding notions of community – are to be normatively differentiated, therefore, as dimensions of what it means to be recognized as a person in various practical contexts. What matters most is to see that, despite their multifarious and complex interdependence, none of these spheres may substitute the other: ethical relations cannot take the place of law and morality, and vice-versa. Therefore, the question as to *which person* and *which kind of community* ought to be central to a theory of justice should not be answered in an one-dimensional, either liberal or communitarian, way. Persons are always members of different communities and are at the center of different normative obligations to justify their actions. It is thus not an ideal of the fully recognized person that lies at the center of the analysis of four contexts of recognition, but a reconstruction of four contexts – ethical, legal, political and moral – of justification and their corresponding criteria of validity (cf. Forst 1994:ch. V). Rather than speaking of a priority of the right or the good, this analysis presupposes the priority of the principle of reasonable, context-related justification; and only in this way can it be the basis for a theory of justice. A theory that aims at completeness has to do justice to all these *contexts of justice*; it has to show where the 'good' or the 'right' provide appropriate answers to a normative question.

(Translated from the German by Amós Nascimento & Rainer Forst)

Notes

1 I have developed a more elaborated view of these theoretical levels in Forst (1994). In what follows I draw upon this view – often in a very abbreviated way.
2 Cf. the notion of a 'situated' self in Taylor (1979:15) and (1985a).
3 On the notion of the moral person see especially Rawls (1971:§§ 4, 77).
4 In 'Atomism' (1985b) Taylor misses this point.
5 See Spelman (1978), Darwall (1978). Especially informative is the analysis of different forms of recognition (love, law, solidarity) by Honneth (1992:ch. 5).

6 In this sense, Hannah Arendt – alluding to the meaning of the Latin word *persona* as 'mask' – speaks of the 'protecting mask of a legal personality' (1965:108).

7 The insufficient distinction between questions of justice and questions concerning the good forced Nagel to take back his epistemological argument (1991:163, n. 49).

8 See the discussion in Forst (1994:ch. I.1). For theories of general justification cf. Waldron (1987), Larmore (1987) and Ackerman (1989). The problem with Ackerman and Larmore, however, is their strict dichotomic separation between ethical values and general norms. This seems to reduce the process of argumentative generalization to a minimization of conflicts by means of the appeal to a minimal normative consensus.

9 Cf. Hegel, *Grundlinien der Philosophie des Rechts*, § 273 and Taylor (1979:133ff.). Cf. also the model of a community integrated through rights and the model of a participatory political community in Taylor (1989b).

10 This point is stressed by MacIntyre (1984), even though he does not present an adequate moral basis of that kind of moral responsibility.

11 This is the starting point for a critical theory of democracy. See Offe (1989); Offe & Preuss (1991); Buchstein (1992).

12 In Taylor's 'The Politics of Recognition' (1992) there is a detailed discussion of different aspects of political recognition. His attempt to connect the recognition of ethical difference and the recognition of the equal dignity of citizens leads him to a plead for the recognition of the distinction of Quebec and its claim to cultural self-preservation. What remains for those who are not francophones within Quebec then is the protection of their 'different' identity by means of basic liberal rights, while the whole political community of Canada is presented according to a 'thin' liberal procedural model. Both points contradict Taylor's thesis that a procedural liberalism is 'inhospitable to difference'. On the one hand, Taylor is therefore forced to include a procedural liberalism in his conception of a politics of good life (within Quebec) in a stronger way than he would admit, while on the other hand he leaves indeterminate how the limits between personal liberty and the demands to 'cultural preservation' are to be drawn in a specific community without leading to new forms of discrimination. Given the cases he discusses, one may question whether the ethical and cultural identity of immigrants, for example, is treated justly.

13 Herein lies the main methodological difference between the above account and Axel Honneth's elaborate theory of recognition based upon a formal, yet teleological and anthropological conception of three dimensions of recognition. Cf. Honneth (1992) as well as my critique and proposal of four contexts of justice and recognition (Forst 1994:ch. V.3). The main problem of Honneth's approach lies in its lack of both adequate *criteria* to justify claims to recognition in terms of reciprocal justice and a reason for the morally *binding* character of norms of justice if they are merely understood as part of a theory

of the good. Apart from this general difference, Honneth's conception of political recognition as solidary esteem 'in light of values [...] that make it possible to see the capabilities and characteristics of each other person as meaningful for the common practices' (Honneth 1992:209f.; 1993) differs from the one I propose here. Compared to the ethical esteem of a particular person (on the basis of a shared conception of the good), political recognition is more formal. It is a 'second-order esteem', to be understood as a sense of mutual responsibility that enables the development of ethical communities (as well as of ethical recognition) without political and social exclusion, while not itself being a form of ethical recognition.

14 The debates about the question of international justice show to which extent the context of humanity is an important context of justice (cf. O'Neill 1991).

References

Ackerman, B. (1989), 'Why Dialogue?', *The Journal of Philosophy* 86, 5-22.

Apel, K.-O. (1973), 'Das Apriori der Kommunikationsgemeinschaft und die Grundlagen der Ethik', *Transformation der Philosophie* 2, Suhrkamp: Frankfurt.

Arendt, H. (1949), 'Es gibt nur ein einziges Menschenrecht', *Die Wandlung*, 754-770.

— (1965), *On Revolution*, Viking Press: New York.

Aristotle, *Nichomachean Ethics*, Oxford University Press [1923]: Oxford.

Barber, B. (1984), *Strong Democracy*, University of California Press: Berkeley.

— (1989), 'Liberal Democracy and the Costs of Consent', in Rosenblum, N. (ed.), *Liberalism and the Moral Life*, Harvard University Press, Cambridge (MA).

Baynes, K. (1992), 'Liberal Neutrality, Pluralism, and Deliberative Politics', *Praxis International* 12, 50-69.

Benhabib, S. (1989), 'Liberal Dialogue versus a Critical Theory of Discursive Legitimation', in Rosenblum, N. (ed.), *Liberalism and the Moral Life*, Harvard University Press, Cambridge (MA).

Buchstein, H. (1992), 'Perspektiven kritischer Demokratietheorie', *Prokla* 86, 115-136.

Cohen, Jean and Arato, A. (1992), *Civil Society and Political Theory*, MIT Press: Cambridge (MA).

Cohen, Joshua (1989) 'Deliberation and Democratic Legitimacy', in Hamlin, A. and Petit, Ph. (eds.), *The Good Polity*, Oxford University Press: Oxford.

Darwall, St. (1977/78), 'Two Kinds of Respect', *Ethics* 88, 36-49.

Dworkin, R. (1990), 'Foundations of Liberal Equality', in Peterson, G.B. (ed.), *The Tanner Lectures on Human Values* XI, University of Utah Press: Salt Lake City.

Forst, R. (1994), *Kontexte der Gerechtigkeit. Politische Philosophie jenseits von Liberalismus und Kommunitarismus*, Suhrkamp: Frankfurt.

— (1996), 'Politische freiheit', in *Deutsche Zeitschrift für Philosophie* 44, 211-227.

Forst, R. (1997a), 'Gerechtigkeit als Fairneß: ethisch, politisch oder moralisch?', in Philosophische Gesellschaft Bad Homburg & Hinsch, W. (Hrsg.) *Zur Idee des politischen Liberalismus. John Rawls in der Diskussion*, Suhrkamp: Frankfurt.

— (1997b), 'Foundations of a Theory of Multicultural Justice' in *Constellations* 4, 63-71.

Fraser, N. (1989), *Unruly Practices*, Minnesota University Press, Minneapolis.

— (1990), 'Rethinking the Public Sphere: A Contribution to the Critique of Actually Existing Democracy', *Social Text* 8/9, 56-80.

Friedman, M. (1990), 'Feminism and Modern Friendship: Dislocating the Community', in Sunstein, C. (ed.), *Feminism and Political Theory*, Chicago University Press: Chicago.

Galston, W. (1991), *Liberal Purposes*, Cambridge University Press: Cambridge.

Habermas, J. (1983), 'Diskursethik: Notizen zu einem Begründungsprogramm', *Moralbewußtsein and kommunikatives Handeln*, Suhrkamp: Frankfurt.

— (1991), 'Vom pragmatischen, ethischen und moralischen Gebrauch der praktischen Vernunft', *Erläuterungen zur Diskursethik*, Suhrkamp: Frankfurt.

— (1992), *Faktizität und Geltung. Beiträge zur Diskurstheorie des Rechts und des demokratischen Rechtsstaats*, Suhrkamp: Frankfurt.

Hegel, G.W.F. (1821), *Grundlinien der Philosophie des Rechts*, Ullstein [1972]: Frankfurt, Berlin, & Vienna.

Honneth, A. (1992), *Kampf um Anerkennung. Zur moralischen Grammatik sozialer Konflikte*, Surhkamp: Frankfurt.

— (1993), 'Posttraditionale Gemeinschaften. Ein konzeptueller Vorschlag', in Brumlik, M. and Brunkhorst, H. (Hg.), *Gemeinschaft und Gerechtigkeit*, Fischer: Frankfurt.

Kant, I. (1793), 'On the Proverb: That May Be True in Theory, But Is of No Practical Use', *Perpetual Peace and Other Essays*, Hackett [1985]: Indianapolis.

Korsgaard, C. (1993), 'The Reasons We Can Share: An Attack on the Distinction Between Agent-Relative And Agent-Neutral Values', *Social Philosophy & Policy* 10, 24-51.

Kymlicka, W. (1990), *Contemporary Political Theory*, Clarendon: Oxford.

— (1992), 'Two Models of Pluralism and Tolerance', *Analyse & Kritik* 14, 33-56.

Larmore, Ch. (1987), *Patterns of Moral Complexity*, Cambridge University Press: Cambridge.

Macedo, St. (1990), *Liberal Virtues*, Oxford University Press: Oxford.

MacIntyre, A. (1981), *After Virtue*, Duckworth [2nd ed., 1985]: London.

— (1984), *Is Patriotism a Virtue?*, The University of Kansas: Lawrence (KS).

— (1988), *Whose Justice? Which Rationality?*, Duckworth: London.

MacKinnon, C. (1989), *Toward a Feminist Theory of the State*, Harvard University Press: Cambridge (MA).

Manin, B. (1987), 'On Legitimacy and Political Deliberation', *Political Theory* 15, 338-368.

Marneffe, P. de (1990), 'Liberalism, Liberty and Neutrality', *Philosophy and Public Affairs* 19, 253-274.

Michelman, F. (1988), 'Law's Republic', *Yale Law Journal*, 97 1493-1537.
Minow, M. (1990), *Making all the Difference*, Cornell University Press: Ithaca (NY).
Nagel, Th. (1987), 'Moral Conflict and Political Legitimacy', *Philosophy and Public Affairs* 16, 215-240.
— (1991), *Equality and Partiality*, Oxford University Press: Oxford.
Offe, C. (1989), 'Bindung, Fessel, Bremse. Die Unübersichtlichkeit von Selbstbeschränkungsformeln', in Honneth, A., McCarthy, Th., Offe, C. and Wellmer, A. (Hrsg.), *Zwischenbetrachtungen. Im Prozeß der Aufklärung*, Suhrkamp: Frankfurt.
Offe, C. and Preuß, U.K. (1991), 'Democratic Institutions and Moral Resources', in Held, D. (ed.), *Political Theory Today*, Stanford University Press: Stanford.
Okin, S.M. (1989), *Justice, Gender, and the Family*, Basic Books: New York.
O'Neill, O. (1989), *Constructions of Reason. Explorations of Kant's Practical Philosophy*, Cambridge University Press: Cambridge.
– (1991), 'Transnational Justice', in Held, D. (ed.), *Political Theory Today*, Stanford University Press: Stanford.
Rawls, J. (1971), *A Theory of Justice*, Harvard University Press: Cambridge (MA).
— (1980), 'Kantian Constructivism in Moral Theory', *The Journal of Philosophy* 77, 515-72.
— (1985), 'Justice as Fairness: Political not Metaphysical', *Philosophy and Public Affairs* 14, 223-51.
— (1987), 'The Idea of an Overlapping Consensus', *Oxford Journal of Legal Studies* 7, 1-25.
— (1988), 'The Priority of Right and Ideas of the Good', *Philosophy and Public Affairs* 17, 251-76.
— (1993), *Political Liberalism*, Columbia University Press: New York.
Raz, J. (1986), *The Morality of Freedom*, Oxford University Press: Oxford.
Rödel, U., Frankenberg, G. and Dubiel, H. (1989), *Die demokratische Frage*, Suhrkamp: Frankfurt.
Rössler, B. (1992), 'Der ungleiche Wert der Freiheit. Aspekte feministischer Kritik am Liberalismus und Kommunitarismus', *Analyse & Kritik* 14, 86-113.
Sandel, M. (1982), *Liberalism and the Limits of Justice*, Cambridge University Press: Cambridge.
— (1989), 'Moral Argument and Liberal Toleration: Abortion and Homosexuality', *California Law Review* 77, 521-538.
Scanlon, T. (1982), 'Contractualism and Utilitarianism', in Sen, A. and Williams, B. (eds.), *Utilitarianism and Beyond*, Cambridge University Press: Cambridge.
Sen, A. (1987), *The Standard of Living*, Cambridge University Press: Cambridge.
Shils, E. (1991), 'Was ist eine Civil Society?', in Michalski, K. (Hrsg.), *Europa und die Civil Society*, Klett-Cotta: Stuttgart.
Spelman, E. (1978), 'On Treating Persons as Persons', in *Ethics* 88, 150-161.
Sunstein, C. (1988), 'Beyond the Republican Revival', *Yale Law Journal* 97, 1539-1590.

Taylor, Ch. (1979), *Hegel and Modern Society*, Cambridge University Press: Cambridge.
— (1985a), 'What is human agency?', *Human Agency and Language* [Philosophical Papers I], Cambridge University Press: Cambridge.
— (1985b), 'Atomism', *Philosophy and the Human Sciences* [Philosophical Papers II], Cambridge University Press: Cambridge.
— (1986), 'Die Motive einer Verfahrensethik', in Kuhlmann, W. (Hg.), *Moralität und Sittlichkeit*, Suhrkamp: Frankfurt.
— (1989a), *Sources of the Self. The Making of the Modern Identity*, Harvard University Press: Cambridge (MA).
— (1989b), 'Cross-purposes: The Liberal-Communitarian Debate', in Rosenblum, N. (ed.), *Liberalism and the Moral Life*, Harvard University Press: Cambridge (MA).
— (1991), 'Die Beschwörung der Civil Society' in Michalski, K. (Hrsg.), *Europa und die Civil Society*, Klett-Cotta: Stuttgart.
— (1992), 'The Politics of Recognition', in A. Gutman (ed.), *Multiculturalism and the 'Politics of Recognition'*, Princeton University Press: Princeton.
Waldron, J. (1987), 'Theoretical Foundations of Liberalism', *The Philosophical Quarterly* 37, 127-150.
Walzer, M. (1977), *Just and Unjust Wars* [new ed., 1992], Basic Books: New York.
— (1983), *Spheres of Justice*, Basic Books: New York.
— (1987), *Interpretation and Social Criticism*, Harvard University Press: Cambridge (MA).
— (1990a), 'The Communitarian Critique of Liberalism', *Political Theory* 18, 6-23.
— (1990b), 'What Does It Mean to Be an 'American'?', *Social Research* 57, 591-614.
— (1990c), 'Nation and Universe', in Peterson, G.B. (ed.), *The Tanner Lectures on Human Values XI*, University of Utah Press: Salt Lake City.
— (1991), 'The Idea of Civil Society', *Dissent*, Spring 1991, 293-304.
— (1992), 'Chantal Mouffe im Gespräch mit Michael Walzer', *Prokla* 87, 286-297.
— (1993a), 'Exclusion, Injustice, and the Democratic State', *Dissent*, Winter 1993, 55-64.
— (1993b), 'Objectivity and Social Meaning', in Nussbaum, M. & Sen, A. (eds.), *The Quality of Life*, Oxford University Press: Oxford.
— (1994), *Thick and Thin. Moral Argument at Home and Abroad*, University of Notre Dame Press: Notre Dame.
Young, I. (1990), 'Polity and Group Difference: A Critique of the Ideal of Universal Citizenship', in Sunstein, C. (ed.), *Feminism and Political Theory*, University of Chicago Press: Chicago.

Plurality and cognitivism in light of Anglo American pragmatism

3 Pluralism and universalism in discourse ethics

Cristina Lafont

The universalist core of discourse ethics rests on the possibility of defending the cognitive status of moral questions. From the outset Habermas has argued for this possibility by underscoring the analogy between questions about moral rightness and questions about truth. Without a doubt, the scope of this analogy is controversial. Habermas himself has repeatedly warned against an all too strong parallel (or even assimilation) between these two different kinds of questions. It is not always clear from his own explanations to exactly what extent these two kinds of questions are similar – and evidently to settle this would be an extremely difficult task. But recently, as a result of Thomas McCarthy's (1991 and more recently 1996) criticism of Habermas, it has become apparent that at least some of the common features underlying the logic of moral questions and the logic of questions about truth have to be pinned down if the universalist core of discourse ethics is to be defensible at all. In reply to McCarthy, Habermas (1996a) has brought together these central features under the heading 'the premise of "a single right answer"'. A defense of the cognitive status of moral questions necessarily involves showing that, to (clearly stated) moral questions, there can only be 'a single right answer' – just as we suppose to be the case for questions about truth. That there is something to be known about certain questions means that there is a fact of the matter as to their answers, that what can be known is either one way or the other – and therefore it cannot be the case that an answer and its opposite are both correct.

However, against this – I think, unavoidable – consequence, McCarthy argues that the premise of 'a single right answer' involves, as a 'regulative idea' for moral discourse, that there has to be only *a single correct interpretation* of moral questions. Thus the premise implies excluding certain kinds of pluralism and disagreement as perfectly rational alternatives to rational agreement on practical questions.

In what follows I will try to question this implication by showing that it follows only from the peculiar way in which Habermas has tried to defend the 'premise of "a single right answer"'. It seems to me, though, that it is perfectly possible on the basis of Habermas' account of communicative rationality to specify the content of this premise in such a way, that the unwelcome consequences pointed out by McCarthy can be avoided and still maintain the universalist sense of moral questions. This amounts to an attempt to determine to what extent pluralism can have a place in a universalist perspective on moral questions.

My argument is structured in three steps. First, I will try to specify the common presuppositions implicit in the use of normative terms such as 'truth' and moral 'rightness'. Showing their structural similarities will help to justify the correctness of 'the premise of "a single right answer"'[1] espoused by Habermas. Second, I will briefly refer to Putnam's defense of the possibility of a plurality of interpretations for theoretical questions concerning truth. This defense allows us to see in which sense a pluralism could also be accepted for practical questions of moral rightness without undermining their universal dimension. Finally, in order to defend this point it will be necessary to distinguish two different senses in which 'the premise of "a single right answer"' can be understood. Once these two senses are distinguished the apparent incompatibility between universalism and pluralism vanishes.

Cognitivism and universalism

Habermas' *cognitivist* account of moral questions relies on a formal-pragmatic reconstruction of the communicative rationality implicit in everyday communication practices. More precisely, it draws on the structural similarities of these practices when questions about truth and moral rightness arise. Whenever we make assertions concerning these kinds of questions, we claim that our assertions are *justified*. This only makes sense if we presuppose that such questions can be decided in a rational way, that there is a correct answer to them which can be *known*. Consequently, a cognitivist position has to provide an account of the internal relationship between knowledge and justification (or rational acceptability).

Habermas' formal-pragmatic analysis of the unavoidable presuppositions implicit in our communicative practices intends to show that knowledge is involved not only when we assert the truth of a statement but also when we defend the moral rightness of a norm. He argues for this position by showing that 'truth' and moral 'rightness' are both universal validity claims in so far as they can be (and usually are) redeemed in a theoretical or a practical discourse (i.e. the peculiar form of communication in which validity claims that have become problematic are examined for their justification).

The formal-pragmatic characterization of discourse is thus, at the same time, a discourse-theoretic interpretation of the notion of justification or rational acceptability. This shows that the rational acceptability of our knowledge becomes the more contingent on the rationality of our argumentation *procedures* the less it can rely on any *substantive content* a priori precluded from being problematized. In this sense, there is no essential difference between a theoretical and a practical discourse with respect to the *formal* features of rationally acceptable argumentation-procedures. The difference between them thus depends on the *content*, on the different senses of the notions of 'truth' and moral 'rightness': the knowledge involved in our assertions of true statements depends on the existence of certain states of affairs in the objective world, whereas the knowledge involved in our defense of morally right norms depends on the existence of generalizable interests shared by all the individuals in the social world. Habermas explains in his *Erläuterungen zur Diskursethik* (1991):

> Just as the assertoric mode can be explained through the fact that the asserted states of affairs exist, so the deontological mode can be explained through the fact that the demanded actions are in the common interest of all possibly affected (1991:130).

The parallel between the two kinds of questions, therefore, does not depend on an assimilation between the assertoric mode and the deontological mode of our speech acts. Rather, it depends on the possibility of looking for the right answer to these questions by means of our grasp of the *necessary and sufficient conditions* for the satisfaction of both validity claims. As much as we know the necessary and sufficient condition for 'truth', which can be expressed through the so-called 'Convention T': '"p" is true if and only if p', we know also the necessary and sufficient condition for moral 'rightness', which can be expressed through a 'moral principle': a norm N is morally right if and only if it is equally in everyone's interest.[2]

Grasping the meaning of these validity claims is what enables the participants in a theoretical or a practical discourse to know what they have to look for in them – what, from the point of view of the content, 'rationally acceptable' means in each case. But if we look at the discourse-theoretic explanations of the meaning of the validity claims 'truth' and moral 'rightness', we find that both become, in turn, dependent on a kind of condition very different from the ones mentioned before. For both are redefined in terms of the notion of 'idealized rational acceptability':

1 The validity claim 'truth' is redefined in the article 'Wahrheitstheorien' (1984b) in the following fashion: 'The truth condition of statements is the potential agreement of everyone else [..]. The truth of a proposition means the promise to reach a rational consensus over what is said' (1984b:137).

2 The validity claim to moral 'rightness'[3] is redefined by explaining[4] the moral principle mentioned before through the discourse principle: 'Just those action norms are valid to which all possibly affected persons could agree as participants in rational discourses' (1992:138).

The striking parallel between the definitions seems to be the evidence that gives support to Habermas' defense of the structural similarity between questions of truth and moral rightness. But, at the same time, it is precisely this parallelism that makes both redefinitions seem counterintuitive *as explanations of the meaning of 'truth' and moral 'rightness'*. Had we not been told before that the agreement in the first case has to be an agreement *on the existence of states of affairs in the objective world* and, in the second case, *on the generalizability of the interests* safeguarded by the norm at issue, we would have never known by means of the definitions just given alone how the participants in discourses can tell what they have to look for in these different cases.

The plausibility of these definition as explanations of *what may be considered rationally acceptable decision procedures concerning truth and moral rightness* (in posttraditional societies) gets lost if, at the same time, they are to be understood as explanations of *what 'truth' and moral 'rightness' mean*. But, if that is correct, the structural similarities between the two kinds of questions cannot be derived by way of assimilating 'truth' and moral 'rightness' to an 'idealized rational acceptability', as Habermas seems to suppose.[5] On the contrary, they show only the *internal* relationship between the two validity claims *and the claim of rational acceptability*. A defense of a cognitivist view of both kinds of questions consists precisely in an account of this internal connection.

As many critics have already remarked, the participants in a theoretical or practical discourse indeed need to know how to find out a right answer which could be accepted as correct by everyone. But whenever they find a valid answer, its validity is not derived from the agreement of the participants. On the contrary, the agreement of the participants, if it is to be considered as a rationally motivated agreement, has to be based on the satisfaction of the necessary and sufficient conditions mentioned before: they will have to believe that the statement in question is true not because everyone happens to agree to it, but *because* it expresses an existing state of affairs; similarly, if the norm in question is morally right, it is not because everyone agrees to it but *because* it is equally in everyone's interest (which is especially important to distinguish a *cognitivist* from a merely *decisionist* account of moral questions). Habermas seems to acknowledge this, when he explains in his 'Reply' (1996a):

> On the one hand, substantive reasons are what convince us that an outcome is right; on the other hand, the soundness of these reasons can be *demonstrated* only in real processes of argumentation, namely in defense against every objection that is actually raised (1996a:1508).

In light of this distinction, it seems clear that the internal connection between our validity claims and the discursive practices does not require defending the counterintuitive thesis that truth (or moral rightness) means or depends on argumentative agreement,[6] but rather acknowledging that our claims of truth or moral rightness are always already claims of *knowledge* as well. And the knowledge claims as such, depend not only on truth (or rightness) but, more importantly, on justification or rational acceptability.

Habermas' pragmatic analysis of the validity claims involved in our communicative practices indeed contains an account of the internal connection between knowledge and rational acceptability. This analysis shows that our commitment when we *assert* that a particular statement is true (or a particular norm is morally right) unavoidably goes beyond just the commitment to the truth of the statement or the validity of the norm. As Habermas explains in 'Wahrheitstheorien': 'truth is a validity claim that we attach to statements when we assert them [..] In asserting something I make the claim that the statement that I assert is true. *This claim I can make with reason or without reason*' (1984b:129, my emphasis).

What this pragmatic analysis of communication shows, thus, is the unavoidable interdependence[7] of *two* different claims involved in our speech acts: with them, as Habermas explains, we claim not only that the statement happens to be *true* (or the norm morally *right*), but – what is more important – that we *know* it, that we are justified in believing it and could, if necessary, redeem our claim with arguments. It is precisely due to this further claim to *knowledge* that it is not enough, for our assertion to be acceptable, that the statement happens to be true or the norm right. It is also required that we be able to justify here and now that this is the case.

It is precisely this further claim that compels us to enter, if necessary, into a theoretical or a practical discourse in which we prove our validity claims. In such a discourse, we prove the – never definitively redeemable – claim to the truth of the statement at issue (or to the moral rightness of the norm). But we do that by proving a redeemable knowledge claim, i.e. the claim that we are justified *here and now* in believing in the truth of a particular statement or in the moral rightness of a particular norm in light of the best available arguments (it may also happen that we see that our arguments are not yet good enough for deciding the question one way or the other).

The interdependence between 'truth' (or moral 'rightness') and 'rational acceptability' becomes evident if we pay attention to the components of our notion of 'knowledge'. As commonly expressed, the necessary and sufficient conditions[8] for establishing that someone knows something are the following:

S knows that P if and only if,
(1) S believes that P
(2) P is true
(3) S is justified in believing that P.[9]

The irreducibility of these conditions is evident: that my statement is *de facto* true (2) does not imply that I must know what is expressed in it, that is, that I can give reasons for my belief in it, and therefore that this statement is justified or rationally acceptable (3). Conversely, it is not sufficient that I have good reasons that support my belief in such a statement (3) for it to be true (2). However, the rationale of this irreducibility is perhaps not so evident. On the one hand, the irreducibility of truth to justification (or rational acceptability) expresses the context-transcendent validity of the former as opposed to the latter. This context-transcendence leaves open the possibility of finding out – perhaps later on, on the light of new information, a new interpretative strategy or even an entirely new categorization – a way of defending the validity of a particular statement or norm, which here and now appears to be utterly unjustifiable. On the other hand, the irreducibility of justification to truth is what compels us to *prove* our claims to truth (or moral rightness) to be acceptable as justified, and therefore it compels us to withdraw our *knowledge* claim as long as this proof is not available – as long as our reasons or justifications are not intersubjectively convincing.

In light of this classic analysis of the notion of knowledge, it becomes clear that is not necessary to defend the counterintuitive thesis that the truth of a statement depends on the possibility of agreement about it, in order to defend the evident thesis that our *knowledge* claims are dependent on argumentative practices, in which we prove the convincingness of our reasons and arguments by exposing them in a public discussion, to all the available counterarguments. As Habermas explains in his *Theory of Communicative Action*: 'the learning processes by which we acquire theoretical knowledge and moral insight, revise and extend our evaluative language, overcome self-deceptions and difficulties of understanding, depend on argumentative practices' (1984a:44). But, for this very reason, the argumentative practices which direct our learning processes can only *entitle* us to hold our beliefs as valid but not *guarantee*[10] their 'truth' or moral 'rightness'. As Habermas has recently pointed out: 'the rationality of a judgment does not imply its truth but only its justified acceptability in a given context' (1996b:69). It appears that in order to defend the view that our *knowledge*[11] claims are contingent on *rational acceptability* (as well as on truth or moral rightness), it is not necessary to maintain the counterintuitive position that truth and moral rightness themselves are also contingent on rational acceptability.

The central intuition of the discourse-theoretic interpretation of rational acceptability seems to be the following: as long as we do not have a direct access to truth (or to reality in itself) we are only left with the possibility to *infer the truth of our beliefs from the convincingness of our reasons*. Thus, someone is justified in believing something if his or her reasons are (or would be) convincing for everyone else, and unjustified if her reasons are merely subjective or idiosyncratic. Consequently, if the discourse theory is correct, we cannot but infer the convincingness of our reasons from the results of a discursive process taking place under the conditions of an ideal speech situation. Justification or rational acceptability in this inter-subjectivist sense is therefore essential to our epistemic practices in so far as it enables us to distinguish between reasonable and unreasonable ways of achieving knowledge. This is why we do not count a 'true belief' automatically as 'knowledge',[12] since 'knowledge' also involves an evaluation of the reliability of the way one acquires (and justifies) the beliefs at issue. In order to allow for the (more than likely) possibility of a general[13] mistake (and the subsequent learning process), to bear in mind that the inference mentioned before *can fail*, it is essential to avoid identifying 'justified belief' and 'knowledge'. This is the reason why our notion of 'knowledge' recognizes a logical gap between justification and truth (or moral rightness).

One of the essential factors that precludes the identification of the truth of the statement (or the moral rightness of the norm) with the rational acceptability of our assertion of it, is the *unconditional validity* that we suppose the former but not the latter to have. This difference goes back to two characteristic traits of our use of the notion of 'truth' (or moral 'rightness') – traits which cannot be found in the use of the notion of justification (or rational acceptability): first, the *binary* use of the opposition true/false (or just/unjust) in contrast to the *gradual* use of the notion of justification; second, the *fixed* character that we ascribe to truth (or moral rightness) in contrast to justification or rational acceptability, i.e. the fact that we consider truth or moral rightness properties that statements or norms *cannot lose*.

It is precisely the combination of these two features that results in the 'premise of "a single right answer"': we cannot say that a statement was true and now is false or that a norm was just and now is unjust. This explains why we cannot say that we *knew* something that turned out to be wrong whereas we can say without contradiction that we were *justified* – i.e. epistemically responsible – in believing something that it turned out to be false (or morally wrong). This impossibility is precisely what suggests the context-transcendence of the validity of such absolute notions.

However, if we try to explain this context-transcendence by appealing to the notion of 'idealized rational acceptability', we have to transfer the unconditional validity of 'truth' (or moral 'rightness') to the epistemic notion of 'idealized rational acceptability'. In so doing, we have to consider our particular interpretations and ways of justifying the statements that we hold to be true (and the norms that we hold to be morally right) as also endowed with absolute validity. Our evaluation of these interpretations also has to be considered as constrained by the characteristic binary use of the notion of 'truth' (or moral 'rightness'), i.e. by the *either-or* of the premise of 'a single right answer': just as we are required to presuppose that 'if a statement is true it cannot be false at the same time', we are required to accept that 'if a statement is rationally acceptable under ideal conditions it cannot be false at the same time'.[14] The consequence of closing up the gap between truth and rational acceptability – even if only counterfactually – is that, in such a case, it is not only valid that if a statement is true it cannot be false but also that our particular way of justifying the statement cannot be wrong either. Thus the particular interpretation (or theory) through which we understand and justify the truth of the statement must be *absolutely* correct, the *single correct interpretation*. It is in this sense that the notion of 'idealized rational acceptability' seems to involve unavoidably the anticipation of the end of the argumentation process: so understood, the claim of rational acceptability for our reasons and arguments implies – at least from the perspective of the participants – anticipating that they 'will stand up to all possible objections' (1996a:1508). Therefore, these reasons belong to the definitive ones, they come from the *single correct interpretation.*[15] In this sense, rational acceptability is related, not to our capacity to reason under the conditions of an ideal speech situation (i.e. our capacity to be epistemically responsible), not to the *procedure* of argumentation, but to its *content*. Obviously, if what is rationally acceptable under ideal conditions possesses also the *absolute* validity that we ascribe to 'truth' and moral 'rightness', our commitment to rationality is unavoidably a commitment to incorrigibility.

According to this strategy, accepting the premise of 'a single right answer' indeed seems to imply accepting the further (epistemic) commitment to the premise of 'a single correct interpretation'. But precisely because of this epistemic commitment, the difficulties of this strategy go further than just the counterintuitive explanation of the meaning of 'truth' and moral 'rightness'. They concern the problematic move of reading antifallibilist idealizations into the notion of rational acceptability.

However, if we pay attention to *our use* of the notion of rational acceptability (in contrast to our use of notions such as 'truth', moral 'rightness' or 'knowledge'), we realize that it does not actually imply any unconditional validity: it admits a *gradual* use and *changes over time* (as opposed to the binary use of notions like 'knowledge', 'truth' or moral 'rightness', for which we presuppose a fixed value). It is important to keep in mind the rationale of such a use: if we want to be able to redeem our claim of being justified *at a given time*, we are committed to being *reasonable* – in the sense that our reasons have to be convincing for everyone as the best available reasons – but not to being *successful* – so that our reasons also happen to establish the truth.[16] As Habermas explains in his 'Entgegnung' (1986:327-405): 'that our reasons are *really* good reasons and are sufficient for convincing us of the truth does not alter the fact that, in principle, what we take to be – definitively – true may turn out to be wrong' (1986:352).

When we claim to be justified in believing something, what we commit ourselves to is not that we have the ultimate reasons or arguments, the actually correct ones. On the contrary, whenever we claim rational acceptability for our beliefs, we rely on our epistemic responsibility rather than on a – mysterious – guarantee of success. Our commitment thus involves only that our reasons can (or could) be considered *as good reasons by everyone* – of course, only as long as no counterargument (or counterevidence, etc.) appears. In order to prove the soundness of our arguments, we commit ourselves to presenting them to all possible participants in a discourse, to adopting a hypothetical attitude toward their validity, and to following exclusively the logic of 'the unforced force of the better argument'. These commitments make clear the normative (or idealized) content of the notion of justification or rational acceptability. The use of such a notion can only be meaningful under the presupposition that, if all these conditions were fulfilled (i.e. under the conditions of an ideal speech situation), 'the unforced force of the better argument' would have a *universal* force.[17] As Habermas puts it: 'each person, who participates in argumentative practices in general, can in principle arrive at the *same* judgments about the acceptability of norms' (1983:131) – or of statements.

The notion of 'justification' or 'rational acceptability' (in its intersubjective sense) seems to concern more the *soundness* of our *procedures* of achieving knowledge than the *absoluteness* of a (hypostasized) ultimate *content*. Therefore, in order to be really operative in the evaluation of our argumentative processes (of what can be considered valid for us at a given time) it is not necessary to overburden the notion of 'rational acceptability' with the unconditional validity characteristic of notions like 'truth', moral 'rightness' or 'knowledge'.

Thus the question seems to be how to explain the unconditional validity of these notions, on which the correctness of the premise of 'a single right answer' depends, without appealing – not even counterfactually – to the absoluteness of the presupposition of 'a single correct interpretation'. In my opinion, all the necessary elements of such an explanation can already be found in Habermas' own analysis of communicative rationality.

As pointed out before, the absolute or unconditional validity implicit in the binary use of notions like 'truth' (and moral 'rightness'), can be explained as a consequence of the following trivial condition: if a statement is true, it cannot be false at the same time. By using the opposition true/false (and the same holds for moral 'rightness' or 'knowledge'), we commit ourselves to accepting that the statement at issue *either is true or is false* and, hence, that our evaluation of the reasons supporting such a statement will have to be directed toward the exclusion of one of the two possibilities. This logical condition seems to be a consequence of the presuppositions of existence implicit in the meaning of the notions of truth and moral rightness mentioned before: the truth of the statement depends on whether the described state of affairs exists, and the moral rightness of the norm on whether the regulated actions are in everyone's interest.

Due to these existence presuppositions, whenever we use such binary notions we have to accept – in advance – the correctness of the premise of 'a single right answer'. But precisely because these *existence* presuppositions have *no epistemic content*, our commitment to the premise of 'a single right answer' – and therefore to the context-transcendent validity of these notions – does not include an epistemic consequence such as the premise of 'a single correct interpretation'. That is, this commitment does not predetermine *in how many epistemic ways* we will be able to express *the same existing states of affairs*, or to safeguard *the same existing generalizable interests*. In this sense, the (logical) premise of 'a single right answer' *per se* does not imply the (epistemic) premise of 'a single correct interpretation'.

In what follows I will try to show, using Putnam's arguments, how this epistemic pluralism, which seems to be defensible for theoretical questions of truth, can analogously be accepted for practical questions of moral rightness.

Cognitivism and pluralism

Putnam's debate with B. Williams in *Realism with a Human Face* (1990:chap. 11, especially section on 'Absoluteness', 170-174) can be reformulated for our purposes as an attempt to make clear that, in order to defend the rationale of the premise of 'a single right answer', we do not need to introduce the presupposition of 'a single correct interpretation' or – in Putnam's terms – of an 'absolute conception of the world'. In his defense of this thesis Putnam appeals to the actual state of the empirical sciences:

> At the level of space-time geometry, there is the well-known fact that we can take points to be individuals *or* we can take them to be mere limits. States of a system can be taken to be quantum mechanical superpositions of particle interactions [..] or quantum mechanical superpositions of fields states. [..] Not only do single theories have a bewildering variety of alternative rational reconstructions (with quite different ontologies), but there is no evidence at all for the claim [..] that science converges to a *single* theory. [..] That convergence to one big picture is required by the very concept of knowledge is sheer dogmatism. Yet, without the postulate that science converges to a single definite theoretical picture with a unique ontology and a unique set of theoretical predicates, the whole notion of 'absoluteness' collapses (1990:171).[18]

If this is correct, a defense of the premise of 'a single right answer' does not seem to require accepting the epistemic presupposition of 'a single correct interpretation'. We only need to be able to recognize, across the different ontologies contained in the different theories or interpretations at issue, that these alternative interpretations are interpretations of the *same* phenomena, and therefore that the truth-values of (in this sense) equivalent statements will have to be distributed across these alternative conceptualizations or theories *in the same way*. As Putnam puts it in *Renewing Philosophy*: 'If a sentence in one version is true in that version, then its correlate in the other version is true in the other version' (1992:118). This requirement, derived from what Putnam calls the 'useful idealization' of 'the principle of bivalence' (1992:123), underlies our use of the opposition true/false. However, this is not to be understood as if, in order to be equivalent, the sentences of two different theories had to be (in a trivial sense) synonyms, as if they were not – so to speak – *genuine alternative* ways of conceptualizing the same phenomena – as if they were in the end just one theory. As Putnam shows, they are not synonyms at all. They cannot preserve *meaning* since they can only acquire their meaning in the holistic context of their respective theories or conceptualizations, and these indeed cannot be reduced to one: 'But to ask if these two sentences have the same meaning is to try to force the ordinary-language notion of meaning to do a job for which it was never designed. [..] We should simply give up the idea that the sentences we have been discussing preserve something called their "meaning" when we go from one such version into another such version' (1992:119). As Putnam makes clear later on, what they actually preserve is *reference*: 'Seemingly incompatible words may actually describe the same situation or event or the same physical system' (1992:24).

Only by taking this possibility into account can we recognize the fallacy of considering the epistemic premise of 'a single correct interpretation' as necessarily contained in the premise of 'a single right answer'. We can thus recognize that epistemic pluralism does not necessarily entail relativism. As Putnam points out: 'The fact that the real system allows itself to be talked about in these two very different ways does not mean either that there is no real physical system being talked about, or that there are two different physical systems in two different Goodmanian worlds being talked about. [..] It is absolutely clear, it seems to me, that the two descriptions are descriptions of *one and the same world*, not two different worlds' (1992:122). Putnam concludes: 'The whole point [...] is that very *different* sentences can describe the very same state of affairs' (1992:117).

It is this possibility that leads Putnam to draw the further conclusion that we have 'to recognize that there are many true descriptions of the world in many different vocabularies, without trying to privilege one of those descriptions as the "absolute" one' (1992:103). As long as we can 'claim that our conceptual schemes are just different "descriptions" of what are in some sense "the same facts"' (1992:110) – which is always a revisable claim –, we can concede that 'there is no one uniquely true description of reality' (1992:110), that is, we can give up the doubtful presupposition of an 'absolute conception of the world'.

In order to maintain such a claim, it is not necessary to postulate the possibility of having access to reality in itself. On the contrary, we only need to be able to recognize the different conceptualizations as conceptualizations of the same phenomena. Habermas explains in his 'Reply' (1996a) what this capacity involves, in the following terms:

> If we want to do justice to the transcendental fact of learning then we must indeed reckon with [..] a communicative reason that no longer prejudges the contents of a particular view of the world. This entirely procedural reason operates with context-transcending validity *claims* and with pragmatic *presuppositions* about the world. But the presupposition of an objective world that is the same for all participants in communication only has the formal meaning of an ontologically neutral system of reference. It only implies that we can refer to the same – reidentifiable – entities, even as our descriptions of them change (1996a:1527).

The connection between this formal capacity and the possibility of learning becomes clear if we take into account that such a capacity is the condition of possibility of discourse as such. It is what is required to evaluate the rational acceptability of alternative interpretations in a theoretical discourse, since it is precisely the capacity which allows the participants in a discourse to adopt a hypothetical attitude toward their own interpretations or conceptualizations. As Habermas explains in his *Theory of Communicative Action*:

> Validity claims are in principle open to criticism because they are based on *formal concepts of world*. They presuppose a world that is identical for *all possible* observers, or a world intersubjectively shared by *all members* of a group, and this *in an abstract form, freed from all specific contents* (1984a:82).

If we recognize the *formal* character of these existence presuppositions, we can see that the premise of 'a single right answer' derived from them does not include any epistemic presupposition of absoluteness for the particular *contents* at issue; that is, it does not imply the premise of 'a single correct interpretation'. But, for this very reason, these formal existence presuppositions, in so far as they constitute a condition of possibility of discourse in general, are operative as much in theoretical as in practical discourses.

The particular *content* of the formal system of reference (or existence presupposition) linked with the practical discourse is different from the one operative in theoretical discourses for obvious reasons. But its *formal role* as condition of possibility of discourse is actually the same. Just as the presupposition of the existence of states of affairs in the objective world is the condition of possibility for a meaningful discussion about the truth of statements, the presupposition of the existence of generalizable interests shared by all the members of the social world is the condition of possibility for a meaningful discussion about the moral rightness of social norms. This existence presupposition is indispensable for practical discourse, not because it is necessarily the case that there are such interests among all human beings, but because if we came to the conclusion that this presupposition makes no sense (which is, obviously, an open, empirical question), the discussion about the moral rightness of social norms would also become meaningless. As Rousseau indicates in *The social contract*:

> If the establishment of societies was made necessary because individual interests were in opposition, it was made possible because those interests concur. *The social bond is formed by what these interests have in common; if there were no point at which every interest met, no society could exist.* And it is solely on the basis of this common interest that society must be governed (1994:63, my emphasis).

Or put in the terms of discourse ethics: if, as a matter of fact, there were no common interests shared by all human beings, we would not understand what it means to consider a norm morally right or wrong (just or unjust). But as long as we can reasonably presuppose that there are such interests, as long as we consider it meaningful to find out which norms are 'equally in everyone's interest', there can only be one right answer, i.e. every norm either safeguards these interests or it does not.

As in the case of questions about truth, maintaining the commitment involved in the use of the binary opposition 'morally right/morally wrong' in the evaluation of social norms requires only that the participants in a practical discourse, with the help of their own – perhaps different – interpretations of their common interests, try to reach a consensus about the *either-or* concerning the moral rightness of the norm at issue. This agreement, though, is not contingent on a previous agreement on their own interpretation of the reasons why the interests safeguarded by the norm are worth having, unrenounceable or what have you.

McCarthy's argument against the meaningfulness of the premise of 'a single right answer' has cogency only on the assumption that this premise necessarily implies the premise of 'a single correct interpretation'. The central argument seems to be that, because our access to our own needs and interests is symbolically (i.e. culturally) mediated, whenever our descriptions and interpretations of these needs and interests are (to whatever extent) different, we have to conclude that they cannot be different descriptions or interpretations of the *same* interests and needs, that there is no way of considering the symbolically interpreted needs as the same ones across all alternative interpretations. Only if the participants in practical discourses did not have this possibility available, only if they operated under the premise of 'a single correct interpretation', the pluralism of ethical interpretations (characteristic of multicultural societies) would lead them, unavoidably, to accept relativism.

Habermas seems[19] to see this when in his answer to McCarthy's criticism in *Erläuterungen zur Diskursethik* (1991) he points out:

> It remains an empirical question how far the sphere of strictly generalizable interests extends. Only if it could be shown in principle that moral discourses *must prove unfruitful*, despite the growing consensus concerning human rights and democracy, because there is no way at all of *identifying common interests as such in the light of incommensurable languages*, would the deontological endeavor to uncouple questions of justice from context-dependent questions of the good life have failed (1991:202-3).

However, if we grant the possibility of identifying the same needs and interests even under (relatively) different interpretations of them, then it is not clear that the premise of 'a single right answer' requires presupposing 'the premise that a single correct interpretation has to be found' (1996a:1498). The only requirement seems to be that, independently of the different cultural ways of understanding and interpreting these interests and needs historically, the participants in practical discourses be able to reach an agreement about the norms to be considered morally right – insofar as they safeguard the common, unrenounceable interests that all of them happen to have. As long as the participants find it feasible to identify the interests safeguarded by the norms at issue as the same common interests that they share, it is meaningful – even if perhaps extremely difficult – to look for an agreement on the social norms which can be considered morally right (even if they accept the plural ways of articulating these common interests by different cultures). The hermeneutic task, required from the participants in practical discourses, of bridging the gap between the different interpretations and of identifying, even if under alternative conceptualizations, the same unrenounceable interests is already difficult enough.[20] It would be just hopeless if the participants were further required to reach an agreement on the particular way of interpreting and understanding the interests at issue.

Pluralism: the right and the good

Even if we acknowledge the formal (non-epistemic) content of the premise of 'a single right answer', there is a further aspect involved in the discussion about the cognitivism implicit in it that has still to be settled. The line between pluralism and relativism has to be drawn in a more precise way.

As we know from Habermas' defense of the cognitivism implicit in discourse ethics, the premise seems to involve the additional requirement that the participants in a practical discourse have to agree about the moral rightness of a norm *for the same reasons*. I think that this is correct but have the impression that there is an ambiguity in this formulation which makes it difficult to distinguish between the premise of 'a single right answer' and the premise of 'a single correct interpretation'. However, in this context such a distinction seems to be crucial for Habermas' defense of the autonomy (*Entkoppelung*) of questions of rightness from questions of goodness.

The requirement in question can be understood in two very different ways. In my view, one of these ways is important for discourse ethics. The other way, I suggest, provokes the criticism of the absoluteness of the premise of 'a single correct interpretation'. Like this premise the second way of understanding the requirement does not belong among the normative presuppositions of a universalist or cognitivist point of view. This way of understanding the requirement seems to imply that the participants in a practical discourse can come to share conclusions only if they share the evaluative backgrounds or ethical self-understandings from which they take the reasons for the justification of moral norms. In multicultural societies, however, the participants in practical discourses are not likely to have these evaluative commitments in common. It follows that in discussions of whether a norm is 'equally in everyone's interest', even if the participants come to common conclusions they do not do so *for the same reasons*.

However, a universalist or cognitivist perspective on moral questions does not rest on such a strong (or substantial) view of the requirement. Such a perspective requires only:

1 that all participants agree on the moral rightness or wrongness of the norm at issue;

2 therefore that all of them assent to the validity of the norm *for the reason* that the norm is morally right, i.e. preserves a generalizable interest, is 'equally in everyone's interest' (as opposed to being a fair compromise or an efficient regulation, for example).

This first level of agreement expresses only what it means for a norm to be just; in this sense it is identical with the unavoidable requirement that the participants in a practical discourse have to be able to adopt the moral point of view. But beyond this level of consensus it is not necessary that they agree also about the further, substantial reasons as to why the needs or interests regulated by the norm are worth safeguarding, unrenounceable or whatever. The universalist or cognitivist in fact recognizes that the value of morally right social regulations can be understood only from the internal perspective of such an ethical self-understanding. Such a perspective, *as the interpretative framework through which the participants are aware of their own needs and interests*, is a necessary condition of participation in practical discourse. However, participants need not share these interpretative frameworks, for they could agree that the norm at issue preserves the interests they all happen to have, even if they describe and interpret these interests by recurring to the different symbolical constructions contained in the different cultural traditions.

In fact, discourse ethics excludes the absolute presupposition that the participants cannot agree on the moral rightness of a particular norm (by evaluating whether it preserves a generalizable interest or not) if they do not agree at the same time in the particular way of understanding these interests at large. It does so precisely to the extent that it defends the (relative) autonomy of questions concerning rightness from questions about the good.

But for that reason, it seems possible to keep an epistemic pluralism of interpretations without collapsing into a relativist point of view only if we explain our universalist intuition about the unconditional validity of the moral 'rightness' of social norms in terms of the existence of common interests among all human beings. Because (and so long as) there are such interests among all human beings, we can in principle find norms able to preserve these interests; only these norms can be considered morally right. The either/or of the absolute opposition between morally right and morally wrong need not be extended beyond the norms at issue to the interpretations themselves in the light of which the participants understand their own needs and interests.

As pointed out before, the presupposition of common interests is unavoidable just to the extent that, without it, it makes *no sense* at all to attempt to determine whether or not a norm is 'equally in everyone's interest'. In this sense, the issue does not seem to be whether such a presupposition is implied by our claims to moral rightness, for the participants do not have such a choice. Rather, the issue seems to be whether the participants have to presuppose not only the existence of such common interests (however they may be interpreted), but also that, among the different ways of understanding these interests by different people and at different times, just one and only one particular interpretation is correct.

In fact, some participants in communicative practices may naively presuppose that their own interpretation is the only correct one. However, as soon as they are confronted by *alternative* interpretations *of the same matter at issue* (as is unavoidable in multicultural societies), in order to enter into discourse they would have to adopt a hypothetical attitude towards their own interpretation. But this in turn requires them to distinguish intuitively between competing interpretations and that of which they are interpretations (whatever this may be in the different cases). That is, they must be able to identify, across these different interpretations, the *same interests* that they themselves are trying to articulate with the help of their own interpretations.[21]

It seems clear that the premise of 'a single right answer' makes sense only under the presupposition of common interests shared by all human beings. This presupposition is what makes the principle of bivalence operative in our use of the absolute opposition between moral right and wrong. However, regarding the different (ethical) interpretations in the light of which the participants in a moral discourse understand the sense, value and motivation of the interests safeguarded by the norm at issue, as long as they may be considered interpretations of the *same generalizable interests*, they do not have to be considered constrained by the premise of 'a single correct interpretation'. *This kind of absoluteness* is actually neither required nor desirable for a consistent defense of a cognitivist position concerning moral questions.

Notes

1 In what follows, I try to show that the structural similarities between questions of truth and questions of moral rightness are due not to a similarity of content but to the unavoidable connection between the 'premise of "a single right answer"' and any *knowledge* claim whatsoever. Therefore my analysis focuses on this connection and pays no attention to their undeniable dissimilarities.

2 The parallel I am referring to does not depend on any similarity of *content* between such a 'moral principle' and 'Convention T' but rather on the fact that they *exhaust* the normative meaning of both validity claims, i.e. they express their necessary *and sufficient* conditions. This is precisely what allows these questions to be considered as cognitive – or, put in other terms, this is something we lack with respect to other kinds of questions (say, questions of taste) which, for that reason, cannot be considered *cognitive* or *discursively reedemeable* questions, i.e. questions related to *universal* validity claims.

3 Felmon Davis has pointed already to the ambiguity between the two different definitions of moral 'rightness' (1994:125-142). I agree thoroughly with his analysis of the realist presuppositions implicit in discourse ethics, but I draw very different conclusions concerning the internal relationship between them and discourse.

4 In *Faktizität und Geltung* (1992:135ff., esp. 140), Habermas recognizes the obvious non-identity between the moral principle and the discourse principle, but he does not seem to have recognized also the consequences of this. If the moral principle has obviously a *different content* than the discourse principle then the latter can not *explain* the former or, put in other words, rational acceptability cannot be a *condition* for the *validity* of moral norms but rather – as he himself makes clear – for 'the possibility of *rational decision* of practical questions' (1992:142); precisely its *procedural* character makes it logically dependent on the *content* of the moral principle (and in the case of theoretical discourses of the *content* of the notion of truth).

5 As I will try to show in the following, it is not that the notion of 'rational acceptability' or justification, as a normative notion, does not contain any idealization, but that the idealization implied in it is of a very different nature than the one implied in the notions of 'truth' and moral 'rightness'. See note 17 below.

6 This thesis is at the basis of Rawls' critique of Habermas (1995) concerning the distinction between procedural and substantive conceptions of justice in his 'Reply to Habermas' (1995:170-180). Rawls interprets discourse ethics as attempting to offer a procedural notion of 'justice' and provides convincing arguments against the plausibility of such an attempt. Basically, he argues that the conditions for agreement in practical discourse can be at most conditions for the legitimacy of its outcome but not for its justice (i.e. moral rightness). He thus concludes that it is not the notion of justice but the more general notion of legitimization that is procedural. Even though Rawls' interpretation gets some support from the inconsistencies of Habermas' exposition discussed here, it is

clear that his criticism misses the real point of Habermas' theory of communicative rationality. As already indicated, what the theory actually offers is indeed not a procedural interpretation of the notion of 'justice' (or 'truth') but of the notion of 'rational acceptability'. This notion is not only more general than the notion of justice (as Rawls observes), but more importantly, it does not have any *specifically moral* content. And this is precisely the virtue of Habermas' construction and not its vice. For, one of the crucial aims of Habermas' theory is to show that the redemption of *both* our truth-claims *and* our claims concerning the justice of norms, depends on *one and the same basic conception of rational acceptability understood in procedural terms* (i.e. as the outcome of a discussion taking place under the conditions of an ideal speech situation). In this sense, the discourse-theoretical interpretation of 'rational acceptability' can simultaneously explain both the notion of theoretical *justification* and the notion of moral *legitimation*. That is, it can explain at the same time the conditions under which answers to questions concerning the truth of statements can be *justified*, and the conditions under which answers to questions concerning the justice of norms can be *legitimized*. It is precisely on the basis of this explanatory strategy that Habermas can claim that moral questions are as *cognitive* as theoretical questions. He explains this in '"Vernünftig" versus "wahr" – oder die Moral der Weltbilder' as follows: 'I agree with Rawls' remarks about procedural vs. substantive justice (Reply 170-180); these reflexions, though, fail to capture the sense in which I use the expressions "procedure" and "procedural rationality" when I affirm that an argumentative practice organized in a particular way justifies the supposition of *the rational acceptability of its outcomes*' (in 1996c:119, my emphasis).

7 By the way, this internal connection between 'truth' and 'knowledge' is what cannot be reached by a semantic explanation of the meaning of 'truth', which – as present deflationism is making clear – can only come to reformulations of 'Convention T'. The trouble is not that 'Convention T' is not a correct explanation of the meaning of 'truth', but that our philosophical interest in an explanation of truth was always to know the epistemic value of such a notion in the context of our practices of achieving and revising beliefs. This further perspective is not accessible from a *semantic* analysis of the notion of truth as such but requires a *pragmatic* analysis of the process of communication in which it becomes clear that our claims of *truth* of *statements* are *at the same time always already* claims of *knowledge* concerning the *beliefs* expressed in such statements. This unavoidable connection between knowledge and truth (or moral rightness) is where the connection between these validity claims and the notion of rational acceptability comes from.

8 In this context I do not consider the difficulties pointed out by E. Gettier (1963: 121-123) because they are intended to show the *incomplete* nature of these conditions whereas my argument is exclusively based on the unquestionable *irreducibility* of the same.

9 It is easy to specify these conditions also for the case of the discussion about the moral 'rightness' of a norm:

S knows that N is morally right iff
(1) S believes in the rightness of N
(2) N is morally right
(3) S is justified in his belief about N.

10 Precisely that there is no such guarantee is what is expressed in our understanding of the notion of 'knowledge' as depending on three analytically independent necessary conditions, i.e. in our considering none of them alone as sufficient condition for knowledge. Only thanks to this understanding can we maintain a *fallibilist* attitude towards any belief candidate to knowledge.

11 The epistemic dimension of 'validity for us' (1996a:1509) which Habermas seeks originates not in truth or moral rightness being contingent on our judgments or agreement but in knowledge being unavoidably related to us. This obvious circumstance is expressed by the first of the three conditions for knowledge: in order *for me* to know something *I* have to believe it. Knowledge (as opposed to truth) can only be knowledge *for us*. But for the very same reason the context-transcendence implicit in the absolute validity of truth (or moral rightness) should not be sought in the epistemic dimension of 'validity for us'.

12 The intuition that truth cannot be a sufficient condition for knowledge is our only way of avoiding that the fortune-teller may be considered a truth-teller, even if some of his or her statements happen to be true.

13 For example, the case in which (retrospectively seen) nothing was particularly idiosyncratic with our reasons but we had just a wrong categorization of the question at large, or we lacked the abductive creativity for developing a correct explicative paradigm capable of producing true statements (like in cases where the result of a learning process is not the internal correction of the arguments available by a particular explanation or theory but a change of paradigm). In such a case we consider the former beliefs *unjustified* not in the sense that our reasons for supporting them were *not convincing* (i.e. we were *epistemically irresponsible* or irrational) but only in the sense that they were *incorrect* or *insufficient for establishing the truth*. Concerning these two different senses of justification see R. Fogelin (1994:24f.).

14 In 'Realism and Reason' (1978:123-140) Putnam explains the internal connection between such a notion of 'idealized rational acceptability' and the idea of 'an absolutely "unrevisable" truth as an idealization' (1978:138), when he says: 'The supposition that even an "ideal" theory [...] might *really* be false appears to collapse into *unintelligibility*' (1978:126). He has recently rejected such an epistemic conception of truth (as 'idealized rational acceptability') precisely because of its antifallibilist consequences (see 1994:242-295).

15 But if that were the commitment we would never dare to claim rational acceptability for our beliefs (and, consequently, we would not be able to distinguish between epistemic responsibility and irresponsibility, between sound and unsound justifications). Habermas seems to recognize that when he writes: 'Who agrees with opinions that turn out to be false is not thereby irrational; a person is only irrational if she insists dogmatically on her opinions and clings to them even

after having seen that she is not able to justify them. For an opinion to qualify as rational, it is enough that it can be held true for good reasons in a given context of justification, i.e. that it is rationally acceptable' (1996b:69)

16 If whenever we raised validity claims, we would presuppose – even from the internal perspective of participants in a communication process – that we have the correct arguments, that we are not only rational but successful, we would not have any reason for entering into a discourse or adopting a hypothetical attitude towards our beliefs. The rejection of such a fundamentalist presupposition (in posttraditional societies) is precisely what makes possible the procedural notion of rational acceptability as it is explained by the discourse theory.

17 Or, in other words, that under such conditions all the participants would evaluate the convincingness of the arguments *in the same way*. Obviously the use of a notion like 'rational acceptability' implies the possibility of a transcultural convergence in our criteria of rationality. The universalism implicit in such a presupposition about the *unity of reason* can be considered already controversial, but at least not so much as it would be if it had to support also the further presupposition of the *necessary success of our reason*. Our fallibilist intuitions tell us that there is no guarantee of such a success.

18 Putnam continues his argumentation by drawing the consequences for ethical knowledge in the following terms: 'It is, indeed, the case that ethical knowledge cannot claim absoluteness; but that is because the notion of absoluteness is incoherent. Mathematics and physics, as well as ethics and history and politics, show our conceptual choices; the world is not going to impose a single language upon us, no matter what we choose to talk about' (1990:171).

19 Habermas seems to recognize the non-epistemic origin of the premise of 'a single right answer' at different places of his 'Reply', for example when he writes: 'Each national constitution represents a historically different way of construing *the same* – theoretically reconstructible – basic rights, and each positive legal order implements *the same* basic rights in a different form of life. But the identity of the meaning of these rights – and the universality of their content – must not be lost in the spectrum of these different interpretations' (1996a:1498).

But under his use of the expression 'identity of the meaning' is concealed the epistemic premise of 'a single correct interpretation', as becomes clear when he continues: 'This contest of interpretations makes sense only on the premise that it is necessary to find a single correct reading that claims to *exhaust* the universalistic content of these rights in the present context' (1996a:1498).

The claim that identity of the content of human rights comes from an ideal, identical *sense* or interpretation of them, waiting to be discovered, seems dubious to me. I think rather that the identity of the content of human rights depends on their *reference* to the interests presupposed as existent among all human beings. That is just what it means to say that different interpretations can express the *same* interests.

20 Obviously not so much as it may sound. It would be hopeless if it should take place at this abstract level, if it should be a general – once for all – ethical

agreement about the admissible alternative interpretations of the common interests of all human beings (as opposed to the inadmissible ones). The fact that practical discourses are centered on social norms (on prohibited or permitted actions) gives to the participants a (relatively independently) operationalized way of *identifying their own interests* by attending to the consequences of a general observance of the norm at issue, as is made clear by the discursive interpretation of 'U'. Precisely because this identification is not fixed once and for all – especially if it has to take place through different cultural interpretations – the decision about the moral rightness of a norm depends on the possible acceptance of all affected by it.

21 Whenever they are not able of identify the same interests in the different interpretations from which the different participants in the discussion of a particular norm justify its moral rightness (like at the moment seems to be the case in the discussion on abortion, for example), they may (temporarily) conclude that – for that reason – it may not be a moral issue at all, but rather an ethical one.

References

Davis, F.J. (1994), 'Discourse Ethics and Ethical Realism: A Realist Realignment of Discourse Ethics', *European Journal of Philosophy* 2 (1994), 125-142.

Fogelin, R. (1994), *Pyrronhian Reflexions on Knowledge and Justification*, Oxford University Press: New York.

Gettier, E. (1963), 'Is justified true belief knowledge?', *Analysis* 23/6 (1963), 121-123.

Habermas, J. (1983), 'Moralbewußtsein und kommunikatives Handeln', *Moralbewußtsein und kommunikatives Handeln*, Suhrkamp: Frankfurt.

— (1984a), *Theory of Communicative Action*, vol. 1, Beacon Press: Boston.

— (1984b), 'Wahrheitstheorien', *Vorstudien und Ergänzungen zur Theorie des kommunikativen Handelns*, Suhrkamp: Frankfurt.

— (1986), 'Entgegnung', in Honneth, A. and Joas, H. (Hg.): *Kommunikativen Handelns*, Suhrkamp: Frankfurt.

— (1991), *Erläuterungen zur Diskursethik*, Suhrkamp: Frankfurt.

— (1992), *Faktizität und Geltung. Beiträge zur Diskurstheorie des Rechts und des demokratischen Rechtsstaats*, Suhrkamp: Frankfurt.

— (1995), 'Reconciliation through Public Use of Reason: Remarks on John Rawls' Political Liberalism', *The Journal of Philosophy* 92/3, 101-131.

— (1996a), 'Reply', *Cardozo Law Review* 17/4-5 (1996), 1477-1558.

— (1996b), 'Sprechakttheoretische Erläuterungen zum Begriff der kommunikativen Rationalität', *Zeitschrift für Philosophische Forschung* 50/1-2 (1996), 65-91.

— (1996c), *Die Einbeziehung des Anderen*, Suhrkamp: Frankfurt.

McCarthy, Th. (1991), 'Practical Discourse: On the Relation of Morality and Politics', *Ideals and Illusions*, MIT Press: Cambridge (MA).

McCarthy, Th. (1996) 'Legitimacy and Diversity: Dialectical Reflections on Analytical Distinctions', *Cardozo Law Review* 17/4-5 (1996), 1083-1127.

Putnam, H. (1978), 'Realism and Reason', *Meaning and the Moral Sciences*, Routledge & Kegan Paul: London.

— (1990), *Realism with a Human Face*, Harvard University Press: Cambridge (MA).

— (1992), *Renewing Philosophy*, Harvard University Press: Cambridge (MA).

— (1994), 'Comments and Replies', in Clark, P. and Hale, B. (eds.), *Reading Putnam*, Blackwell: Cambridge (MA).

Rawls, J. (1995), 'Reply to Habermas', *The Journal of Philosophy* 92/3, pp.132-180.

Rousseau, J.-J. (1994), *The Social Contract*, Oxford University Press: Oxford.

4 Are moral concerns irreducible to ethical concerns?

Habermas and the cognitive content of morality

Wilson P. Mendonça

This essay is concerned with a distinction which plays a very prominent role in discourse ethics, namely between the moral and the ethical points of view. My main overall contention is that the irreducibility claim implied by that distinction cannot be maintained on rational grounds. I shall devote a good deal of attention to a recent paper by Jürgen Habermas (1996), where he articulates again the main tenets of his version of discourse ethics. A large part of the task is to clarify Habermas' standpoint and critically follow its implications for moral theory.

Moral insights *versus* ethical insights

Discourse ethics adopts the viewpoint of an 'egalitarian universalism' first, by way of a 'rational reconstruction' of everyday moral intuitions in modern, pluralistic societies. Besides that, it aims to provide a context-independent theoretical justification of the moral point of view itself from which the basic norms underlying our (first level) moral judgments can themselves be judged (on a higher level) in an absolutely impartial way. As to the task of reconstructing the moral language game in modern societies, Habermas argues for the differentiation between at least two ways through which practical reason effectively binds our will through 'insights' or 'epistemic reasons'. According to this distinction, 'ethical insights' guide rational choice in contexts defined by questions of the good or not misspent life, 'which arise in the context of a particular collective form of life or of an individual life history' (1996:341), whereas 'moral insights' concern the more abstract question of what is equally in the interest of *all* human beings, including, of course, those human beings who form their individual and collective identities in cultures (or subcultures) which do not share with my culture (or subculture) the same ethos and conception of the good. As Habermas puts it, the moral question '*goes beyond* the context-bound ethical question of what is best "for me" or "for us"' (1996:342).

The difference is said to be 'semantic' (1996:341) and concerns the binding character of (ethical) values on the one hand, and (moral) obligations and duties on the other. Values are defined by their 'less binding character' (1996:348). What is morally right in that proprietary sense of 'moral' claims 'categorical validity', while what is ethically worth striving for is only 'conditionally valid'. The difference should become manifest when we approach questions of justice and solidaristic responsibility for everyone. Habermas thinks that an adequate philosophical account of our 'intuitive understanding of justice' should conceive justice 'as a context-independent standard of impartial judgment', not 'as just one value among others (however pronounced)' (1996:338). This is supposed to be the point where all contemporary 'neo-Aristotelian' moral theories based on the concept of the good go astray. Under the ethical point of view, however articulated, the right can only be the road to the good and refers in general to the more or less concrete demands which others impress upon us. There may be good reasons for us to take account of these demands, but *as ethical reasons* they remain, according to Habermas, confined to local community bounds, being, therefore, dependent on the substantive conception of the good shared by me and those who happen to be equally situated in the same historical tradition. And this is so, as already mentioned, on conceptual or 'semantic' grounds. By contrast, the universalistic potential of the cognitive content of everyday morality, as revealed by an adequate philosophical reconstruction, points to 'an ethically neutral conception of justice' (1996:342) which accords the right an *absolute* priority over the good. Here, at least, moral theory should 'uncouple the horizontal perspective in which interpersonal relations are regulated from the vertical perspective of my or our own life-project and treat moral questions separately' (1996:342). Otherwise, moral thinking runs into trouble when considering justice in 'societies characterized by a pluralism of worldviews' or dealing with 'the just regulation of international relations between states, [...] cosmopolitan relations between world citizens and [...] global relations between cultures' (1996:342).

Even a socially extended ethical perspective, which looks for a more inclusive conception of the good capable of being shared by a community more generous than my actual community in the recognition of others as my equals, is no real alternative for Habermas. First of all, it seems to him simply *improbable* that one could devise a conception of the good substantive enough to be both a conception *of the good* and also equally recognized by all human beings, as this would be required by the universal morality of equal respect. Of the utmost importance for him, however, is the circumstance that the limits for a tentative universalization of any conception of the good are not merely empirical, but, again, *conceptual*: the projection of a globally shared collective good would involve 'the abstraction from all local contexts' and this, in turn, 'would destroy the concept of the good itself' (1996:342).

Overcoming contextualism?

Two questions are immediately relevant here. The first one concerns the ties between conceptions of the good and local contexts defined by inter-subjectively shared experiences and interests. There can be no doubt that, for Habermas, these ties are 'internal' in the sense that they are constitutive of conceptions of the good. The question is how *narrow* these ties are in reality, or, in other words, how *concrete* the interests are which define the local contexts, or, again, how *particular* the forms of life are which supposedly give conceptions of the good all the meaning they can have. Discourse ethics draws on a rather narrow view of these matters. Conceptions of the good are in Habermas' view always substantive standards, traditionally anchored, and so dependent for their individuation on communitarian practices and more or less rigid ways of living that even *within* modern, pluralistic societies (nations) they prove to be essentially not generalizable. If they cannot be extended beyond the narrow limits set by traditionally evolved cultural arrangements without losing their very identity, one cannot appeal to them in order to ground the more universalistic aspects of the moral language game or the demands of universal respect. The moral philosopher is then, according to Habermas, confronted with two mutually exclusive alternatives. She can adopt a revisionist attitude *vis à vis* our universalistic intuitions, downgrading the claims of justice and universal solidarity to values 'more important for one person than they are for another and [...] of greater significance in one context than in another' (1996:341) (Habermas tell us that this is what neo-Aristotelians, as radical 'contextualists' in the wake of Aristotle and Wittgenstein, are doing). Or she can take seriously the complete range of the presumed cognitive content of everyday morality, acknowledging the reality of context-independent standards for deciding moral questions (Herewith the moral philosopher's attitude embodies, according to Habermas, an insight originally due to Kant). Be that as it may, it is clear that the whole scenario described by Habermas is based on a quite narrow view of conceptions of the good in their relations to local contexts or intersubjectively shared traditions, which are, moreover, taken to be incommensurable.

I shall argue that Habermas has overlooked some real possibilities to generalize over values. It is true that individuals are located in social complexes which are connected with other complexes in such a way that we can expect not only cooperation but also conflicts involving the most constitutive values competing, in the social world, for the individuals' vital allegiance. I may belong to some particular communities and more or less institutionalized forms of life to which you do not belong. There are, then, some obligations explicit and implicit in the social positions I hold which have force for me, not for you. Some of these obligations go very deep in the structure of my personality, so that I can conceive myself mainly in terms of how well or badly I have discharged them in the course of my life history. In the sense that obligations may be said to presuppose socially accepted norms, our personal identities are deployed within the frameworks of not entirely commensurable sets of norms. Accordingly, the values in whose light I understand myself and which ultimately determine how I should live may differ in important respects from *your* values. Habermas holds that these differences are now so great as to make it virtually impossible, especially for *philosophers qua philosophers*, to address questions of the good life for human beings. From his point of view, matters of self-realization and self-understanding simply do not yield to general theory. But of course it does not follow from partially incommensurable specific views concerning the good for human beings, each bringing with it a distinct set of norms, that there can be no substantial agreement between them. I shall argue that there is a substantial core which can be described in general terms and on which even discourse ethics itself has ultimately to rely.

One possible counter to this argument is the claim that we have only to enlarge our view and consider cultural complexes in a historically broader perspective to see that, whatever common elements there may happen to be in today's well established, practicable specific conceptions of the good, they are not really universal anthropological constants, but still context-dependent, particular constellations of values or, as Habermas puts it, 'historically changing images of self and world of individuals and groups which stands in need of interpretation' (1996:346). But now the counter to the counter is the question whether this same broadening strategy could also reveal that the moral principle proposed by Habermas, based as it is on the idea of discourses between *individuals* who conceive themselves from the beginning as *autonomously legislating* subjects, embodies a non-neutral value. Is the 'republican' ideal of legitimation of norms through a process of deliberation in which each concerned individual counts as one culturally invariant feature, a metaphysically necessary telos for humanity? The discourse theoretical reinterpretation of the categorical imperative does make morality dependent on a prior commitment to communicative rationality: 'the moral point of view can only be realized under conditions of communication which ensure that each individual tests the acceptability of a norm, implemented in a general practice, also from the perspective of his own understanding of himself and of the world' (1996:347). Moreover, 'moral norms could win the agreement of all concerned on the condition that they jointly examine in practical discourse whether a corresponding practice is in the equal interest of all' (1996:349). Since no 'norm' that may compel us to join rational discourses as a way of solving social conflicts can, without vicious circularity, be said to win our considered allegiance on the same grounds, it is plausible to interpret it as the expression of broad liberal-democratic values characteristic of a 'eurocentric' view of social living.

To see what is at stake here, we need only to consider the principle of universalization (U) which in discourse ethics operationalizes the moral point of view. It says that

> a norm is valid when the foreseeable consequences and side effects of its general observance for the interests and value-orientations of each individual could be freely accepted *jointly* by *all* concerned. (1996:354)

Moral reasoning is here conceived in terms of the rational consideration of individuals' interests, which, apart from the circumstance that they may destructively interfere with the interests of other individuals, are simply taken for granted. Besides, discourse ethics takes the 'yes' or 'no' stances of each individual involved in discourses of normative justification to be 'non-substitutable' (1996:348). The operative idea here looks very much like a value. And the circumstance that this value may be now so cherished by (many of) us that we are, as a rule, not prepared to question it when adjudicating many other conflicting values makes no difference in this connection.

The point of these remarks – to which I have to return later – is *not* that moral philosophy should do whatever is possible to supplant Habermas in the search for a really neutral point of view beyond all contexts infected by values. Rather, moral philosophy, as any other theoretical endeavor, must start somewhere in the middle of things and resist the 'Cartesian' temptation to look for 'absolutes', which could make it in principle immune to any logically possible critique of ethical contextualism. Before turning to this point, however, I shall state the second question of the two mentioned above.

Moral knowledge and moral motivation

The question revolves round a certain tension within discourse ethics. On the one hand, Habermas describes the predicament in which modern human beings find themselves in terms of the impossibility to restore a consensus, lost for ever, on the fundamental values which should determine how they understand themselves and, ultimately, how they should conduct their lives: 'their initial impulse is [...] to engage in deliberation and work out a shared ethical self-understanding. But under the differentiated social conditions of pluralistic societies they will soon realise that their strong evaluations lead to competing conceptions of the good' (1996:352). The members of modern societies are then in a sense obliged to learn to leave behind conceptions of what is better for them and to resort instead to some 'ethically neutral' circumstance where they might find the normative elements with which their living together can be morally regulated. This is what it means to say that the right has absolute priority over the good. On the other hand, Habermas himself acknowledges the fact that even self-consciously deliberating men and women looking for justice and the right ultimately have to fall back on common features they already share with other men and women. They still draw on 'a particular self-understanding', characteristic of human beings who currently participate in a certain community to which 'all individuals who have been socialized into any communicative form of life' belong (1996:343). This introduces a *prima facie* not-negligible degree of qualification in the asserted ethical neutrality of moral categories in general and justice in particular. Indeed, Habermas even recognizes a genuine, albeit heuristic, value in 'the intuition that issues of justice evolve from an idealising extension of the ethical problematic' (1996:342f.). There is for him after all a 'remnant of the good at the core of the right' (1996:343), for it is only as members of an admittedly broad, but still *particular* community – the community of the deliberators, so to speak – that individuals can expect equal respect from the others.

To be sure, Habermas restricts immediately the range of the good at the core of the right: it is only a 'formal good' which can not begin to compete with the 'commonalities' of traditionally structured forms of life. The formal good has its roots in a form of life, actually in a certain 'practice of deliberation which we call "argumentation"'. This form of life is supposed to have 'no functionally equivalent alternative' and to be 'found in all cultures and societies' (1996:355). But what makes it 'ethically neutral' is the purported fact that it offers no strong support for our self-understanding, which always needs a more substantive view of the good. *In that sense* the normative features intrinsic to the practice of deliberation, however they prove to be, are no real alternative to the strong evaluations rooted in traditionally shared conceptions of the good. In other words, we simply cannot refer the sense of a personal identity to those aspects of our culture which define the practice of deliberation itself – even if these aspects are (indeed: *because* they are) as Habermas supposes they are: culturally universal and non-substitutable. As Habermas points out, by adopting, even if only counterfactually, the point of view of this form of life, each deliberating human being definitely 'transcends the limits of any actual community'. But this is the move she ought to make if she likes to find some universal duties and obligations which go beyond 'the boundaries of a concrete lifeworld, be it that of a family, a neighborhood, a city, or a state' (1990:201f.).

Now, according to the statement quoted at the end of the first section, this 'abstraction from all local contexts' should 'destroy the concept of the good itself'. The position which Habermas is now urging us to accept admits that there remains after all some good at the core of the right. Characterizing this good as formal or, which is the same, saying that it cannot be the source of an encompassing *value*-consensus in pluralistic conditions – that it cannot play the role of a 'hypergood' (Ch. Taylor) over and above competing conceptions of the good – may resolve the apparent tension in this corner of Habermas' moral theory. However, some other problems arise in other corners. It should be noticed, for instance, that whatever guidance can be derived from the presumed 'ethically neutral' practice of deliberation itself remains formal, that is, detached from our moving sense of personal identity and the stuff of ethical life. Habermas is fully aware of this consequence: 'The appeal to moral contents must be replaced by the self-referential appeal to the form of this practice' (1996:353f.). But under these conditions it is not easy to understand why he still attributes to ethical values, as those normative elements rooted in full-blooded conceptions of the good, a 'less binding character' than the merely formal moral obligations which should emerge from the intrinsic make-up of the practice of deliberation itself.

If I am convinced that something is really good for me, I have *ipso facto* bound my will. There is no need for an additional explanation for the fact that I now have *both* a direction *and* an overriding motive to act. On the other hand, an additional explanatory story has to be told or is somehow tacitly assumed if I offer the apprehension of some facts as a reason why I act in a certain way. As long as the apprehension of facts is conceived as in principle detached from my beliefs concerning my full-blooded good, it owes whatever motivating force it has to the cravings, desires, interests and, in some decisive cases, the sense of personal identity with which it is only contingently associated. And it makes no difference whether the facts in question are 'empirical' or 'formal' in character – whatever that means exactly. Knowing and reasoning, as Hume argues, can never be by themselves an 'influence motive of the will'. Kant, on the contrary, tried notoriously to impress on us the idea that pure reason can be practical in the sense that it has in itself features which would be action-directing absolutely, not contingently on the agent's desires. So he ends up conceiving respect for the moral law as an emotion or a sentiment which is '*self-produced* by a rational concept', in opposition to the rather 'empirical' sentiments originated in the self-love, which determine the will from without.[1]

The Kantian Habermas has no sympathy for Kant in this regard. From his point of view, only an uncritically accepted 'Platonistic' premise to the effect that insight into the moral reality is intrinsically motivating could have led Kant to the assumption that a cognitivist position concerning moral judgments should cover also their illocutionary force (1992:136). Habermas proposes the elimination of the offending premise and with this, consequently, the uncoupling of moral knowledge from moral motivation. This is, in a sense, only the reverse side of the fact that the concept of morally right action has been detached from any full-blooded conception of the good: 'It is true [...] that the uncoupling of morality from questions of the good life leads to a motivational deficit [...] Discourse ethics even intensifies the intellectualist separation of moral judgment from action by locating the moral point of view in rational discourse. There is no direct route from discursively achieved insight to action' (1996:348). Indeed neither the normative presuppositions of discourse, whatever they are, nor the moral principle based on them can motivate us to take part in discourses or to follow moral insights justified in and by discourses. To avoid the charge of circularity in his attempt to ground discursively the moral point of view, Habermas refers all normative presuppositions of discourse 'to the process of argumentation itself, not to interpersonal relations *outside* of this practice' and eliminates from these normative presuppositions 'any *immediate* practical significance for actions and interactions beyond rational discourse' (1996:357; cf. also 1992:135). But by the same token 'we lose the strongest motive for obeying moral commands' (1996:348). Emptied from any content, moral insights, so conceived, determine the will only when embedded in the richer contexts of institutionalized, socially legitimated full-blooded forms of life which furnish us with the right motives to act (1990:207). It therefore turns out that, despite the initially asserted greater binding character of moral insights, they have only a weak motivating force, derived as it is from our ethical and pragmatic concerns: 'When we know what is morally right to do, we know that there is no good (epistemic) reason to act otherwise. But that does not prevent other motives from prevailing' (1996:348).

Even this concession is misleading, as it suggests that moral motives can be overridden by 'other' motives. What really follows from Habermas' division of the practical landscape into moral concerns and ethical concerns is that motives can now be found only on the ethical side of the fence. Under the perspective of a cognitivism expunged of all 'Platonistic' internal ties between moral knowledge and motivation, moral attitudes contain in themselves no more than the inert intellectualist apprehension of facts. Embedded in the right affective context, they may be *reason-giving*, but *per se* they are not *determining*. As if ignoring this, Habermas observes again in a misleading way that the autonomous will is bound by moral insights, although it could decide otherwise (1992:136). Given the non-orthodox cognitivism defended by him, it would be more adequate to acknowledge that ethical and pragmatic reasons do actually all the binding or determining here, *even when the will decides in accordance with moral reasons*. For, as he concedes, it is only as backed by ethical and pragmatic concerns that moral insights become practically effective. Anyway, the whole *impetus* for the decisions of the will does not come from intellectual insights, but is at best directed by these – as Hume pointed out.

Cognitivism

The last remarks put the semantic difference between ethical reasons, on the one side, and moral reasons, on the other, which Habermas is so eager to render prominent, in a new light. The purported higher validity of moral judgments is purchased by discourse ethics at the price of an abstraction from the contents of our ethical life. Practical reason in its moral version, we are told, is a power opposed to 'pre-existing interests and context-dependent value-orientations through pragmatic and ethical reasons' (1996:346) and which should impose restrictions on them. But the net result of making moral judgments independent of more mundane weak and strong evaluations is their characterization exclusively along an intellectualist dimension. And this, as I argued, makes them in an important sense powerless. Strong evaluations rooted in substantive conceptions of the good, on the contrary, are immediately effective. They are *internally* connected to the interests and self-understanding of socially situated agents and answer to their need of self-realization. What makes them ultimately objectionable for Habermas is the fact that they furnish only 'subject-centered' reasons for acting, whose very meaning depends on the particular life stories and traditions in which the agents in question happen to be contingently situated. As such they do not yield strictly universal prescriptions, as this would be required by an 'egalitarian universalism' in the spirit of Kant. Strong evaluations, as ethical reasons in general, put the will under 'contingent, subjective determinations' and the imperatives they yield are merely conditional, since they depend on 'subjectively given interests or intersubjectively shared traditions'. The will is then said to be determined 'from without'. Only the elimination of all these 'residues of compulsion' would make it possible for the will to be determined 'from within' (1996:345). Of course, saying so only occasionally makes it so. With these statements Habermas more assumes than proves that there is some determination left when reason abstracts from everything that gives content to the ethical life. The natural continuation of this line of reasoning would be an argument to the effect that there is some real substitute for Kant's non-empirical moving interest, born in reason itself and capable of setting an aim in itself which everyone has to realize, independently of her actual preferences and inclinations. However, Habermas wants nothing of the sort. He so intellectualizes moral reasons that they end up entirely devoid of any determining force. The addressee of categorical imperatives, so interpreted, may indeed *know* that she has no reason to act otherwise; but as categorical imperatives now are no more immediately action-guiding, this still leaves open the *practical* decision to act in the way indicated by morality.

That this view should be termed 'cognitivism' is again misleading. *Non-cognitivist* accounts in ethics are usually based on the thesis that moral terms have primarily a non-descriptive meaning. Rather than referring to objective entities which could be proper objects of knowledge, they are taken to conventionally express either subjective attitudes or prescriptions and recommendations by the utterer of moral judgments. Moral talk would then be more a matter of expressing decisions than putting forward claims of knowledge. *Naturalistic* accounts, on the contrary, hold that moral words are descriptive in meaning, but descriptive of relations between actions and some 'natural' human wants and interests. Here we would have knowledge and truth, for it is an objective, although not-easily solvable matter, not a question of choice or decision, whether a certain course of action brings, in the short or perhaps only in the long run, more satisfaction than distress (I am drawing in this paragraph on Mackie 1977:32f.). Yet, by making the action-guiding aspect of moral judgments dependent on conditions defined by the needs and possible satisfactions of the persons whose actions are to be guided by then, naturalistic approaches leave no room for absolute standards of evaluation over and above 'natural' desires. In particular, they leave aside categorical imperatives. This seems to go against the ordinary understanding of the moral language game as viewed from the inside by the participants themselves. *Prima facie*, at least, the moral judgment of an action is about the action itself, not about its relation to the utterer of the judgment or to anyone else. Naturalistic approaches imply therefore revisionist reconstructions of the moral language game. But non-cognitivist approaches are revisionist too. Why would we still engage in moral disputes if we did not believe that there is some 'matter of fact' involved in them? It seems that in these disputes we intuitively appeal to something 'external' to us, which has objectively authority over our desires.

Cognitivism proper – not the mitigated form advocated by Habermas – opposes both non-cognitivism and naturalism and take these features of ordinary morality at face value. It maintains that moral words have a descriptive meaning, not of some 'inert' fact, but of something intrinsically evaluative and prescriptive, something whose determining aspects are not contingent upon our desires and inclinations. Moral terms would then be instrumental to the aim of introducing objectively prescriptives into our talk about action and choice. Apprehension of moral properties and relations would be reason-giving *and* determining in one.

As J. L. Mackie points out (1977:ch. 1), this view is at least implicitly held by the main stream of European moral philosophy from Plato onwards. It is offered as the best explanation for the very *practicality* of moral statements, which is taken to be one with the 'fact' that moral statements have illocutionary force as an integral part of their meaning, i.e., that their directive component is not really distinguishable from the descriptive aspects that make them 'right' or 'wrong' – or even 'true' or 'false'. This view is embodied in Kant's claim that through rationally justifiable categorical imperatives reason prescribes ends absolutely and necessarily, irrespective of our self-centered interests – indeed, *against* our self-centered interests. It is also part of both Sidgwick's thesis that to be morally, objectively good is to be 'good from the point of view of the universe' and Moore's assumption of a non-natural property as that which is picked up by the word 'good'. In a sense, we deal in this connection only with variations of the Platonic theme that acquaintance with the Idea of the Good would not only tell us to pursue the good, but automatically make us pursue it.[2]

The tenability of the many admittedly different cognitivist positions is not in question here – and fortunately so. The point I am trying to make is rather that Habermas' 'cognitivist' approach in moral philosophy, far from representing a possible solution for the problem which cognitivism proper tries to solve, simply passes over it. For the problem is to give an account of the *prima facie* intrinsic prescriptivity of moral judgments. The assumption of objectively prescriptives may prove in the end to be very hard to justify. Such would-be abstract entities are ontologically and epistemologically very odd. Yet one can see how this assumption, if it could be made good, would solve the problem at hand. Alternatively, one can try one's hand at the non-cognitivist denial that moral terms have a descriptive meaning or at the naturalistic recourse to existing needs and satisfactions. And maybe there are other possibilities, other theoretical moves which could be successful. Anyway, to hold with Habermas a 'cognitivist' position tailored to the non-motivational aspects of morality is, in the context of the debate on the practicality of moral judgments, *simply uninteresting*.

Habermas apparently commits himself with cognitivism proper when he observes that a valid moral judgment (in his sense of 'moral') *means* an obligation. However, the commitment is more verbal than substantial, as this obligation is conceived as a purely intellectual affair, which depends for its force and efficacy on a motivational background contingently associated with it. 'For unless discourse ethics is undergirded by the thrust of motives and by socially accepted institutions, the moral insights it offers remain ineffective in practice' (1990:207). On the motivational background itself discourse ethics is silent. It leaves us, therefore, with no positive account of the practicality normally associated with moral judgments. As such, its 'cognitivism' does not oppose naturalistic reactions to cognitivism proper. Indeed, I shall explore in the last two sections of this paper the possibilities of a naturalistic interpretation of Habermas' position.

Ethical reasoning and ethical understanding

I now turn to the details of Habermas' account of how ideals of good living operate in practical reasoning. As against Kant's 'failure' to sufficiently distinguish questions of ethical self-understanding from the prudential concerns having to do with given preferences and goals of a more or less unchanging self, Habermas points to a 'layer of traditions in which identities are formed' (1996:346). At this level of reflection, my subjective preferences are submitted to a scrutiny with the aim of determining what is *really* good for me. Accordingly, I have to turn from the question of which course of action would best satisfy my actual desires to the question of which desires should go into the habits of action defining my own character. Hence, not what I have or would like to have, but what I am or would like to be constitutes the subject-matter of an ethical inquiry. This difference is one of complexity and manifests itself clearly, as Dewey stresses (Dewey 1980:ch. VI), whenever my actual ends prove to be incompatible. For if my ends cannot be made homogeneous, if my choice cannot be guided by a single type of end, a question almost inevitably arises concerning the relation of my ends to my character. The decision about the best course of action turns out then to be a decision about what sort of character disposition is most valuable and shall be reinforced. If we also assume, again with Dewey, that we, as socially situated agents, 'cannot separate the idea of ourselves and of our own good from our idea of others and of their good', since 'it is as difficult to determine what is really good for oneself as it is to discover just where the good of others lies and just what measures will further it' (Dewey 1980:158), then we can see, now with Habermas, that ethical questions, although formulatable in the first person singular, go much beyond the 'pragmatic' concerns of a particular person who takes her likes and dislikes as a datum. 'In these questions the first person perspective no longer signifies an egocentric restriction to my preferences; it points rather to the totality of an individual life history which is always already embedded in intersubjectively shared traditions and forms of life' (1996:340).

To a certain extent, insights into what is really good for humans are, according to Habermas, amenable to a rational control. *Initially* at least, his moral theory seems to admit the possibility of *something like* ethical knowledge. The provisos are, however, carried so far by Habermas as to virtually annihilate any genuine knowledge claims in this connection. 'Ethical knowledge' exists first and foremost as 'intersubjectively shared know-how which has gained acceptance in the lifeworld and has "proved" itself in practice' (1996:340). Out of this state, it can be retrieved, so Habermas claims, by some sort of reflection on the material 'sedimented in evaluative vocabulary and in the rules for the use of normative sentences' (1996:339f.). But this is to be sharply distinguished from 'the acquisition of factual knowledge', as the retrieval in question inevitably takes the form of a hermeneutic reappropriation which brings nothing really new to the fore: 'reflexively achieved "insight" only makes explicit the pre-theoretical knowledge which communicatively socialized individuals have already acquired in the lifeworld' (1996:339). Moreover, there is no cognitive controlling of a claim concerning what is good for us in anything approaching the manner of a scientific testing, since any such claim 'enjoins "objectivity" in virtue of its social diffusion and acceptance' (1996:340).

Habermas' recourse to double quotes in this context is no accident. He starts with a distinction between the form of reflection with takes an agent's own interests, desires and inclinations as a datum and the form of reflection aiming to determine the agent's real good. In the first case, the perspective is egocentric; and my attitudes, my private feelings about people and actions, my likes and dislikes have authority for me just by being mine. In the second case, by claiming and trying to justify that something *is good*, I appeal or seek to appeal to a higher and more authoritative standard. This breaks the narrow egocentric barrier. However – and this is the important point – the shift from the purely personal concerns of any individual agent to ethical standards of good living brings us only, according to Habermas, to institutions and values accepted in the society to which the agent and those with whom she establishes communication equally belong. Ethical reasoning 'unfolds *within* the horizon of unquestioningly recognized norms' (1996:338). Hence, the ultimate source of the authoritative ethical standards which any socialized agent can expect others and herself to recognize as well as the source of the specific contents of ethical evaluations is to be located in the context of historically conditioned forms of life. Being dependent on a contingent ethos, ethical evaluations are valid on the condition of given interests. These may be widely *intersubjectively* shared. But as even wide intersubjectivity alone still does not make for objectivity, ethical evaluations are 'objective' only in a figurative sense. And if the hermeneutic articulation of our shared ethos points beyond the subjective world of private preferences and is not narrowly egocentric, it still adheres to an intuitively held particular point of view. That is why Habermas speaks here of '*self*-understanding' or '*self*-clarification'. Again, this is only figuratively 'knowledge'.

The practical meaning of ethical reasoning is characterized by Habermas as deriving 'from the idea of a consciously guided and coherent course of life where the authenticity of a life-project can be understood as a higher level validity claim' (1996:341). This characterization picks up only a *form*, since, as Habermas seems to assume, the very value of authenticity, embodied as it is in forms of social life, changes as these forms change (for a similar thesis see MacIntyre 1966:7). On this account, the validity claim raised by the ideal of an authentic life cannot have the last word. It would be indeed preposterous, in trying to *impartially* assess (sufficiently ethical) forms of life, to appeal to the form common to them. Thus the guidance afforded by even the most rational ethical consideration gives us no *neutral* stand by reference to which a reasoned choice between substantive ideals of good living could be made.

So much for Habermas on ethical reasoning. In what follows I shall not dispute his main contention that ethical ideals constitutive of our self-understanding (or socially embodied conceptions of the good in general) may differ from each other, beyond expressing some doubts about whether in that case the recourse to an ethically neutral stand would be really possible.

Are moral needs ethically neutral?

The question which I shall be concerned with comes to a head in connection with the requirement – which Habermas takes to be moral *par excellence* – 'that each person should stand in and answer for a stranger who has formed his identity in completely different circumstances and who understands himself in terms of alien traditions'. With reference to such situations, Habermas writes:

> Socialized individuals are particularly vulnerable in their integrity and are consequently in special need of protection because they can only stabilize their identities in relations of reciprocal recognition. They therefore need to be able to appeal to an authority beyond their own community (1996:343).

The problem here is to give a practical sense to Habermas' use of 'therefore'. If the 'alien tradition' with which a socialized individual is confronted is constituted by ethical values more or less congruent with the values of his or her own community, there seems to be no need to appeal to a higher authority. In that case there is *ex hypothesi* agreement between the respective social conceptions of the good on which individuals draw their self-understanding; and the confrontation with an alien tradition does not represent a threat to the stabilization of identities. On the other hand, if traditions begin to radically diverge in the values in whose light their respective members understand themselves and their lives, there may follow out of their encounter some bad consequences for the personal integrity of those carried by the ensuing conflict. Consider, for instance, the case of a tradition whose concrete conception of the good looks, from my point of view, 'perverse', so that I may doubt whether we are talking about the same subject-matter when we are explaining and practically exemplifying our ideals of good living. Viewed from their, let us say, 'super-spartan' stand, the very demand that I should be protected and actively supported in my efforts of self-realization, *conceived in my terms*, should be met with contempt, rather than with recognition. If the conflicting ideals and values are such that those subscribing to them are willing to tolerate some constraints upon the means by which they strive to reach their good, the case is not very different from the first one and we could appeal to *that* as part of a strategy for the consensual resolution of practical conflicts, eventually modifying or extending our self-understanding. But if there is no common ground in that respect, if the traditions confronting each other are really alien and the circumstances in which identities are formed are completely different, then it is plausible to assume that there is nothing short of force to which those afflicted with the feeling of destabilization in their identities could still appeal. For there can be even no necessary guarantee that what is, from one point of view, a clear case of destabilization of identity will be perceived as such by the other conflicting party, rather than as a 'natural' consequence of a 'crazy', 'vicious' way of living.

The crucial point which begins to emerge is that there seems to be no ethically uncontroversial way to specify those features of a societal life which form the locus of the moral. Of course, Habermas would gainsay this emphatically. According to him, the fundamental human needs to which morality answers have to do with the 'unconspicuous necessity for participants [in social interactions] to become more and more individuated'. Habermas takes it as established that such individuation, in the case of normal human beings, is possible only through a specific kind of socialization mediated by language: to form the inner center of his or her personal identity, the human subject has no choice but to participate in increasingly differentiated interpersonal relations through language. This in turn is the source of a special sort of vulnerability, which is taken to be more serious than 'cruder threats to the integrity of life and limb'. Finally, the socialized individuals' need to stabilize their structurally fragile personal identities plays in Habermas' philosophical ethics the role of a defining criterion for moral concerns. Accordingly, moral judgments refer essentially to this need: 'Moral intuitions are intuitions that instruct us on how best to behave in situations where it is in our power to counteract the extreme vulnerability of others [...] In anthropological terms, morality is a safety device compensating for a vulnerability built into the socio-cultural form of life' (1990:199). To know then whether a judgment should be counted as genuinely 'moral' – as opposed to 'ethical' and 'pragmatic' – we have to ask whether its subject-matter is the satisfaction of the 'universal' need to stabilize a personal identity. Also, by referring to the their implications for the satisfaction of this need, we could tell right and wrong judgments.

But what to say of the identification of the need in question? Is *this* concrete event a case of destabilization of identity calling for a special "moral" regulation or rather one 'ethical' affair, i.e., one of those 'clinical questions of the successful and happy, or better, not misspent, life' requiring the 'critique of self-deceptions and of symptoms of a compulsive or alienated mode of life' (1996:341)? The considerations above may have suggested that in crucial cases there is no clear-cut answer to this question. In such cases the categorization of an event as destabilization of the inner center of identity cannot be less dependent on the constitutive values of a collective life than the very process of forming a personal identity. Indeed, this categorization *is* an ethical judgment in Habermas' sense. For it may be the object of a dispute which Habermas himself would have to classify as ethical.

It should be noticed that the argument above could proceed along pretty immanent lines. It centers on Habermas' observation that personal identity, far from being an absolute datum, is determined by socially and historically situated strong commitments and evaluations which make up the framework within which an 'ethical' orientation towards what is good or how one should live is possible. But then a similar observation must be made concerning whatever is taken to be the most fundamental needs of the human self: what we are prepared to recognize as a fundamental need of human beings in each case keeps pace with the varying set of constitutive values of modes of living, i.e., with historically changing ethical outlooks. And any choice between ethical outlooks is simultaneously a choice between rival conceptions of human needs and the preferred ways to satisfy them. Habermas *formal* delimitation of the moral domain in terms of a special vulnerability of socialized human beings makes it look as if we had no need to fix *first* an interpretation scheme *and then* see where the personal vulnerability lies – and with it also how to locate our moral obligations. But if Habermas is right on the forming of identities, there is such a need and the relevant interpretation can again only be fixed in the context of historically conditioned forms of social life. The upshot of all this is that there are not two independent forms of practical deliberation, 'discourses of self-clarification' and 'discourses of normative justification', by reference to which we could separate ethical from moral questions (1996:347f.).

On the character of norms justified under 'the moral point of view'

The discourse theoretical delimitation of the moral domain in terms of conditions defined by the need to stabilize structurally fragile personal identities lends itself to a 'naturalistic' interpretation. This vitally connects moral principles with the material of conflicts of action which grow out of everyday life. It allows the treatment of morality not as an abstraction or an 'empty' formalism, but as part of our efforts in behalf of important ends. In particular, the correctness of moral judgments or moral norms can be assessed, under a naturalistic interpretation, by reference to their consequences for the satisfaction of certain real necessities of human existence.

The bearing of this view on our main problem – namely, whether moral concerns can be understood and pursued independently of any conception of the good life – can be better appreciated if we separate two levels of analysis. First, we have to consider the character of the norms justified under the 'moral point of view' whose most general articulation is the rule of argumentation (U). Do norms selected in accordance with this rule necessarily avoid any reference to elements pertaining to the good life? Second, we have to consider the proposed 'moral point of view' itself. Is there an 'ethical choice', an implicit reference to a vision of the good living, behind Habermas' privileging a certain procedure for the moral resolution of conflicts?

Habermas' attitude at the first level is stated in conditional form:

> If the participants remain steadfast in their resolve to engage in deliberation and not abandon the moral regulation of their coexistence for a negotiated *modus vivendi*, they find that, in the absence of a substantive agreement on particular norms, they must rely on the 'neutral' circumstance that each of them participates in *some* communicative form of life. (1996:353).

As we had opportunity to comment, participation in *some* practice of deliberation, although a common feature shared by those entangled in conflicts of action, is in Habermas' view a 'formal' trait, *not* the common denominator – which according to Habermas may not exist at all – of the substantive conceptions of the good giving rise to conflicts. It is a 'formal good' out of which the 'moral good' should be gained, *not* the minimal basis for a compromise or value-consensus – which again may not be possible. The claim is therefore that the search, guided by the rule (U), for morally satisfying norms will lead to results which abstract entirely from any factors positively referring to the good life.

Habermas is doing here what he otherwise considers to be definitely wrong: to *anticipate* in moral philosophy what only real practical discourses should establish. From his point of view, the object of moral theory is to fix the standpoint which allows for participants in discourses to find *themselves* the constitutive norms of their interaction (1992:124). This is accomplished in discourse ethics by the specification of a rule of argumentation (U) out of which alone *no* moral obligation follows. Rather, any moral obligation as such 'attaches to the special objects of practical discourse, that is, to the input of norms to which the reasons mobilized in deliberation refer' (1996:357). Now, the rule of argumentation in question says nothing whatsoever about the necessity of 'transcending' conceptions of the good or finding an 'ethically neutral' circumstance on which moral duties and rights can be based – so as to better assure the stabilization of personal identities. It states only that norms should be tested by each individual from the perspective of his or her interests and jointly accepted by all. Hence any claim to the effect that morally satisfying norms will contain no reference to elements pertaining to the good life goes *beyond* what is 'logically' implied by the rule of argumentation (U) and stands in need of an extra, 'empirical' support.

Still, whether transgressing or not his own methodological maxims for moral philosophy, Habermas *could* be right in his anticipatory claim. The important point to be kept in mind, however, is that considerations to be adduced for this claim have to show their value by connecting it with the fundamental needs in behalf of which morality has a point and a function. It is indeed possible to justify with considerations of this sort some general assumptions about the results of practical discourses without running them in 'real time'. For instance, it is safe to assume that norms selected according the rule (U) will stand up to what Mackie calls the first stage of universalization (the elimination of numerical differences in the sense of individual reference to persons, groups, nations, and so on) and also the second stage (the elimination of principles which differentially favor those who happen to have certain characteristics or certain positions). That the constraints imposed by the first stage will be satisfied if morality is to fulfill the function assigned to it by Habermas is more or less evident. This sort of universalization is now almost part of the meaning of moral terms and statements. Satisfaction of the second stage constraints have a less 'logical' status, but can be well supported by arguments dealing with the distinctively 'moral ends': to give their potentially and actually endangered personal integrity a safe basis, it is strongly advisable for serious deliberating human beings to adopt norms which reflect the ability to put themselves sincerely in the place of another, to see things from the standpoint of his or her social position. This procedure will naturally lead to prescriptive principles that will not resist application to numerically different individuals *irrespective of such characteristics as rank, race, sex, and so on.*

However, if norms satisfying the constraints of the second stage call for an 'intersubjectively extended perspective' and rationally compel each participant to adopt the perspective of others, they do not take sufficiently into account the whole gamut of varying values and ideals: when putting herself in the place of another according to the second stage of universalization, each individual initially only asks for real possibilities of realizing *her* given values and ideals if she were to occupy the social position of another. If this were all there is to practical deliberation, it may easily lead, as Habermas puts it, to 'the marginalization of worldviews of particular individuals or groups' (1996:354). It may make us insensitive to the intrinsic worth of activities that are not attractive from the point of view of our values, which in turn may have bad consequences for the personal integrity of social actors.

To prevent such a development, participants in discourse could tentatively go in for Mackie's third stage of universalization: taking full account of all the interests that anyone has, including interests arising from the ideals and values that they do not actually share. This corresponds exactly to the utilitarian's injunction to put our desires and dispositions in agreement with what they would be in the mind of an impartial observer. However, as Mackie shows, the attempt to put oneself thoroughly into the other person's place, so as to take on not only his more 'external' social position, but also and especially his ideals and values, is not feasible. For it then 'hardly makes sense to talk of putting *oneself* in his place; hardly any of oneself is retained' (Mackie 1977:93). Of course, conflicts of action would be peacefully solved (or would perhaps not even really arise) if we could rely on norms positively expressing an absolute agreement of all points of view, i.e., norms subsuming in themselves all different systems of values. But the fact is that systems of values differ and individuals may not be willing to eliminate completely the differences, as this may amount in their view to giving up important elements of their identities. 'People do have specific and divergent ideals and values, and it is not possible genuinely to adhere to an ideal and at the same time to subordinate it to some resultant of all ideals' (Mackie 1977:154).[3] It now goes without saying that disagreements of this sort also have a necessary reflex in disagreements concerning aspects of procedures for the resolution of conflicts.

Habermas would surely agree with this negative appraisal of attempts to a full-blown universalization on values and ideals. Also, he would use it as evidence for the claim that participants in discourse will ultimately set out for features which only 'refer negatively to the damaged life instead of pointing affirmatively to the good life' (1990:205). Also, since there can be no real universalization along the dimension of values, participants in discourses will have to 'disengage problematic actions and norms from the substantive ethics of their lived contexts, subjecting them to hypothetical reasoning without regard to existing motives and institutions' (1990:207). All this would be equivalent to a vindication of the conditional statement quoted above. But refraining from any engaging entanglement with conceptions of the good is *not* the only alternative to the impracticable all-inclusive ideal of a benevolent observer. Participants in discourse could instead work out a rationally acceptable compromise between not entirely homogeneous systems of values. A compromise of this sort is not to be generally confounded with the arbitrary imposition of one point of view in detriment of others by means of persuasion. Rather, it could be motivated by what Dewey calls 'intelligent sympathy', whose main point is to widen and deepen our concern for the consequences of our acts on the social welfare (1980:107). Under some favorable conditions, this could lead to morally defensible *negative* constraints on the means by which individuals and groups strive to reach their aims. What is more important in the present connection: it could also lead, again on favorable conditions, to the recognition and active endorsement of some aims and goals *positively* contributing to the well-being of all concerned.

There is of course no *a priori* reason why these conditions do not obtain. Habermas would counter with the observation that this presupposes something like a 'shared ethos', which is rapidly desintegrating in a society characterized by the pluralism of worldviews. However, it is implied in what is brought out in the last section that there are limits for the desintegration of a shared ethos in that sense. Trespass of these limits cannot be compensated by any amount of 'discursive' intentions, for under such conditions we would very likely only discover that discourses are just impossible.

That an intelligent compromise between systems of values characterized partly by cooperation, partly by conflict can fulfill any function reasonably assigned to morality is an insight explored in the ethics of Dewey (1988:part IV) and Mackie (1977:ch. 8, section 1).[4] They work in frameworks differing from each other and also from the framework of Habermas. In particular, their conceptions of the fundamental needs which give morality its point cannot be brought to absolute coincidence. Nevertheless, they share an insight that can be profitably mobilized in the critical evaluation of Habermas' moral theory. Accordingly, participants in discourses organized around the rule of argumentation (U) are *not* coerced either by the rule itself or by the relevant facts to rely on the ethically neutral, 'formal' circumstance that they have been socialized in communicative forms of life. This is not the only common ground where they can reasonably expect to find a normative system capable of guaranteeing their structurally endangered personal integrity. They could as well (or even better) take recourse in their deliberations to Dewey's consideration that

> there are common human affections and impulses which express themselves within every social environment; – there is no people the members of which do not have a belief in the value of human life, of care of offspring, of loyalty to tribal and community customs, etc., however restricted and one-sided they may be in the application of these beliefs. Beyond this point, there is always, on whatever level of culture, the possibility of being on the alert for

opportunities to widen and deepen the meaning of existing moral ideas. The attitude of *seeking* for what is good may be cultivated under any conditions of race, class, and state of civilization (1980:143).

Why should these ideas be less characteristic of human life than the fact that human beings speak *some* language which can be put (ideally? always? only under special circumstances?) to an argumentative use? That it should be easier discursively to get effective action-guiding principles deserving the eulogistic title 'moral' with their help than with the help of recondite formal presuppositions of 'communication as such' is evident. And even recognizing that these ideas cannot be given a fixed meaning once and for all, since they are internally connected to changing social arrangements, participants in practical discourses could still argue for and against proposed substantive interpretations of these ideas with a view to best satisfy the 'moral ends'.

Any such substantive interpretation, if minimally acceptable, can be viewed as the expression of a negotiated *modus vivendi*. Now, in the passage quoted at the beginning of this section, Habermas seems to oppose radically the moral regulation of coexistence to negotiated *modi vivendi*. But under this reading, the claim that moral norms selected by discourses with the help of the rule of argumentation (U) will contain no positive reference to elements pertaining to the good life is tautologically uninformative. Habermas' position here can be rationally assessed only if negotiated *modi vivendi* are not excluded *a priori* from the legitimate options to be examined in discourses. As such, negotiated *modi vivendi* are not objectionable. They can be more or less intelligent (in Dewey's sense of intelligence). It is open to discourses to tell them apart.

Compromises and the justification of 'the moral point of view'

Compromises of the sort mentioned above can be an effective way of adjudicating between rival claims originated in irresolvably diverse conceptions of the good. Habermas wants to restrict their range of application to cases where 'exclusively particular interests are at stake', as opposed to 'generalizable interests' (1990:213, n. 10). But there is no good reason for such a restriction, based, as it seems to be, on the assumption of a hard and fast line of separation where there may be none. Compromises do not have to accept any characterization of interests 'as is'. They work by bringing the parties first of all to avoid seeing the issues dividing them in polarized terms. 'Moral inquiry', as Dewey calls the working out of intelligent compromises, is the search for fruitful standpoints from which rival descriptions begin to make sense. Particular problems are put in a larger context and interests are redescribed in more general terms, so as to render possible the rational evaluation of alternatives that might otherwise be overlooked. Compromises are, therefore, systems of *positive morality*, enabling the determination of concrete rights, liberties and duties. These will never be absolute, as they are made stable by a body of considerations which require vindication by the event. But that does not make them 'particular' in any pejorative sense.

Nor is it mandatory to view the framework of ideas within which compromises are worked out as calling for some 'higher' justification to be provided by specific 'decontextualized' arguments (1990:205). Compromises must take care of themselves. The 'local' adjudication of conflicts will naturally make use of general ideas or general principles which allow a fair, i.e., acceptable weighting of the claims involved – after submitting them to all sorts of proper (again: acceptable) redescriptions. Such principles are among the most important considerations to be brought into the debate about what rights and duties should be created, modified or preserved in the concrete instance. While playing this role, they are frequently assigned a special status which puts them, at least *for the time being*, aside of the subject-matter of the dispute in question. From a Deweyan, naturalistic point of view, however, they are still 'hypotheses with which to experiment', 'instrumentalities' or 'methods by which the net value of past experience is rendered available for present scrutiny of new perplexities' (Dewey 1988:165f.). Hence, not only can general ideas become the subject-matter of a dispute to be settled by a new compromise – in which case *other* general ideas are taken for granted – they are indirectly tested and eventually revised by their working in the background of fair, successful compromises.

This can now be brought to bear on Habermas' interpretation of the moral point of view. A naturalistic acceptable justification of the rule of argumentation (U) is to be found in the fact that it expresses an idea which has been increasingly effective in previous, acceptable judgments of conduct and now can be actively employed in the working out of fair compromises. Of course, the moral development of our societies cannot be viewed as a rule-governed argumentative practice, a succession of discourses or intelligent compromises reached by the strict compliance of principles of legitimate inference. Still, a case can be made, as Habermas puts it, for 'the emergence, after a long seesawing struggle, of a *directed* trend toward the realization of basic rights' (1990:208). A naturalistic moral theory – as the meta-theory of successful moral judgments – would reconstruct this historical process, thereby isolating and making more significative its main operative ideas. This is no purely descriptive affair, since explicit consideration of the rather implicit valuings of approved sociopolitical movements transforms them in *values*, i.e., items requiring our endorsement as effective means to make more stable the goods which we are interested in.

There is much to be said, from this point of view, for a principle which binds up the acceptability of social norms with agreement of those affected by it. We may have learned 'by trial and error' that the stability of compromises on a large scale depends on the fact that conflicting interests are given an adequate say *first of all from their own perspective*. Cooperation in social bodies sufficiently similar to ours and loyalty to their political forms stays and falls together with institutions whose function is to assure potentially conflicting interests a proper hearing. On the other hand, individuals are now located in so many different communities of interests that the best way – as shown by experience – to achieve this is to let them, at least in principle, speak for themselves. Further, what is suggested by a tortuous experience can be enhanced in meaning by reflection. Thus, we come to the ideal of a discourse in which no other contributions are allowed than those which can be defended by each concerned agent herself with a view to ensure fair conditions for the pursuit of her own good. This is a powerful idea, appeal to which recommends itself as an outstanding way to find and establish in the concrete situation satisfactory norms for coexistence. It is not universally applicable. First, there are in our societies some contexts in which positive moral development does *not* even suggest the device of discourses based on the non-substitutability of the stances of all concerned. Family life is obviously a case in point. Second – and more to the point – it is an historical product which holds on more or less specific conditions: pluralism of conceptions of the good, a certain degree of 'individualism', etc. Still, it is a powerful idea which can be justifiably put to work in the concrete working out of fair compromises.

It is highly significant that support for a 'naturalistic' justification of the moral point of view as sketched above can be found in some statements by Habermas. He prefaces the passage on basic rights referred to above with the claim: 'Moral universalism is a *historical result*'. Accordingly, the task of rendering plausible the principle of universalization (U) is said to involve 'genealogical arguments which rest on assumptions of modernization theory' (1996:357). More emphatically, he observes that this principle is initially 'nothing more than a hypothesis arrived at in an abductive fashion' (1996:354). The abductive confirmation of the rule (U) presupposes of course that it can be put to practical use in an experimental basis. Habermas accepts that: 'It must first be *shown* that a practice of justification conducted in this manner succeeds in selecting norms which are capable of gaining general agreement – e.g., those that enshrine human rights' (1996:355).

For an ethical naturalist this is as far as one can go – as far as one *should* go. For Habermas, however, it is not far enough. At this point he parts company with the naturalist, but also *with the participants in discourse themselves*, who, as Habermas concedes, 'will perhaps be content with this (or a similar) rule of argumentation as long as it proves its usefulness and does not lead to counterintuitive results'. Fearing then that 'ethnocentric assumptions, and hence a specific conception of the good which is not shared by other cultures may have insinuated themselves into the abduction of "U"', Habermas requires of the moral theorist 'a final step in justification', namely the dispelling of 'the suspicion that the understanding of morality operationalised in "U" reflects eurocentric prejudices' (1996:355).

The discourse theoretical approach *presumes* that this final step can be made good if the moral theorist, so to speak, 'goes transcendental', taking recourse to the purported normative content of communicative presuppositions of argumentation as such. Since I cannot possibly go here into the details of Habermas' extensive contributions to the program of a final justification, I will finish this paper with three short remarks.

1 In the absence of a final justification in that sense – and Habermas never claims to have *accomplished* it – our present agreement on fundamental-rights norms as well as the historical realizations in which Habermas sees 'the gradual embodiment of moral principles in concrete forms of life' (1990:208) should be assigned at best the status of *tacit compromises*. For they *may* just reflect, of course without our being aware of it, "intuitions of a particular culture or epoch" or 'the prejudices of adult, white, well-educated, Western males of today'. For the time being, we do not know whether this is the case or not. 'As long as the moral principle is not justified [...] the ethnocentric fallacy looms large' (1990:197). But this is to concede that the principle hypothetically posited by discourse ethics may be *au fond* the expression of an ethical value constitutive of a concrete form of life. Further, it also implies that compromises can now be

regulating pretty general interests. For the task I set myself in this essay this is a significative result.

2 Habermas never tells us how it would be, if the search for an ethically neutral foundation for morals should lead us to the unexpected *denial* of the idea expressed by the rule (U). Would we then have to recognize that some of our most central moral intuitions are all *wrong*, i.e., not moral at all? *If* there is a final step in justification to be made, it cannot be wholly determined by the justification reached at by merely abductive means. It must be possible for the yet to be accomplished final justification to collide with the less final one. The question of the final justification must be open even for unexpected outcomes. Otherwise, we may legitimately suspect that the device of a justification beyond the abductive one is only another manifestation of the nowadays so unpalatable philosophical hankering for an absolute certainty leading only to 'foundations' that have, however, to be supported by what they should carry. But again: can we make sense of a 'moral point of view' which goes against the core of our historically confirmed moral intuitions? If unexpected outcomes are excluded from the very beginning: what is laying foundations for what?

3 Let us, though, suppose that a rule of argumentation *has been* successfully derived in an unobjectionable way from presuppositions of argumentation as such. The question is: What difference does it make for participants trying to regulate morally their coexistence? They now have a rule of argumentation which can be used to set apart some norms of action as valid. But are the norms so selected also *moral*, i.e., *morally* justified? To see whether this is the case, participants have to apply them, to check the consequences of following them against their past experiences, their well-considered expectations, their intuitions. In short: they have to see whether the selected norms fulfill the function assigned to morality independently of the derivation of the rule of argumentation in question. But this is exactly the procedure of abductive justification; in which case the final justification does not add much. In this process, participants may be called to work out all sorts of compromises with a view to a 'locally' more satisfactory determination of rights, liberties and duties. Let us suppose that they explicitly refer in their deliberations to the principle (U). If a situation now arises in which the practical meaning usually associated by them with this principle reveals itself as part of the project of a privileged form of life, a form of life excluding others, their working out of a more inclusive compromise will involve at the same time the submitting of the

principle to a novel, fairer interpretation. Doing this they will be giving the idea behind (U) a new meaning – in each case a new meaning. Moreover, they will be here on their own: no amount of *a priori* considerations about pragmatic presuppositions of discourse can fix in advance and for all cases the meaning of a principle of universalization.

Notes

1 Here I quote Paton's translation of Kant's *Grundlegung* (1948:66).
2 Mackie (1977:33f.) makes a very strong case for the claim that a cognitivist view is now part and parcel of the ordinary understanding of morality. In a passage at least Habermas seems to follow suit. By separating moral knowledge from moral motivation, he concedes, discourse ethics cannot 'defend the full moral content of "comprehensive doctrines"' (p. 347). In this regard, discourse ethics does not accept without revisionism everyday moral intuitions.
3 A similar point is made by Dewey (1980:114): 'Complete universality of interest is, of course, impossible in the sense of equality of strength or force of quantity; that is, it would be mere pretense to suppose that one can be as *much* interested in those at a distance with whom one has little contact as in those with whom one is in constant communication'.
4 In his *Theory of the Moral Life*, (1980:112), Dewey states that the idea of 'a *standard* upon the basis of which approbation and disapprobation, esteem and disesteem, *should* be awarded [...] implies something universally applicable'. This, however, 'does not eliminate the element of favor and hostility to certain modes of conduct. But it introduces the regulation of these manifestations by something beyond themselves'.

References

Dewey, J. (1980), *Theory of the Moral Life*, Irvington Publishers: New York.
— (1988), *Human Nature and Conduct*. Southern Illinois University Press: Carbondale.
Habermas, J.(1996), 'On the Cognitive Content of Morality', in *Proceedings of the Aristotelian Society*, 46, pp. 335–358
— (1990), 'Morality and Ethical Life: Does Hegel's Critique of Kant Apply to Discourse Ethics?', *Moral Consciousness and Communicative Action*, MIT Press: Cambridge (MA).
— (1992), *Erläuterungen zur Diskursethik*, Suhrkamp: Frankfurt .
Kant, I. (1948) *The Moral Law. Groundwork of the Metaphysics of Morals* [Trans. H.J. Paton], Routledge: London.
MacIntyre, A. (1966), *A Short History of Ethics*. Macmillan: New York.
Mackie, J. L. (1977), *Ethics. Inventing Right and Wrong*, Penguin Books: London.

The postmodern discourse on the Other in the French context

5 Lyotard's conception of conflicting claims to validity and its insufficient Kantianism

Dietmar Köveker

The philosophical discussion of the last years is largely dominated by the question of whether it is possible to make the validity of universal, non-contextual, and non-relative standards of rationality as well as moral and social commitments intelligible or not. Whereas this debate found its specific Anglo American form in the controversy between liberals and communitarians, its European variant is pretty much focused around the discussion between the German defenders of the so-called Neo-enlightenment such as J. Habermas and K.-O. Apel and its French discourse-critical opponents like, for instance, J. Derrida or J.-F. Lyotard. As if it were not interesting enough that *both* of the participating sides are to a large extent referring to Kantian theorems and considerations, Lyotard's main thesis of a general, unavoidable conflict between different types of discourse that cannot be settled in any circumstances, relies fundamentally on a specific interpretation of (parts of) Kant's *Critique of Pure Reason*.

This essay pursues two major aims: it tries to elucidate this dependence on Kant's *opus magnum*, which is due to the close relationship between the problem of the *différend* and the questions discussed by Kant particularly in the 'transcendental dialectic' of the first *Critique*; and it seeks to identify the point in which Lyotard deviates from the Kantian arrangement of these problems. This far-reaching reference to the *Critique of Pure Reason* is obviously opposed to the current preoccupation with Lyotard's interpretation of the *Critique of Judgment*. Together with, nevertheless, Lyotard's astonishing negligence of one of Kant's main arguments for a solution of the *différend* which is found in the 'antinomy of pure reason', a more minute and exhaustive look on Kant's 'solution', especially of the 'conflict of pure reason with itself' as well as its comparison with the *différend* as such, becomes strongly desirable. This is the major consequence of the hermeneutic situation just described, giving rise to a thorough reexamination of the proposition of a general *différend* which is held to characterize postmodern societies.

In order to introduce and establish this thesis I will proceed in three steps. After (1) a reconstruction of the main aspects of Lyotard's conception of a *différend* I will (2) compare it with the Kantian reflections on the topic. The last step (3) will consist of a summary of the results of this discussion.

The conception of differend

'*Mon livre de philosophie*' (Lyotard 1983:cover-text). This is how Lyotard refers to his work on the differend. The initial phrase of the book immediately provides us with something like a working definition of what this expression means.

> As distinguished from a litigation, a differend [*différend*] would be a case of conflict, between (at least) two parties, that cannot be equitably resolved for lack of a rule of judgment applicable to both arguments (Lyotard 1995:xi).

What does this mean? The following 260 pages of the book try to develop this statement in the direction of a general insufficiency of human efforts to reach understanding in the course of communication. This lack of a common, all-embracing metalanguage 'in general' (1995:xii) in which every particular statement could be translated holds also for wider contexts and leads to the thesis of an unavoidable moral and social differend as such. Even if Lyotard seeks to restrict himself methodologically by saying that 'the A.'s only rule here is to *examine* cases of differend and to find the rules for the heterogeneous genres of discourse that bring about these cases' (1995:xiv, italics mine), his main thesis about the differend contains quasi-universal claims. In fact, the quoted methodological modesty is in conflict with Lyotard's contention 'that a universal rule of judgment between heterogeneous genres is lacking *in general*' (1995:xi, italics mine)

Lyotard could now try to resolve this problem by reference, for instance, to the Kantian distinction between laws or rules being 'universally' valid [*die allgemein gelten*] and others being valid just 'in general' [*die im Allgemeinen gelten*] (Kant 1902 V:36, and 1902 VIII:348 fn.). But this is obviously not what Lyotard has in mind, since he does not want to say that a differend just happens in most of the cases [*im Durchschnitte am öftesten* (see Kant 1902 V:36)]. Much more than this, he is adopting the perspective that people's efforts to communicate their ideas and thoughts *inevitably* lead to a differend. Following Lyotard, this can be seen most clearly if we consider the irritating problem that appears to be in the background of the whole topic: the difficulty of proving the existence of Nazi-extermination camps. The surviving victims do not only suffer from the humiliations and violations they were subjected to, they also have to face the structural difficulty, if not impossibility of providing proof for the existence of these camps.

> To the privation constituted by the damage there is added the impossibility of bringing it to the knowledge of others, and in particular to the knowledge of a tribunal. Should the victim seek to bypass this impossibility and testify anyway to the wrong done to him or to her, he or she comes up against the following argumentation: either the damages you complain about never took place, and your testimony is false; or else they took place, and since you are able to testify them, it is not a wrong that has been done to you, but merely a damage, and your testimony is still false (Lyotard 1995:§ 7).

As Lyotard states in the following paragraph, this problem, in its structure, resembles a 'dilemma'.

> Either you are the victim of a wrong, or you are not. If you are not, you are deceived (or lying) in testifying that you are. If you are, since you can bear witness to this wrong, it is not a wrong, and you are deceived (or lying) in testifying that you are the victim of a wrong. Let *p* be: you are the victim of a wrong; *not p*: you are not; *Tp*: phrase *p* is true; *Fp*: it is false. The argument is: either *p* or *not-p*; if *not-p*, then *Fp*; if *p*, then *not-p*, then *Fp*. The ancients called this argument a dilemma (1995:§ 8).

The fact that it is *not only* a dilemma brings us closer to Lyotard's own and genuine view on the problems which we are facing here. Everything depends on the *question of time* that is at play. Quite similar to the Aristotelian characterization of a contradiction, a genuine dilemma – taken in its original signification as an (unfortunate) alternative choice –, is dependent on the options available as an *immediate* alternative. That is, options which have to be chosen *hic et nunc* – at the same time and in the same regard (see Aristotle, IV.3, 1005b 19f.). As we have already seen, Lyotard shares this perspective on the 'dilemmatic' structure of the differend in so far as he conceives the latter as being constituted by alternative 'phrases' *excluding* one another: 'Phrases from heterogeneous regimens cannot be translated from one into the other' (Lyotard 1995:xii). This and the relation of exclusion between the various *régimes de phrases*, at the same time and in the same regard, becomes clearer when Lyotard focuses on the question of how to proceed after a certain régime de phrases has been chosen – or 'has arrived'.

> A phrase "happens" [*Une phrase «arrive»*]. How can it be linked to? By its rule, a genre of discourse supplies a set of possible phrases, each arising from some phrase regimen. Another genre of discourse supplies another set of other possible phrases. There is a differend between these two sets (or between the genres that call them forth) because they are heterogeneous. And linkage must happen "now"; another phrase cannot not happen. It's a necessity; time, that is. There is no non-phrase. Silence is a phrase. There is no last phrase (1995:xii).

We can see clearly from here that Lyotard in fact initially adopts the classical Aristotelian perspective on contradictions and dilemmas. The choice is unfortunate in so far as none of the alternative *régimes de phrases* can be translated into the other (i.e. does harm to significations contained in others), and the choice has to be taken at the same time [*maintenant*] and in the same regard (namely between *régimes de phrases*). The already mentioned corresponding inevitability of this structure relies on the fact that we cannot escape from being significant and from taking part in communication. The last sentence of the previous quotation, as well as various other formulations,[1] state this continuum of significance. This is the well known specific double-bind structure of human communication analyzed by the Palo Alto School (see Watzlawick/ Beavin/Jackson 1967, who, by the way, talk also of a 'schizophrenic dilemma') that underlies these statements, as summarized in the simple proposition: 'one's silence makes a phrase' (Lyotard 1995:xi).[2]

But this sentence also throws a certain light on Lyotard's view of the role of time in the constitution of a differend. In his thesis about the necessary emergence of a differend, Lyotard does not simply say that there exists a *necessity* for the linkage of phrases which, by the way, is a further indication of hidden 'universal' implications in his 'examination' of performative structures. He rather advances the question of time to the center of our interest, namely by identifying it with the necessity already mentioned. In fact, the consideration of time-inherent necessities is of the greatest importance for Lyotard's scrutiny of the differend. It is his first

'Notice', on Protagoras, which reveals this circumstance in all its important aspects.

The Protagorean argument

Lyotard introduces the well-known controversy between Protagoras and his student Euathlus as an example of the problems with which we are dealing. Having never been successful with complaints at court, the student went to Protagoras who should teach him how to argue convincingly.

> The master and the pupil have concluded a contract: the former will be paid only if the latter has been able to win, thanks to the teaching he receives, at least one of the cases he will plead before the tribunals during the period of said teaching. The alternative is simple and the judgment easy: if Euathlus has won at least once, he pays; if not, he is absolved (1995:Protagoras Notice, § 1).

One day Protagoras came to the student and asked him to pay his debt. The latter rejected by pointing to the fact that he had never won even with the teaching that he had received. Protagoras contradicts him by stating that he did in fact succeed once – i.e., in the very argument directed against Protagoras and maintaining Euathlus' missing success – *thereby* providing the precondition for the student's factual success.

> How can it be affirmed that Euathlus won when he always lost? It suffices to include the present litigation between him and Protagoras among the series of litigations to be considered in order to decide whether he always lost. In every previous litigation, he lost. Therefore, in the case against Protagoras who maintains that he won one time, he triumphs by ascertaining that he never won. But, if he thereby prevails in a litigation against Protagoras, he has *indeed* won at least once (1995:Protagoras Notice, § 1, italics mine).

According to Lyotard, this 'sophistication' used by Protagoras can be analyzed under three main aspects: self-reference, totality, and time-logic.

Self-reference. The first aspect concerns a peculiarity of ordinary language: it is capable of referring to outer properties of the world as well as to its own 'inner' components, that is, to itself. In other words: the 'paradox' is based on the fact that a phrase can serve as its own referent (1995:6). This sounds very 'structuralistic' in the sense that an abstract happening is executed by an anonymous power which is represented by a nameless structure. Speaking of the faculty of a *phrase* to refer to itself,

Lyotard seems to adopt this understanding of French structuralism which helped to overcome the metaphysical subjectivism of the traditional *philosophie de la conscience*. But this is just one way to put the problems in dispute, and it leads to some serious theoretical as well as practical difficulties. For instance, the self-referential, reflective question on how this purported insight into the elementary structure of, say, grammatical language can be possible on the ground of its own premises. If the 'universal' validity of the assumed, anonymous structure rules out by definition any *analyzing* access to it (which still must be conceptualized in terms of the properties and capacities of a mere consciousness): then how can *we* find it out? Who tells us about it? One of the corresponding practical problems would be how any kind of responsibility for human actions and its consequences could be maintained within the framework of such a structuralist essentialism.

Lyotard must have felt uneasy about this, since in the course of his further elaboration of this first peculiarity of the differend he returns to a language in which human actors can still be identified: '*Protagoras* confuses the modus (the declarative prefix: Euathlus says that) with the dictum, the negative universal that denotes a reality (Euathlus did not win once)' (1995:Protagoras Notice, § 2, italics mine). However, the last two quotations draw our attention to the range of possible points-of-view on the differend, a range which is still enlarged by Lyotard's indication that it was this ability of self-reference that forced B. Russell to develop his 'theory of types' in an attempt to avoid such 'confusions' (1995:6f.). With reference to the current philosophical debates mentioned in the introductory remarks of this essay it seems worthwhile to add here that it was exactly this bifurcation as a general property of speech-acts which, under the name of the 'performative-propositional double-structure' of every speech-act (see Habermas 1971:101ff.), served as one of the main sources of inspiration for the Habermasian project of a theory of communicative action. This represents a view on the phenomena under discussion here, which is obviously diametrically opposed to the one brought up by Lyotard.

Totality. The second aspect under which the differend between Protagoras and his student could be analyzed according to Lyotard presupposes the former distinction between *modus* and *dictum*. It is by this step that we reach Lyotard's more Kantian considerations. In an interesting preceding paragraph he already introduced the distinction between 'objects of cognition' and 'objects of an idea'.

> The difference, though, between communism, on the one hand, and a virus or a nebula, on the other hand, is that there are means to observe the latter – they are objects of cognition – while the former is the object of an idea of historico-political reason, and this object is not observable (1995:§ 5).

This is very much like the Kantian distinction between 'objects of possible experience' (or understanding) on the one hand, and 'objects of an idea' (or reason) on the other, which is deeply rooted in the architectonic of Kantian epistemology (among the numerous works on the topic cf. Buchdahl 1966/67 and Köveker 1996) and which provides the background for the vast discussion about principles of significance (see e.g. Rorty 1971). Still within the horizon of Kant's general treatment of these questions, Lyotard adds that no generally acknowledged procedures exist in order to prove the reality of an 'object of an idea'.

> For example, even in physics, there exists no such protocol for establishing the reality of the universe, because the universe is the object of an idea (1995:§ 5).

If there are still doubts concerning the question of whether Lyotard is inspired by the Kantian treatment of these questions or not, they should be entirely dispersed by Lyotard's choice of this example. It was exactly this 'cosmological' question about the nature or reality of the universe that caused, in Kant's view, the so-called 'antinomy of pure reason'. And just like Kant did in his chapter on the 'transcendental ideas' (Kant 1968:B 377ff.), Lyotard now introduces a concept that can be regarded as one of the key-words of his whole thinking: the concept of totality.

> As a general rule, an object which is thought under the category of the whole (or of the absolute) is not an object of cognition (whose reality could be subjected to a protocol, etc.). The principle affirming the contrary could be called totalitarianism (Lyotard 1995:§ 5).

How many ways this conception of totality and totalitarianism guides his thinking will become clear in the course of the following discussion on Lyotard's approach.[3] In our present context, to begin with, this conception deploys an impressive 'critical' power which is backed by profound epistemological restrictions. Adopting the Kantian 'transcendental-logical' argument against the 'natural' inclination of reason to infer from the concept of condition that there must be a totality of conditions – i.e. the unconditioned – and doing this before the background of a certain interpretation of Wittgenstein (Lyotard 1995:xiii), Lyotard's statements gain a specific air of skepticism that is pertinent to his interpretations (as well as to the one's of his deconstructivist and postmodernist fellows).

> If the requirement of establishing the reality of a phrase's referent according to the protocol of cognition is extended to any given phrase, especially to those phrases that refer to a whole, then this requirement is totalitarian in its principle (1995:§ 5).

I think this sentence contains, in a nutshell, one of the main characteristics of Lyotard's thinking. In view of the desperate history of the twentieth century, making him think of 'terror' (1995:§ 159), on the one hand, and the fatal weakness of reason, if not its very contribution to this history, on the other hand, all that seems to be expected from reason boils down to a kind of self-denouncing and self-limitation by the aid of its 'better' – the critical tradition. This can be seen as the motivational background responsible for a huge part of Lyotard's writings which can be easily detected when he goes on:

> That's why it is important to distinguish between phrase regimens, and this comes down to *limiting the competence* of a given tribunal to a given kind of phrase (1995:§ 5, italics mine).

In one of the most impressive paragraphs which also reveals the mentioned fusion of motives, driven by the deep distrust against simple 'rational' promises of consensus, comprehension and so forth, Lyotard applies these anti-totalitarian principles on the paradigm-case which he has in mind. He starts with the consideration that there can be no 'passage' from the phrase-universe of a Nazi-victim to the one of his torturer. But in order to state that, Lyotard adds, it has been inevitable to affirm an embracing plural, giving rise to the illusion that 'we' nevertheless come together: you, the reader, and me, the writer, as well as victim and torturer (see 1995:§ 158). It is *this* 'transcendental illusion' that must be seen as the main objective of Lyotard's critical thinking.

Time-logic. According to Lyotard the third aspect under which the sophistication 'committed' by Protagoras can be analyzed is that of its 'serial' time-structure. A closer look at it reveals the way in which the three aspects together constitute the differend. Firstly we should remember that the issue in question between Protagoras and his student is the failure of the latter in the course of his juridical controversies. Their succession builds a 'totality' which provides the proper subject of what the student's and Protagoras' contract is about. But while the former just thinks of his past controversies, the latter adds their present litigation [*litige*] to it. Exploiting the characteristic ability of linguistic self-reference, Protagoras claims that the student did in fact succeed once, *thereby* creating the precondition for the differend between the two. However disputable it may be as to whether Protagoras' behavior can be morally justified or not, his factual success, that is the possibility to reckon in the present controversy in their obviously 'moving' totality, reveals the later's 'serial' structure.

> The totality upon which the argument bears is serial: there are n litigations, the "current" litigation between master and pupil is added to the preceding ones, $n + 1$. When Protagoras takes it into account, he makes $n = n + 1$. It is true that this synthesis requires an additional "act": $(n + 1) + 1$ (1995: Protagoras Notice, § 3).

This serial structure of the differend[4] renders a mere logical analysis unsatisfactory, which makes a consideration of time-relations necessary. This is where a proper 'logic of time' has to be applied (Lyotard 1995:Protagoras Notice, § 3). Lyotard's elaboration of this point throws a specific light on the role of time-operators and in particular on that of the operator 'now'. Similar to language as such, it is characterized by a certain deictic capacity of self-reference. This property allows him to indicate the initial unit of a time series as well as a part of it – 'to be both the origin of temporal series (before and after) and an element in these series' (1995:Protagoras Notice, § 3), as Lyotard adds with reference to Jean Schneider (Schneider 1980) and Jean-Louis Gardies (Gardies 1975). Moreover, it is by reference to this *maintenant* as the unique point of time where conflicting opinions, argumentations and so on meet,[5] that the cryptic-universal inevitability of such a clash of claims to validity becomes evident. Whether the reasons that gave rise for a certain conflict were properly discussed or not, whether arguments were sufficiently exchanged and solutions in sight or not – in each case, 'linkage must happen "now"' (Lyotard 1995:xii).

In his revelation of the 'dilemma' in which the surviving victims of the Nazi-extermination camps find themselves when trying to provide proof of the existence of such camps, Lyotard referred to the classical origins of this problem, thereby also alluding to the exclusion of time-structures as represented, for instance, in Aristotle's formulation of the principle of contradiction. We took this as a demonstration of the universalistic traits in Lyotard's conception of the differend. If one expected to see this claim to (negative) universality modified or even renounced by the consideration of time-relations, it is a surprise to find the reinforcement of these cryptic-universal structures in an inescapable and 'necessary' compulsion to reproduce the differend even when time-relations are taken into consideration.

Kant on the differend

Even though Lyotard confessed that the most inspiring sources for his philosophy of the differend were 'the Kant of the third *Critique* and the historical-political texts (the "fourth Critique")' and 'the Wittgenstein of the *Philosophical Investigations* and the posthumous writings' (1995:xiii), I would also like to provide evidence for how the *first* Critique has influenced him. This evidence can still be reinforced, if we take into account other, even more striking parallels between Lyotard's 'agonal' conception of communication and Kant's *Critique of Pure Reason* (hereafter *KrV*).

As we already mentioned, one of Lyotard's guiding ideas is derived from the Wittgensteinean theory of language games. Similar to this conceptualization of the *relation* between the various uses of language in different cultures and through different speech-acts, Lyotard lists a variety of 'phrase regimens: reasoning, knowing, describing, recounting, questioning, showing, ordering, etc.' (1995:xii). We have also shown that, even though oscillating methodologically between the attitude of mere description and strong generalizing claims, Lyotard is inclined to maintain the latter cryptic universalism. In the present context this is expressed by the succinct contention: 'Phrases from heterogeneous regimens cannot be translated from one into the other' (1995:xii). Of peculiar interest here are the purported parallels between Lyotard and the Kantian first *Critique*, namely the contention that the conflicting points of view, expressed by the use of different *régimes de phrases*, are vindicating the same legitimacy. Already the initial two sentences of the book state implicitly that conflicting argumentations can show such an equal validity: 'One side's legitimacy does not imply the other's lack of legitimacy' (1995:xi) Even though this sentence only indirectly insinuates this equality without explicitly acknowledging the 'corresponding' legitimacy, Lyotard's further remarks on the topic leave his presupposition of equal (il-) legitimacy beyond a doubt.[6]

It is exactly this assertion of well-distinguished argumentations claiming convincingly equal validity which characterizes Kant's treatment of the so-called 'antinomy of pure reason' in the 'Transcendental

Dialectic' of his first *Critique*. Just as Lyotard presupposes the impossibility of judging who is right by stating 'the absence of a phrase regimen or of a genre of discourse that enjoys a universal authority to decide' (Lyotard 1995:xii), Kant contends that the 'antinomy of pure reason' seems to be irresolvable: it signifies 'the conflict of the doctrines of seemingly dogmatic knowledge (*thesis cum antithesi*) in which no [sic!] assertion can establish superiority over another' (*KrV* B 448).

As I already declared in the initial passage of this essay, my main objective is twofold: to mark the large extent in which Lyotard is relying on Kant's first *Critique*; and to indicate the point at which he deviates from the Kantian argument. I suppose that the previous remarks could already provide sufficient evidence in order to reach the first goal. In fact I consider this evidence to be a necessary hermeneutic prerequisite for reaching the second aim which has to be pursued by a close comparison between the Kantian solution of the antinomy and the differend as such. I would first like to summarize the Kantian 'solution' of the antinomy of pure reason as introduced in four steps.

1 After an application of his basic 'transcendental-idealistic' distinction between 'things in themselves' and (their) 'appearances' (*KrV* B 518-525) on the 'cosmological' questions;

2 Kant secondly separated the *given* appearances of the understanding from the tasks of reason (*KrV* B 525-530). He later summarizes this distinction in the following way.

> Since no maximum of the series of conditions in a sensible world, regarded as a thing in itself, is *given* through the cosmological principle of totality, but can only be *set as a task* that calls for regress in the series of conditions, the principle of pure reason has to be amended in these terms (*KrV* B 536).

3 The third step introduces a further (double) discrimination. Kant begins with the antinomy's outlook as if it were representing two contradicting propositions endowed with equal claims to validity. This is the case of what Kant calls an 'analytical opposition' where one of the two propositions is nothing more than the mere negation of the other. But in the case of the antinomy we are dealing rather with a 'dialectical opposition' of propositions, 'for the one is not a mere contradictory of the other, but says something more than is required for a simple contradiction' (*KrV* B 532; cf. Llewellyn 1964/65). This is explained for example by reference to the statement 'that the world is

either infinite in extension or is not infinite' (*KrV* B 531). One of the two propositions must be false, whereas in the case of 'the world is either infinite or finite (non-infinite)' (*KrV* B 532), both can be false. In short, Kant's third step in his solution of the antinomy of pure reason introduces the distinction between a contradiction of assertions [*Widerspruch* von Aussagen] and a dispute of statements [*Widerstreit* von Behauptungen], holding that the antinomy represents a sample of the latter species.

4 Thus prepared, Kant makes his fourth step, which consists in the introduction of 'the regulative principle of pure reason in its application to the cosmological ideas' (*KrV* B 536ff.). If one reads Kant's elaboration of this principle in section eight of the chapter on the antinomy carefully, one could conceive it as a kind of 'synthetization' of the previous steps. Given that the alternative propositions of the antinomy do in fact stand in a relation of conflicting statements to one another – i.e., the argument just developed in the previous section –, the present passage already opens by relating argument (1) and (2) to the principle of totality (*KrV* B 536). Only a few sentences later, where the 'regulative principle' is introduced explicitly, this allusion to the previous steps appears in its characteristic form.

> The principle of reason is thus [...] a principle of the greatest possible continuation and extension of experience, allowing no empirical limit to hold as absolute. Thus it is a principle of reason which serves as a *rule*, postulating what we ought to do in the regress, but *not anticipating* what is present *in the object as it is in itself, prior to all regress*. Accordingly I entitle it a *regulative* principle of reason, to distinguish it from the principle of the absolute totality of the series of conditions, viewed as actually present in the object (that is, in the appearances), which would be a constitutive cosmological principle. I have tried to show by this distinction that there is no such constitutive principle, and so to prevent what otherwise, through a transcendental subreption, inevitably takes place, namely, the ascribing of objective reality to an idea that serves merely as a rule (*KrV* B 536f.).

This raises the question of *how* the 'greatest possible continuation and extension of experience' [*die größtmögliche Fortsetzung und Erweiterung der Erfahrung*] can be secured. Kant's answer to this question operates with the distinction between the different *modi* of this research: a *progressus in infinitum* and a *progressus in indefinitum*. Both are relevant as far as the advance of knowledge is concerned, but in different cases. Kant restricts the application of the former to cases:

> when the whole is given in empirical intuition [...]; but when a member only of the series is given, starting from which the regress has to proceed to absolute totality, the regress is only of indeterminate character (*in indefinitum*) (*KrV* B 540f.).

The details of this suggestion are highly disputable, and the developments of modern physics, for instance, vote in favor of the *regressus in indefinitum*, especially when small objects, 'given' through direct perception, are concerned (cf. Köveker 1996). But what is much more important for our present discussion is that Kant deals *exactly* with the same problems that Lyotard is concerned with. As we saw earlier, Lyotard is less concerned with the 'antinomic' relation between the *content* of different argumentations but with the formal or 'structural' conflict between them as such. He contends that different points of view, argumentations, hypotheses etc. cannot be brought to agreement without violence. No higher authority helps to join them, understanding is impossible. But since insignificance and non-communication are held to be impossible (s.a.), we are inevitably led to the question of what happens next [*l'arrive-t-il'*] (cf. Lyotard 1983:14f. and § 264)]. Considering the conjunction of the convincingly asserted impossibility of non-communication within the inescapable progression of time and the contended general incompatibility of either part of the differend with the other, one would expect a never-ending misunderstanding. In fact, this is not the perspective of Lyotard, who reckons, however surprising, with the possibility of *future* understanding.

> The differend is the unstable state and instant of language wherein something which must be able to be put into phrases cannot *yet* be (Lyotard 1995:§ 22, italics mine).

In spite of all the experienced failure of understanding and what I have called the cryptic universalism of his thesis of hermeneutic totalitarianism, Lyotard still relies on the capacities of the *process* of communication. 'The invention of a new idiom' (1995:§ 23) is not understood as a continuation of our hermeneutic sufferings and insufficiencies. It is obviously considered as the unconditioned, unlimited possibility of reaching a proper, accurate understanding. Lyotard thinks of 'phrases which are in principle possible' (1995:§ 22).

> To give the differend its due is to institute new addressees, new addressers, new significations, and new referents in order for the wrong to find an expression and for the plaintiff to cease being a victim. This requires new rules for the formation and linking of phrases. *No one doubts that language is capable of admitting these new phrase families or new genres of discourse.* Every wrong ought to be able to be put into phrases. A new competence (or "prudence") must be found (1995: § 21, italics mine).[7]

If we now look back to the Kantian consideration of the relation between 'thesis' and 'antithesis' as contained in the antinomy, we see a very similar view on the *future* dimension of cognition. Whether a 'progressus in infinitum' or a 'progressus in indefinitum' can count as the appropriate procedure for solving a certain epistemological problem, the basic point that Kant has in mind here is undoubtedly that of the possibility of *new* cognitions, i.e. how to *proceed* in the course of knowledge, or, how to relate our past cognitions already 'constituted' to the ones lying before us from now on. Since steps (1) and (2) obviously rule out the possibility of an a priori determination of, for example, whether the world's size is finite or infinite, taking these alternatives as conflicting statements that can be both false (step 3), the road is open for the concrete investigation of the universe here and now *in indefinitum* (4). Even if the details of this question are sometimes arranged by Kant in an unfortunate, misleading, or simply wrong manner (see Köveker 1996:50ff.), we can say that the general accent of his reflections lies on the question of how to proceed adequately, 'backed' by the transcendental considerations and critical restrictions developed in the course of our inquiries until *now*. In this sense, by developing the 'regulative principle', Kant focuses on the epistemological act and moment where all our transcendental reflections inevitably enter and initiate the process of cognition.

We have thus far found astounding parallels between Kant's perspective on the problem of the conflict of reason with itself [Widerstreit] and the view of differend maintained by Lyotard. The even more surprising it is that Lyotard, when reconstructing the Kantian perspective, seems to be blind to its main characteristic which is represented by step (3), which functions like a bracket for the whole solution of the antinomy. This can be clearly seen if we look at Lyotard's own summary of the Kantian 'solution'.

> In the solution to the antinomies of pure reason (KRV), Kant writes that the question of the series resumes in itself all the conflicts that are raised by cosmological Ideas. The "last" phrase synthesizes the preceding ones. Is it or is it not part of their set? Dogmatism answers no, empiricism yes. Criticism remarks that the series is never given (*gegeben*), but only proposed (*aufgegeben*), because its synthesis is always deferred. The phrase that synthesizes the series (the judgment actually born upon the set of Euathlus' pleas) is not part of the series when it "takes place" (as an occurrence), but it is inevitably destined to become part of the series synthesized by the following phrase. The series formed by the world, in particular the world of human history, is neither finite nor infinite (we can argue either one indifferently), but the synthesis of the series, for its sake, is "indefinite" (KRV, pp. 455-548) (1995:Protagoras Notice, § 4).

Remembering the four steps which led to the Kantian 'regulative principle' we can easily see that Lyotard in an explicit way only refers to step (2) and (4) of the Kantian 'solution'. He cites the distinction between the 'data' of the understanding ['the series is never given'] and the 'tasks' of reason ('but only proposed') as well as Kant's 'indefinite' answer to the antinomy. From his earlier discussion of the difference between objects of cognition and objects of an idea we can admittedly deduce his awareness of step (1).[8] But the really surprising result of our comparison is Lyotard's almost entire negligence of step (3), precisely the one which touches the core of the differend. Lyotard's only indication related to this Kantian argument is the short remark that one can argue indifferently for the finite as well as the infinite option ['we can argue either one indifferently']. This clause, besides being hidden in brackets, is the only echo of this crucial reflection within the frame of *Le différend*.

I consider this to be a significant omission in Lyotard's discussion of speech structures in general and the question of whether we can reach understanding and consensus through argumentation in particular. Even though the underlying selectivity in the reading of the Kantian 'transcendental dialectic' is widespread and pertinent to the majority of interpretations (see Köveker 1996:ch. 2), this omission seems to be striking where the core of the interpreter's own approach is affected like in Lyotard's case.

Conclusions

In summarizing the foregoing comparison between Lyotard's conception of the *différend* and the Kantian original treatment of the *Widerstreit* as contained in the chapter on the 'antinomy of pure reason', I think at least three points should be emphasized.

1 Firstly, we have to underline the remarkable difference between the prevailing picture of the importance of Kantian thoughts for Lyotard and the factual influence of the former on the latter. Lyotard himself insinuates that, as far as the Kantian philosophy is concerned, he is occupied with the third *Critique*. This impression is still reinforced by Lyotard's studies on the subject such as his *Leçons sur l'Analytique du sublime (Kant, Critique de la faculté de juger, §§ 23-29)* (Lyotard 1991).[9] Nevertheless, we were able to identify a massive impact of important Kantian epistemological categories stemming from his theoretical philosophy – like, for instance, his distinction between objects of cognition and objects of an idea –, on central considerations of Lyotard.

2 We could also reconstruct deeply rooted connections between what Lyotard calls a *différend* and what Kant treats as a *Widerstreit*. The former concept shares so many features with the latter that it is almost miraculous how Lyotard could fail to realize this likeness and to subject it to proper scrutiny. It is not just the shared equivalence between the claims to validity corresponding to the conflicting 'régimes de phrases' in Lyotard's case, or the 'thesis' and 'antithesis' in the case of Kant, nor Lyotard's specific concept of totalitarianism, obviously relying to a remarkable extent on its Kantian prefiguration. Many further resemblances can be added.

We also heard about the Kantian 'skeptical method' (*KrV* B 451), characterized by its interest less in judging in favor of one of the conflicting sides than in a general understanding of the phenomenon as such. In a quite similar way, Lyotard characterized *le mode* of his investigation of the differend: 'it denies itself the possibility of settling, on the basis of its own rules, the differends its examines'. (Lyotard 1995:xiv) Moreover, within the context of Lyotard's analysis of how Protagoras could succeed in creating a differend, the importance of his inclusion of the present and therefore last controversy into the 'series' was made evident. A similar attention to the serial structure (see Strawson 1966:185ff.; Bennett 1974:§§ 40ff.) of the 'rows' and 'chains' underlying the structure of the antinomy is characteristic of the Kantian approach, leading to the statement that those who are allowed to mount the last offensive will win (cf. Kant 1968:B 450). Is it not quite the same with 'the paradox of the last phrase' (1995:§ 17)?

In this context we should mention a seemingly obvious divergence between Lyotard and Kant. The latter adds in the present passage that the one who attacks will succeed – whereas Lyotard speaks of 'the defense's advantage, as recognized by Aristotle (*Rhetoric* 1402 b 24-25) and by strategists' (Lyotard 1995: § 10), because it is the plaintiff who has to prove, for example, the existence of the Nazi-extermination camps.

> Reality is always the plaintiff's responsibility. For the defense, it is sufficient to refute the argumentation and to impugn the proof by a counter-example (1995:§ 10).

But even here, if we look a little closer to what is said, it becomes less clear whether this provides an example for the divergence between Lyotard and Kant or rather a further affirmation of the resemblance between their positions. In Kant's case it is also a 'reality' (finiteness or infinitness of the world) that is disputed, and whoever the plaintiff may be – in Kant's treatment of the question it becomes quite clear that both sides can play this part –, the *defender* will win (for instance *'par un contre-exemple'*). So even in Kant it is the one mastering '*la dernière phrase*' who will succeed.[10]

However, even if we would throw out all of these examples of how Lyotard relies on Kantian theorems, there remains one 'theoretical' congeniality between the two approaches which alone would justify its thorough investigation: the one between the *différend* and the *Widerstreit* as such, step (3) of the Kantian solution of the 'antinomy' and, as far as the philosophy of the differend is concerned, its most important element. For the time being one of the puzzling questions related to Lyotard's interpretation of Kant is how the former could fail to pay attention to this theoretical relationship. And as if Lyotard's negligence of this point were not remarkable enough, the German translation of *Le différend* into *Der Widerstreit* turns out to be something like the *fait accompli* of this ignorance.

3 I am convinced that the present essay provides enough evidence for the large extent in which Lyotard relies on considerations of Kant's first *Critique*. Adding the quality of this dependence on the Kantian epistemological account, significantly deviating from the prevailing picture of a Lyotardean preoccupation of the third *Critique* as launched by Lyotard himself, a revision of the philosophy of the differend and in

particular its relationship to the Kantian solution seems to be highly desirable.

Since my major aim was to show the necessity of such a new perspective on Lyotard's *opus magnum*, I will not burden future investigations with hasty conclusions about the consequences of the hermeneutic situation described above. But what I hope to have made clear is that the *différend* between Kant and Lyotard is obviously insufficiently articulated, if realized at all.

Notes

1 'Silence makes a phrase' (Lyotard 1995:xi); 'Not to speak is part of the ability to speak' (1995:§ 14); ' silence [...] is a negative phrase' (1995:§ 22); etc.

2 This inevitability of significance does not only hold within the narrow frame of sign-language but, as M. Merleau-Ponty – who was an important philosophical teacher for Lyotard's generation – showed, for the human existence as such. Thus the fact that I cannot stop looking [*je ne peux pas cesser de voir* (Merleau-Ponty 1945: 453)] corresponds to the unavoidable significance of my face, my voice etc. [*un visage* [...] *est toujours condamné à exprimer quelque chose [...], le silence est encore une modalité du monde sonore* (Merleau-Ponty 1945:516)].

3 For a further elaboration of Lyotard's view on the relation between the 'power of totality' and, for instance, 'terror' as well as 'consensus' as a variant of theoretical totalitarianism see Lyotard (1979:last chapter).

4 It might be worth remembering here that Kant talked of chains [*Ketten*] or rows [*Reihen*] of conditions (see Kant 1968: B 377ff.) etc.

5 By the way: Did Lyotard not realize the importance of Merleau-Ponty's phenomelogical approach to time-logic for the conception of the differend [*le présent* [...] *est la zone où l'être et la conscience coïncident* (Merleau-Ponty 1945:484f.)]?!

6 It is admittedly closer to Lyotard's own point of view to restrict oneself in this context to the assertion that he just presupposes an equivalence of (il-) legitimacy. As is pertinent to the French rejection of justificational and grounding discourses since the days of early existentialism, he keeps – or seems to keep – his distance from sharing one or the other of the argumentations in dispute. This seems to be the case even when treating the differend between the victims of Nazi-extermination camps and the 'revisionists' denying their existence like, for instance, the French historian F. Faurisson. Nevertheless it suffices for my argument that Lyotard presupposes equality or equivalence as far as questions of legitimacy and validity are concerned, since this is exactly what Kant reckons with: that the propositions in dispute are 'both false' (*KrV* B 532).

7 See also Lyotard's statement at the end of *La condition postmoderne* that the only legitimation for science would be that it makes new phrases possible (Lyotard 1979:ch. 14).

8 For the purposes of the present essay we do not have to discuss the problem whether this 'transcendental-idealistic' distinction is tenable or not. It is surely not like the criticism of idealism from Hegel through Peirce to Strawson was able to show (cf., for instance, Strawson 1966:38f.). Nevertheless the general intention of this 'critical' distinction can be reconstructed within the logic of discourse (see Köveker 1996: ch. 4).

9 For an interesting treatment of the 'aesthetical' arguments in relation to at least some of the questions discussed in the present essay see Lyotard (1986).

10 This non-equivalence between plaintiff and defender resembles very much the lack of symmetry between verification and falsification procedures as stated by Popper (cf. Popper 1959:32f.). Without explicitly referring to him, it is obvious that Lyotard was aware of the Popperian observation in asserting that 'it cannot be said that a hypothesis is verified, but only that until further notice it has not yet been falsified' (Lyotard 1995:§ 10). With a sense of regret and an appeal to the Heideggerean *Seinsvergessenheit* he concludes: 'This is our way of thinking that reality is not a given, but an occasion to require that establishment procedures be effectuated in regard to it' (1995:§ 10).

References

Buchdahl, G. (1966/67), 'The relation between "Understanding" and "Reason" in the Architectonic of Kant's Philosophy', *Proceedings of the Aristotelian Society*.

Gardies, J.-L. (1075), *La logique du temps*, Paris.

Habermas, J. (1971), 'Vorbereitende Bemerkungen zu einer Theorie der kommunikativen Kompetenz', in Habermas & Luhmann, N., *Theorie der Gesellschaft oder Sozialtechnologie: Was leistet die Systemforschung?*, Suhrkamp: Frankfurt.

Kant, I. (1902ff.), *Gesammelte Schriften* [Hg. von der Königlich Preußischen Akademie der Wissenschaften], de Gruyter: Berlin.

— (1968 [*KrV*]), *Critique of Pure Reason* [Trans. N. Kemp Smith], Macmillan: London.

Köveker, D. (1996), *Grenzverhältnisse. Kant und das »regulative Prinzip« in Wissenschaft und Philosophie*, Duncker & Humblot: Berlin.

Llewelyn, J.E. (1964/65), 'Dialectical and Analytical Opposites', *Kant-Studien* 55, 171-174.

Lyotard, J.-F. (1979), *La condition postmoderne*, Minuit: Paris.

— (1983), *Le différend*, Minuit: Paris.

— (1986), 'Grundlagenkrise', *Neue Hefte für Philosophie* 26, 1-33.

— (1991), *Leçons sur l'Analytique du sublime (Kant, Critique de la faculté de juger, §§ 23-29)*, Editions Galilée: Paris.

Lyotard, J.-F.(1995) [3rd printing], *The differend: phrases in dispute* [Trans. G. Van Den Abbeele], University of Minnesota Press: Minneapolis.
Popper, K. (1959), *The Logic of Scientific Discovery*, Hutchinson: London.
Rorty, R. (1971), 'Verificationism and Transcendental Arguments', *Nous* 15, 3-14.
Schneider, J. (1980), 'La logique self-référentielle de la temporalité' [typoscript], Paris.
Strawson, P.F. (1966), *The Bounds of Sense*, Methuen: London.

6 The limits of solidarity

Discourse ethics, Levinas, and the moral point of view

Max Pensky

'Solidarity' is a term that has recently received a prominent place in a variety of debates in moral and political theory. Yet the term itself, and the philosophical presuppositions that underlie it, often remain obscure. In the following I would like to discuss the idea of solidarity in its relation to the norms of symmetry and reciprocity, specifically as this relation is developed in discourse ethics. I will then present the ethical reflections of Emmanuel Levinas as a way of suggesting that the 'symmetrical solidarity' that discourse ethics discovers in the pragmatic presuppositions of argumentation encounter their limit in the experience of the concrete injurability of an other, which has an inherently asymmetrical character.

One of the enduring difficulties involved in any philosophical discussion of the ethics of solidarity is a basic ambiguity that inheres within the word itself. 'Solidarity' can be taken in either a descriptive or a normative sense. In its descriptive sense, social solidarity refers to the result of a successful process of social integration. In this sense, solidarity merely refers to what members of a community do when they identify themselves and acknowledge each other as members; anomie and isolation, the opposites of social solidarity, describe what individuals cannot do when they are unable to find amongst themselves the elements of a ground consensus on collective identity. Now, this conception of mutual acknowledgment of communal membership is of course far from simply descriptive: witness the number of current political and social questions that hinge on who is acknowledged – and who gets to do the acknowledging – of communal membership. Nevertheless, the sheer fact of membership is in itself not a normative, particularly not a moral question. It is perfectly possible to imagine a high level of mutual recognition of membership to a collective without such recognition implying any special claim to mutual care and protection. In the following it is not so much this descriptive, but rather a normative sense of solidarity that concerns me.

In this normative sense of solidarity, we regard human solidarity to be a disposition among subjects to regard themselves and one another as so mutually and intractably engaged in each others' lives that ethical relationships – of mutual protection, mutual acknowledgment of injurability and need for care and regard – arise as a result. Solidarity in this normative sense entails an active concern for others, an ability to take the role of the other and see the other's interests and welfare as intimately connected with one's own; a willingness to abandon egocentric calculations in order to come to the assistance of others who are threatened with injury or injustice. In this sense, normative solidarity is the thematization, in terms of ethical responsibility, of the experiences of irreducible intersubjectivity, inter-dependence, and injurability or vulnerability [*Verletzbarkeit*]. It is the inability and unwillingness to experience another's injury as unrelated to me. This is why we often use the word 'integrity' to denote not just the process of social integration, the construction of the interconnectedness of different lives into a higher solidity, the wholeness of an ethical life, but also the disposition of individuals to act 'with integrity', that is with a sincerity that is produced out of this whole, out of recognition to the solidarity that is the matrix for all individual moral relationships. Normative solidarity is rooted in the feeling of mutual care, and care arises from the perception of injurability.

In this sense, 'solidarity' seems to differ from the broader category of 'moral relationships' or 'situations of ethical obligation' on two grounds: First, insofar as it relates to the relations of mutual concern and care that should compose the fabric of collective life, solidarity in the normative sense wavers, as it were, in an ambiguous position between purely moral considerations on the one hand, and on the other hand 'ethical' and political considerations that are specific to particular communities at particular times. Secondly, solidarity seems to thematize not just the active concern for the other within a context of interwoven social relationships, but to suggest, in a radical form, the actual undermining of the clear boundaries of individuality itself; for in all its forms, solidarity carries with it the connotation of a 'for-the-other', of a care beyond mere benevolence, in which someone can experience such a direct and complete responsibility for another that the notion of an ethical 'obligation' mediated through the acknowledgment of the validity of a norm seems inappropriate.

This normative feel for the irreducibly shared experience of mutual vulnerability underlies the various attempts to present solidarity – or more generically 'community' in the strong sense – as a set of human relationships that exhibit a structure of symmetry and reciprocity. In this preliminary sense, by 'symmetry' I mean a human relationship or set of relationships structured by mutual acknowledgment and recognition; by 'reciprocity' I mean a relationship or set of relationships structured by mutual, reasonable expectations that everyone's different needs and desires will be taken into account in collective decisions. Symmetry refers to the vision of a collective life that is structured on the fact of complete mutual recognition (whether as 'We white liberals' or 'We members of an ideal communication community'). Reciprocity refers to the vision of a collective life that consists of mutually coordinated interactions.

Most particularist or 'communitarian' ethical theories want to describe the ethical dimension of social solidarity as a feeling of interconnectedness or intersubjective interdependence arising from particular, collectively recognized norms or practices. They thus tend to view symmetry and reciprocity in interpersonal relationships as arising from the facticity of a shared way of life. Discourse ethics, on the other hand, is committed to a formal-ideal criterion of a symmetrical coordination of collective life, grounded in the universal presuppositions of argument. Symmetry and reciprocity in this sense refer not to a concrete form of life, but rather to an intuitively accessible and rationally reconstructible dimension of mutual interdependence that is itself the product of the unavoidable intersubjective reflexivity of ego-development, according to which the very possibility of becoming a human subject is determined as the mutual, simultaneous – 'symmetrical' – constitution of ego and alter. In this manner – specifically by tracing both the moral regard for the individual as the bearer of universal rights to respect and recognition (justice) as well as the ethical 'feel' for mutual protection of common vulnerabilities (solidarity) back to the basic symmetries and reciprocities of language use – discourse ethics argues that the antinomy of individual and collective that have plagued moral theory since its inception can be revealed to be inadequate and correctable.

Solidarity in discourse ethics

Solidarity is a problem for deontological moral theories. The hellenistic-hegelian vision of the concrete immediacy of ethical life, in which collective norms are the organic product of a unique process of collective sociation, presents such theories with the claim that solidarity outweighs freedom; that the latter, as universalized, is underwritten by a doctrine of the autarkic, autonomous, spontaneous self, is itself a moment in a larger process of social solidarization. What emerges is thus a conflict between the freedom of the moral self and the solidarity of the intersubjective group; a conflict between *liberté* and *fraternité*. Enlightenment tradition has tended to respond with the claim that freedom outweighs solidarity insofar as the forms of rational respect and unconditional obligation arising from ascriptions of moral personhood must take priority over any other bases for social solidarity. The Enlightenment view of solidarity is thus curiously doubled: on the one hand, it sees solidarity in its normative sense as a futural predictable side-effect of a universal process of moral-rational and scientific-rational education, in which the cultivation of universal rationality will gradually supplant particular forms of social solidarity for a cosmopolitan solidarity based in the recognition of rational nature alone. On the other hand, solidarity is regarded as a compensation or supplement for the disenchantments and anomic potentials of processes of rationalization.

The discourse ethical approach has responded to this impasse with the argument that both the moral freedom and autonomy that we attribute to individual moral agents (justice) and the acknowledgment of the structures of mutual care, reciprocity and injurability that we understand with the concept of moral solidarity, are not only not opposed to one another, but are in fact two aspects of the same developmental process; the reciprocal respect and recognition that we accord to individuals, to do them justice, and the recognition of another's need for care and protection, of the intimacy of the other's identity with my own, to practice solidarity, are merely the natural consequences of the undistorted developmental path that each person must travel in order to become a competent speaker and hearer.

Habermas, in particular, has argued that the unity of justice and solidarity is ultimately grounded in the symmetry and reciprocity of communicative competencies. Thus symmetrical communicative relationships are explored (a) in the universal pragmatic presuppositions of speaking and hearing as such, (b) in the symmetrical relationships of role-taking that characterize the ontogenetic history of the self, and (c) in the symmetries of undistorted communication that constitute the pragmatically unavoidable idealizations – the 'ideal communication community' – of a postconventional moral consciousness.

The communicative presupposition of symmetrical relations

The symmetrical relationships presupposed by universal pragmatics have been developed and analyzed in great detail and need not be rehearsed at length here. It is sufficient for our purposes to recall that the point of the rational reconstruction of the basic competence of language users is that, in the notion of illocutionary force, utterances carry with them the presupposition of symmetrical interpersonal relationships. The illocutionary force of any utterance is a call or claim that the comprehensibility of the utterance is dependent on a reflective relation with the speaker: to understand an utterance is to be able to place one's self in the role of the speaker; to be willing to hear and take positions on reasons to support the propositional content of the utterance. To be a speaker one must also be a hearer: to be able to take the role of the speaker, the hearer must become the other insofar as the 'otherness' of the other consists of the status of the other as the speaker, as the one who is offering an utterance. To be a hearer is to be able, at least in the context of the speech act in question, to identify with the speaker. The symmetry of speaker and hearer, implied by the illocutionary force of every utterance, is an identity-in-difference between speaker and hearer.

Role-taking as a condition of subjectivity

Such a strong reading of symmetrical communicative relationships is grounded on the Meadean idea that, rather than an opposition between the structures of the individual self and the web of intersubjectivity, 'individuality' itself is always already an intersubjective term; that selfhood is in itself a result of a learning process in which individuals develop identities through processes of internalizing social expectations through role-taking.

For Mead, individuation takes place through mutual and reciprocal socialization in both a cognitive and a moral-practical dimension. Cognitively, 'individuality' invariably presupposes interaction in which subjects learn from others how to take part in symbolically mediated interaction. Ego develops, as it were, first through the other, already as the mirror-reflection of an alter-ego against whom the self must take up a second-person attitude as speaker or hearer. Antecedent to all self-objectifying introspection, then, in which 'I' reflect upon my own experiences, is an immediacy of a me-you relationship, a face-to-face of speaker and hearer in which a social me is constituted through the face of the other. By conforming to a symmetrical relationship with an other, a self learns the meaning of its own utterances through the other's response. What we mean by moral individuality is in itself a moment in a continuous process of mutual and continuous 'face-to-face' encounters.

> The self of an ethical self-understanding is dependent upon recognition by addressees because it generates itself as a response to the demands of an other in the first place. Because others attribute accountability to me, I gradually make myself into the one who I have become in living together with others. The ego, which seems to me to be given in my self-consciousness as what is purely my own, cannot be maintained by me solely through my own power, as it were for me alone – it does not "belong" to me. Rather, this ego always retains an intersubjective core because the process of individuation from which it emerges runs through the network of linguistically mediated interactions' (Mead, quoted in Habermas 1992:180).

And yet, oddly, precisely the symmetry of this relationship also produces an imbalance. Like all true symmetry, the 'sides' of a me-you relationship would be entirely reversible were the self not able to have some recourse, however, dim, to an 'I' that is not identical with the 'me' of symmetricality and thus disturbs this symmetry. For Mead, the 'I' is the moment of self-spontaneity, of action in the sense of *Willkür*. In cognitive self-relation I have a dim access, through memory, of an I that underlay the spontaneous actions and impulses – i.e. the new beginnings in the current of social interaction – that retrospectively a 'me' can attribute to itself. Thus the 'I' is for Mead neither present to consciousness nor absent from it: rather, the absence of a source of unquestioned individual spontaneity persists within the symmetrically generated self as a memory that disturbs that self's totalizing vision of its own essence. This peculiarity becomes more pronounced if, following Habermas' reconstruction, we turn to the I/me relationships in the moral/practical relation to self. As the interiorization of the norms and practices that constitute a solidary community, the practical 'me' of moral self-consciousness is, as Habermas observes, an inherently conservative force. It is the internalization of a 'generalized Other' as the mere abstraction of the sum total of normative expectations.[1] Over against this norm-conforming 'me', a normative 'I' lingers which is the source now of moral spontaneity in the Kantian sense; that is, a non-conceptual selfhood to which we attribute the free will that interrupts the continuum of conventional rule-following for moral principles that transcend the symmetrical structures of mutual expectation. What in cognitive terms served as a peculiar reserve of the interruptive power of retention on the seamlessness of a social self reappears, in a moral self-relation, as the disruptive force of criticism. And if the cognitive 'I' is accessible to the social self only as the interruptive anamnestic trace, so the normative I corresponds to an idealization in which the me projects itself into a community of ideal agents, in whose company alone the acceptability of norms could win unconditional approval.

Thus far Mead's 'me' seems a likely candidate for solidarity – although, as a product and champion of convention, the 'me' would appear to be fit for a merely descriptive solidarity, embedded in the mutual interdependencies of whatever collectivity it finds itself in. This in turn would leave the elusive 'I', grandchild of Kant's noumenal self, as the ultimate subject of rational respect, a being whose existence is diachronic and deferred – preserved through retentional memory in the very me that erases it in a cognitive sense, projected as the pure form of anticipation in a moral sense, against a social self that acts as its conservative brake. The social self offers only a conventional ethical identity; however, the very incompleteness of the symmetry through which the me is created leaves the only access to a moment of moral 'consciousness', a critical idealization through which a universal solidarity can be made practical. In effect, then, the normative I is an 'appeal to posterity' (Habermas 1992:183); that is, the 'I' constitutes (if this is the right word) the ability to think of a self-relation to generalized norms – i.e. the basis for factual social solidarity – as membership in 'a universal discourse that is counterfactually directed into the future' (Habermas 1992:184).

Symmetry and morality

This situation makes the idea of a moral learning process towards a post-conventional moral consciousness plausible as the ability to break from an originary conventional symmetry, and through reflection to aim toward the reconstitution of the form of symmetry itself as a model of interpersonal relationships and intersubjective validity of norms. What Mead had theorized as the futural projection of a community of discourse can now be shown to be what people are already doing insofar as they are capable of mastering the rules of argumentation.

The break-out of an originary symmetry is the impetus for the transition to post-conventional morality, in which the *de facto* authority of conventional norms is abandoned, and along with it the purely factual integrative success of social solidarity. In its place is another symmetry than the one that produced the conventional self. In the move to a postconventional identity, the ego steadily overcomes the conventional contradiction between individual autonomy and collective self-determination. By regarding matters of moral relevance from the formal-abstract perspective of an ideal communication community I place myself counter-factually into another solidarity, in which the bonds between individuals is secured solely through the universal perspective of the conditions of possible understanding.

In this manner discourse ethics argues for the mutuality – or one could say, the symmetry and reciprocity – of justice and solidarity from a post-conventional moral point of view. Once individual integrity and the maintenance of intersubjective structures of recognition are referred to the same vanishing-point (the moral point of view) then the acknowledgment of the inviolability of the individual rights of one person can only be thought possible as one half of a point of view that also always acknowledges the total web of relations of mutual recognition in which 'personhood' arises. 'Moral provisions for the protection of individual identity cannot safeguard the integrity of individual persons without at the same time safeguarding the vitally necessary web of relationships of mutual recognition in which individuals can stabilize their fragile identities only mutually and simultaneously with the identity of their group' (Habermas 1990:116).

Mutual respect for each injurable person is the moral abstraction of the formal symmetries of speech and sociation: it finds its equivalent in an equally formal vision of a network of mutual acknowledgment. Solidarity, not benevolence, thus forms the complement of modern justice; solidarity here is understood as 'rooted in the recognition that each person must take responsibility for the other because as consociates all must have an interest in the integrity of their shared life context in the same way' (1990:118).[2]

Here we can observe the main tension in the discourse-ethical reconstruction of a post-conventional solidarity: on the one hand, modern solidarity as the flip-side of modern justice necessarily abstracts itself from any grounding in a particular *Sittlichkeit*; read through the reconstructed past (of the intimacy of individuation and sociation) and the formalized future (of an ideal communication community) solidarity is the sheer valorization of symmetrical relationships. Modern solidarity has been 'transformed in the light of the idea of a general discursive will formation'. In this sense, the symmetry and reciprocity inherent in any conception of social solidarity, whether modern or pre-modern, moves from a descriptive to a normative sense in a new way. From the implicit universal solidarity that must always be presupposed even in the most particularistic and conventional social collectives (because even such collectives necessarily participate in action oriented toward reaching understanding) universal solidarity is now raised to the level of a conscious ideal against which any form of particular social solidarity must measure itself. Universal solidarity thus serves not only as the mode of integration and integrity for postconventional morality, but also as a continuous test of the limit of particular forms of morality, and thus the continuous demonstration that such conventional limits are always drawn with an element of arbitrariness, of pure contingency.

On the other hand, however, universal solidarity is formal and hence threatened with emptiness. The course of argumentation must make a considerable jump: in order to satisfy the idea that solidarity refers to the lived reality of mutual care and responsibility, and not just to a formal process of argumentation, the argument itself must make a transition from a universal solidarity grounded in the symmetry and reciprocity of communicative relationships to a symmetry and reciprocity of mutual care.

Communicative symmetry and reciprocity presupposes ideally that all members are acknowledged as entitled to participate equally in a discourse, and that everyone's contributions to discourse will be heard. This specifies the form of a communicative practice for the rational justification of norms but says nothing about mutual care. For mutual care to be an intelligible category one must begin with the notion of injurability, derived from the linguistic character of the process of sociation. Individuality is injurable – vulnerable – insofar as the self is produced only through a process of mutual and reciprocal interaction. 'The more the subject becomes individuated, the more he becomes entangled in a densely woven fabric of mutual recognition, that is, of reciprocal exposedness and vulnerability' (Habermas 1990:199). Thus universal solidary defines 'injury' not physically but entirely as the inherent limit of selfhood; that is, that the social limits of the self can be experienced as a threat to that same self. In this sense solidarity is the only way that individual identity can be protected: the 'consideration' that we find in solidarity 'has the twofold objective of defending the integrity of the individual and of preserving the vital fabric of ties of mutual recognition through which individuals reciprocally stabilize their fragile identities' (Habermas 1990:200).

But of what, precisely, does the vulnerability consist? If the 'self' is injurable insofar as it is increasingly enmeshed in deeper and deeper networks of intersubjective interdependencies, then it is not clear how the reciprocal recognition of such dependencies and the mutual concern to protect the integrity of these relationships (solidarity) are to 'stabilize' or protect the individual from injury.

The problem is that a formal conception of symmetrical solidarity must remain empty unless it incorporates a substantial conception of care, which in turn requires at least some approximation to a substantive conception of injurability. As a procedural explanation of the moral point of view, discourse ethics explains injury with very same set of interdependencies and mutual relations of acknowledgment in which it defines solidarity: the 'densely woven fabric of mutual recognition' explains both the need for morality and the satisfaction of this need. There is thus the perpetual risk of a certain circularity in how we conceive of injurability: the vulnerability of the individual and the stabilizing, protective force of symmetrical solidarity are concepts used to define each other. The care for the other, demanded by solidarity, is in fact a care for the fragile networks of reciprocal relationships that constitute the self: care for the other, in other words, is in fact care for a form of interaction for which the injurable other is, so to speak, the ambassador. What is necessarily missing is a substantive conception of the injurability of another person and hence a concrete conception of care as the function of a community of solidarity. But for such a concrete conception of injurability, we may need to step outside of the ideal symmetry and reciprocity of communicative relationships, and attempt another strategy in formulating the ethical content of interpersonal relationships.

Solidarity in the face of the Other: Levinas

In *Totality and Infinity* (1967), Emmanuel Levinas defines ethics as 'the putting-into-question of my spontaneity, by the presence of the Other [*l'Autrui*]' (1967:43). The statement crystallizes much of Levinas' project: first, a critique of the metaphysical tradition in which 'totalizing' thought is condemned as inherently violent due to its origin in the self-preserving and self-reassuring activities of a blindly self-interested subject; second, an attempt to break entirely with the tradition of metaphysics and its obsession with 'Being', from Plato to Heidegger, and the insistence that ethics, not ontology, is the first philosophy; third, the project of supporting the claim for the primacy of the ethical by a phenomenological analysis of the irreducible, 'infinite' appearance of the Other, the stranger, the downcast – a suffering face whose very fragility and injurability constitute an eruption of the infinite into the totalizing system of rational-calculative rationality; fourth, the more complex view that the approach of the face of the Other, and the unconditioned or infinite moment of ethical responsibility conveyed by it, 'puts into question' the very integrity of the intentional ego, undermining its supposedly foundational claim to primacy, contesting the ability of the ego to arrogate to itself the very 'spontaneity' – in the Kantian and Meadean sense of the capacity to inaugurate new beginnings in the phenomenal chain of cause and effect – by which ethical theory has become accustomed to defining moral agency.

The 'approach' of the Other is the confrontation with alterity, and in this initial sense we can define this darling-word of postmodern ethics as that dimension of an ethically relevant relationship with another that cannot be assimilated under a concept or a moral rule. Hence Levinas refers to alterity as an 'excess' or 'overflow' – an infinity – of ethical responsibility in the face of the Other, such that the 'unconditioned' moment of ethical obligation is not universal in the sense of generalizable, but rather in the sense of a context-independent or transcendent moment in the encounter of the suffering face of another. 'Alterity' for Levinas, thus refers to the trace of infinitude, of that element of an ethical encounter that exceeds and resists any and all attempts to capture the essence of ethical relationships in any system of principles.

The 'face' of the Other is thus defined for Levinas as 'the way in which the Other presents himself, exceeding the idea of the Other in me' (Levinas 1967:50). And with this notion of the face, Levinas attempts to thematize in phenomenological terms the paradoxical experience of infinite ethical responsibility: the face of the Other is on the one hand near or proximate; it is not meant as a metaphor but rather as the description of an experience of absolute nearness and also an exteriority that resists all attempts at my appropriation. Rejecting any Heideggerian suggestion that the face of the Other could be thought of as an aspect of *Welterschliessung*, Levinas insists that the face of the other is not 'disclosed' since it was and is always already there: it predates the intentional ego and is prior to its interests. The face – and thus the face-to-face encounter of ethics – is the beginning point and limit of all solidarity.[3]

The face of the other, its skin and its 'nakedness', present me with what about another remains irreducibly other, what can be touched but not grasped or owned, what cannot be 'dealt with' by calculation. This paradoxical simultaneity of proximity and exteriority, of nearness and fairness[4] leads Levinas, in *Totality and Infinity*, to argue for an approach to ethics in which neither sight (as in the metaphysical tradition) nor hearing (as in the later Heidegger) but rather touch (the semiotic dimension of language or discourse) is the medium for the unconditional or transcendental aspect of ethical obligation: the face of the other is irreducibly physical and corporeal, injurable and in need. Discourse originates with the physical nakedness of a face that speaks to me, a face whose very discourse is at every instant subtended by the fleshly categorical imperative not to murder; an infinite command that for Levinas makes discourse as such possible. The inherent vulnerability or injurability of the Other is, for Levinas, the very condition for my sensibility: the Other's fragility and injurability is what I sense insofar as I am able to engage in a face-to-face not already determined by a calculation of needs, where the other appears neither as impediment to my needs, nor as an object of my desires.[5]

The materiality of the face of the other, its skin, is the call to responsibility. Its nakedness and injurability sweep away all other claims upon me. Thus the entire point of Levinas' analysis is the idea that the fundamental experience of ethical obligation is one strongly marked by asymmetry. The experience of responsibility is, for Levinas, one in which the Other remains emphatically other: to approach responsibility by reducing the strangeness of another to a moment of commonality or sharedness is to acknowledge one's inability to discharge responsibility. My responsibility to the Other is prior to any debt. It is the putting-into-question of myself; it is, as Levinas describes it later, the call to feed another with the bread from my own mouth. But such a radical demand implies no reciprocal responsibility, or at least no such responsibility belongs to the presence of the Other itself. Responsibility for Levinas is a 'one-way street'. The face of the other, in Levinas' description, overwhelms the intentional subject; the call to infinite responsibility puts into question or calls to judgment one's own selfhood, a summons to trial in which the self gives up its freedom and autonomy, is rendered 'passive' by the Other – indeed in Levinas' later work the self is described as being 'hostage' [*Geisel*] of the other (Levinas 1984:223).

Responsibility 'consists in taking up a position [...] such that the Other counts more than myself' (1967:247). If the discourse ethic radicalizes the

Kantian formula of the Kingdom of Ends by breaking the pragmatic idealization of a state of symmetrical communicative relationships from Kant's model of autonomous subjectivity, then Levinasian ethics radicalizes Kant's formulation of the Categorical Imperative as the demand to treat the other as an end in him or herself (along with the Hebraic injunction to love the neighbor not because the neighbor is a member of a community but simply because she or he is the nearest) to the point where the very 'solidity' or integrity of selfhood is abandoned in favor of a care and concern that has no bounds, nor 'origin', but is simply and immediately given. The call to recognize the other as an 'End it Itself', for Levinas, exceeds the status of a moral principle, and touches upon the heart of ethics as first philosophy. One cannot, in the final analysis, take this call seriously and remain in a philosophy of the subject.

In his later work, Levinas has tried to discuss this immediacy of an infinite ethical relation in terms of language and discourse. The 'call' of the face of the other is now re-cast as an originary form of communication that is prior to and the condition for all verbal interaction and all systems of signs.[6] Levinas concentrates on the corporeality of the face-to-face encounter – that is, the level of physical intimacy and proximity that lies at the ethical foundation of why and how we speak to one another – to argue that all language finds its basic ethical content in the transcendent, corporeal immediacy of a face-to-face encounter with an injurable other. The heart of any sign is the shared moment of proximity: touch is the origin of signification (Levinas 1987:118). 'The ethical', writes Levinas,

> does not designate an inoffensive attenuation of passionate particularisms, which would introduce the human subject into a universal order and unite all rational beings, like ideas, into a Kingdom of Ends. It indicates the reversal of a subjectivity...an absolute singularity, as such unrepresentable. This is the original language, the foundation of the other one. The precise point at which this mutation of the intentional into the ethical occurs, and occurs continually, at which the approach breaks through consciousness, is the human skin and face. Contact is tenderness and responsibility (1987:116).

This claim amounts to the idea that the physical substratum of speaking constitutes a vocative dimension of communication that takes (ethical) precedence over its locutionary structure, and by implication precedence over the illocutionary dimension of language as well. This claim is particularly interesting, for what Levinas is arguing is that the physical proximity of the Other is not only the origin of ethics – not only the originary locus of identity of *Sein* and *Sollen* – but also the condition for the possibility of speaking and hearing, thus establishing the care for the other as the underlying material, the original language – the physical pre-illocutionary force, as it were, for every successful speech act. In this sense, the asymmetrical ability to open one's self to the presence of an other – to respond through sensibility to the physicality of communication, becomes the transcendent dimension of language in the Kantian sense of providing a condition for the possibility of successful communication. Solidarity as a symmetrical vision of communicative relationships presupposes the asymmetrical capacity to be addressed by an other who remains essentially foreign through the limit of the material. In this sense, the Levinasian challenge to the discourse ethic can be understood as the claim that solidarity, insofar as it is thought as the interlocking web of relationships of reciprocal recognition, is at best derivative, and at worst the concrete loss of, the kernel of our moral 'point of view', in which the injurable other comes first.

Solidarity and the limits of moral philosophy

From a discourse-ethical perspective we may be inclined to reject Levinas' claim of the persistence of a (material) alterity as the foundation of the ethical on several grounds. First and most obvious is the objection that Levinas thematizes 'alterity' and 'difference' or the 'Other' only because he has selected a model of Husserlian intentional subjective consciousness as his starting point, and thus remains tied to this point of departure. The phenomenological impasse of thinking the possibility of the reality of another ego marked a fundamental end-point in the subjectivist paradigm: Levinas' way out is to hypostasize the other ego as the unimpeachable and unrepresentable source of resistance to intentionality. But such a strategy only results, paradoxically, in the mirror-replication of the same structures of intentionality – thematized now according to their failure – that Levinas wants to transcend. From the point of view of Mead's symbolic interactionism, Levinas' radical alterity appears as a phenomenon that is necessarily a *result* of a normal process of individuation – the other as different thus merely refers to what from a Meadean point of view is a successful ontogenesis.

Levinas, of course, means more than this by 'alterity'. He is attempting to capture the specific injurability of the Other, an injurability that engages me on the level of physical affects prior to all moral rules. Here we might object that physical suffering is always something concrete, and thus incapable of being reduced to concepts. Referring to such suffering as the substrate of moral feeling as such cannot appeal to a concept of physical suffering, which could only serve to replicate the suffering itself by reducing concrete suffering to particulars of a general case. Nor can a phenomenological analysis help, since the description of the vulnerability of the other, still caught up within the model of the self-reflective accomplishments of the self (even as the self is being undermined) can only thematize that other's suffering through the category of my sensibility. 'Alterity' thus appears as a fascinating dialectical sibling to the Heideggerian blind invocations of a salvific, generous Being. It is the nostalgic residuum of post-metaphysical regret, explicable, most likely, as a yearning for an irreducibly simple, if subtle, moment of resistance to the structurally inevitable increase in complexity that characterizes the process of modernization.

Finally – and this is the point of this analysis – we may if we wish grant Levinas that a physical substrate, thematized as the vulnerability of the other and my passive sensibility, precedes and resists the entire dimension of language use that is susceptible to rational reconstruction. But this by definition would constitute itself as beyond the frontiers of any moral theory, not just a deontological, cognitivist, formalist and proceduralist one such as Habermas'. We would thus charge Levinas with regressing behind the moral universalism that already belongs to us as citizens of a modern world. Moral theory attempts to reconstruct the bases of the validity of our everyday moral intuitions. But it can do no more than this; it cannot follow those intuitions to the level of bodily movement itself, let alone construct arguments on behalf of a vanishing Other whose signals for help and intervention necessarily resist conceptual reconstruction. It can no more explain the limit-cases of supererogation and sacrifice that Levinas' vision of responsibility seems to require, than it can explicate the grounds of moral motivation. But it seems that this final criticism – that Levinas is exceeding the limit of what is possible in a moral theory – can serve as a basis for a Levinasian response to discourse ethics.

Here we might take up the difficult question of what is involved in the determination of the limit of a moral theory. A Levinasian might readily concede that 'infinite responsibility' cannot be thematized according to reconstructed rules of argumentation, and that the inherent asymmetries of ethical relationships cannot be accounted for in the idea of a social solidarity based entirely on reciprocal communicative practices. But such a Levinasian might well object that this is because discourse ethics draws its own functional limits overly narrowly. It thematizes only the formal-universal procedures through which norms can win intersubjective validity. Leaving aside the now familiar litany of complains concerning the formalism of discourse ethics, it can nevertheless be asked where a Levinasian ethical perspective situates itself at the limit of a discourse ethics. Two thoughts occur to me here.

First, we need to bear in mind that there is no disagreement between Levinas and the discourse ethic concerning the central role of injurability in the origin of ethical relationships. The question is whether the limits of what kind of injury can be coherently discussed in moral theory, and how such a discussion should work, are drawn at the right place. Discourse ethics, we recall, adopts the conception that injury in the sense relevant for moral theory is inherently connected with the fragility of personal identity:

> Because moralities are supposed to compensate for the vulnerability of living creatures who through sociation are individuated in such a way that they can never assert their identity for themselves alone, the integrity of individuals cannot be preserved without the integrity of the lifeworld that makes possible their shared interpersonal relationships and relations of mutual recognition (Habermas 1990:119).

Discourse ethics, as I mentioned earlier, must be willing to pay a price for the introduction of categories of injurability and care into a deontological moral theory: it must make a counterintuitive distinction between physical injurability and what one could call 'relational' injurability of the sociated self; and it must then go on to make a further counterintuitive claim that it is the latter that we mean by injurability in a morally relevant sense.[7] What is lost is the theoretical elaboration of a powerful moral intuition according to which the injurability of an other can be experienced neither through acknowledgment of the other's status as a bearer of rights, nor as the other's membership in a network of relationships, but simply as the vulnerability of the other, period.

A Levinasian, 'asymmetric-non-reciprocal' perspective, claiming this 'period' as the center and condition of ethical relationships themselves, of course runs out of gas precisely at the point where we push it to get a theoretical elaboration of the moment of recognition of vulnerability of an other itself: with his own presuppositions Levinas can say little further about this relationship than to repeat its pre-originary status. Despite its manifest weaknesses, however, such a deliberately overblown vision of the alterity of the vulnerable other might help us raise some questions about the bargain that the discourse ethic makes. Concentration on the elusive and unprincipled materiality of all ethical relationships – and I believe that this materiality is all Levinas means by 'alterity' – might question if the separation of 'injury' into relational and physical is entirely appropriate, and might ask, further, if the origin of morality is really to be located in the former. Moreover, even granting this separation, it seems that one might equally argue that if we are asking about where ethics begins, then reference to mutual injurability and the need for protection might tell us why morality is necessary but not how it is possible .

The question of the possibility of morality is the question of moral motivation and is (rightly) rejected by discourse ethics as being beyond the limit of a universalistic moral theory. Discourse ethics comes on the scene 'too late' to answer such a question; it does not ask why people do, or refrain from doing, harmful or beneficial things to other people, but rather analyzes the procedures that the justification of norms must take if those norms are to be valid (cf. Habermas 1993:70). If this is true, might the Levinasian not speculate that it is not the mutual and reciprocal injurability of a community of consociates, but rather the response to another's physical injurability that lies at the origin of 'moral motivation', a response that itself both makes possible and resists solidarity at the same time?

While Levinasian ethics clearly inhabits a realm of ethical questioning very different than that of discourse ethics, it nevertheless overlaps precisely in the question of solidarity, and serves to test and challenge the limit of what we can contain in the idea of reciprocal recognition. Absolute responsibility to another – not acknowledgment of that other's recognizability as a subject of universal rights or collective belonging, but sensibility of that other's specific, concrete vulnerability and need for protection – this constitutes the limit of (symmetrical) solidarity.

Second, there is the question of the end of morality; the 'why be moral?' question of the cynic. If the question of moral motivation comes 'too early' for discourse ethics, then the response to the 'why be moral' of the cynic 'overtaxes' it: such a question brings moral meta-discourse to its limit in another sense, insofar as it raises a question of the ultimate meaning and value of human life, which must be answered by participants only. And here Rorty must be given his due that philosophy has no advantage over any other kind of collective discourse:

> As to the propaedeutic task of awakening the faculty of moral perception, philosophy is not in a privileged position when it competes with the rhetorically moving, exemplary representation of the novelist or the quietly insistent intuitions of common sense. We learn what moral, and in particular immoral, action involves prior to all philosophizing; it impresses itself on us

> no less insistently in feelings of sympathy with the violated integrity of others than in the experience of violation of our own integrity. The inarticulable, socially integrating experiences of considerateness, solidarity and fairness shape our intuitions and provide us with better instruction about morality than arguments ever could (Habermas 1993:75-76).

I would argue that this admission of the other limit of moral theory – at the end, as opposed to the origin of morality – can also enter into an interesting dialogue with Levinas. Here it is a question of whether the everyday experiences of the 'violated integrity of others' doesn't contain the kernel of a material intuition, a pre-conceptual 'moral point of view', that does not so much lie 'outside' moral theory but actively resists incorporation into any system of philosophical concepts – the intuition that led to Adorno's increasingly desperate attempt to find a paradoxical mode of expression for the non-identical. As the sheer appearance of injurability, the Other is an integrity that appears only in the violation of that same integrity. And yet if, despite Adorno's efforts, that Other cannot be forced to make a conceptual appearance and is hence beyond philosophical limits, then Levinas is justified in describing the 'always-already' of just this appearance (in the face of the Other); it is just that this attempt cannot be understood as philosophy.[8] In this sense it might be instructive to read Levinas as an example of radical moral pedagogy, whose end is not to convince but to sensitize toward questioning where we draw the limits of our moral theory.

A moment of non-theorizable asymmetry underlies every conception of solidarity, both checking its application and questioning its limit. In this sense, the Levinasian argument might be that such non-theorizable asymmetry appears in terms of a particular kind of ethical expertise, rather than the acknowledgment of universal principles of discourse. Such ethical expertise – whether in the form of 'tact', an alertness to the non-discursive dimension of communicative interactions, a sensitivity to the tenuous balance between the force of the better argument and the integrity of the partner of dialogue – is always going on; together with the abstractive achievements of the role-swapping characteristic of the universalistic moral point of view, it is a primary experience of ethical responsibility to an other: Allowing oneself to be constantly – hypersensitively – open to the other's injury means allowing one's relationship to another to enter a moment of radical asymmetry. My question here is whether this constitutes a second moral point of view that is in fact not necessarily in harmony with the moral point of view of impersonality, reflexivity, and universality; indeed, whether such a simultaneity does not appear with all the force of the arguments for the 'unavoidable presuppositions of discourse' that discourse ethics rightly musters on its own behalf. Nevertheless, I have tried to argue that such a harmony between two moral points of view runs into its own limit – and an opening to more questions – at that point when we posit symmetrical solidarity as the quintessence of the experience of morality. (From a Levinasian perspective such a question leads directly to Levinas' own efforts to present a coherent account of justice and 'the third' in *Otherwise than Being* (Levinas 1989); this topic cannot concern us at the moment).

Levinas' moral pedagogy has an oddly unsettling effect: it serves to make us a bit more uneasy about the vision of a symmetrical solidarity. But it seems to me that the results of this pedagogy, this uneasiness, is just what we ought to feel about symmetrical solidarity. Such uneasiness makes us pay particular attention to how and where the limits of solidarity are drawn.

Notes

1 In 'Individualization though Socialization: Mead's Theory of Subjectivity', Habermas writes: 'The "me" characterizes an identity formation that makes responsible action possible only at the price of blind subjugation to external social controls, which remain external in spite of the internalizing effect of role-taking' (Habermas 1992:182).

2 See 'Justice and Solidarity: On Kohlberg's Stage 6': 'Every autonomous morality has to serve two purposes at once: it brings to bear the inviolability of socialized individuals by requiring equal treatment and thereby equal respect for the dignity of each one; and it protects intersubjective relationships of mutual recognition requiring solidarity of individual members of a community, in which they have been socialized. Justice concerns the equal freedoms of unique and self-determining individuals, while solidarity concerns the welfare of consociates who are intimately linked in an intersubjectively shared form of life – and thus also to the maintenance of the integrity of this form of life itself' (Habermas 1990:118).

3 As Stéphane Mosès puts it, 'Das Ethische konstituiert also für Levinas nicht einen von der theoretischen Reflexion getrennten Sonderbereich. Im Gegenteil, das Verhältnis zum anderen Menschen bildet den ersten Horizont jeder spekulativen Philosophie, weil jede Philosophie diskursiv ist und es keinen Diskurs gibt, der nicht – zumindest implizit – an eine andere Person gerichtet ist' (Mosès 1993:366-367).

4 Such a combination of nearness and fairness is also reminiscent of Walter Benjamin's famous conception of aura as 'einmalige Erscheinung einer Ferne,

so nah sie sein mag' in 'Das Kunstwerk im Zeitalter seiner technischen Reproduzierbarkeit' (1977 1:479).

5 'Seiner Form entkleidet, ist das Antlitz durch und durch Nacktheit. Das Antlitz ist Not, und in der Direktheit, die auf mich zielt, ist es schon instaendiges Flehen. Aber dieses Flehen fordert. In ihm vereinigt sich die Demut mit der Erhabenheit. Und dadurch kuendigt sich die ethische Dimension der Heimsuchung an' Levinas, *Spur des Anderen* (1984:222), quoted in Brumlik (1990:129).

6 'Das Antlitz spricht. Die Erscheinung des Antlitzes ist die erste Rede. Sprechen ist vor allem anderen diese weise, hinter seiner Erscheinung, hinter seiner Form hervorzukommen, eine Eroeffnung in der Eroeffnung' (1984:221).

7 See 'Morality and Ethical Life' (1990:199). Here we are referred back to the essay on Gehlen in *Philosophical Political Profiles*, where Habermas writes, 'The profound vulnerability that makes necessary an ethical regulation of behavior as its counterpoise is rooted, not in biological weaknesses of humans, not in the newborn's lack of organic faculties [...] but in the cultural systems that are constructed in compensation. The fundamental problem of ethics is guaranteeing the mutual consideration and respect in a way that is effective in actual conduct'.

8 The move from a hellenistic speculative tradition (of 'totality') toward a Hebraic practical tradition of infinite responsibility is of course precisely what Levinas has in mind. But this is also the opposition, for Levinas, between philosophy and religion. See Brumlik (1990:125).

References

Benjamin, W. (1977), 'Das Kunstwerk im Zeitalter seiner technischen Reproduzierbarkeit', *Gesammelte Schriften*, Vol 1, Suhrkamp: Frankfurt.

Brumlik, M. (1990), 'Phaenomenologie und theologische Ethik. Emmanuel Levinas Umkehrung der Ontologie', in *Parabael* Bd 12, *Levinas: Zur Möglichkeit einer prophetischen Philosophie*, Focus Verlag: Giessen.

Habermas, J. (1990), *Moral Consciousness and Communicative Action* [Trans. Ch. Lenhardt & S. Weber Nicholsen], MIT Press: Cambridge (MA).

— (1992), *Postmetaphysical Thinking* , MIT Press: Cambridge (MA).

— (1993), *Justification and Application*, MIT Press: Cambridge (MA).

Levinas, E. (1967), *Totality and Infinity* [Trans. A. Lingis], Duquesne University Press: Pittsburgh.

— (1984), *Die Spur des Anderen* [Transl. and introd. W.N. Krewani], Alber Verlag: Freiburg (i.Br).

— (1987), 'Language and Proximity', *Collected Philosophical Papers* [Trans. A. Lingis], Martinus Nijhoff Publ.: Dordrecht.

— (1989), *Otherwise than Being or beyond Essence*, [Trans. A. Lingis], Martinus Nijhoff Publ.: Dordrecht.

Mosès, St. (1993), 'Gerechtigkeit und Gemeinschaft bei Emmanuel Levinas', in Brumlik, M. & Brunkhorst, H. (Hrsg.), *Gemeinschaft und Gerechtigkeit*, Fischer: Frankfurt.

The concrete other as subject in feminist perspective

7 Toward a model of self-identity: Habermas and Kristeva

Allison Weir

One of the most important tasks facing contemporary feminist theorists is the task of reformulating and reconstructing our concepts of the self. We need new models of identity, of individuation, of agency and autonomy which will take account of the important critiques of these concepts generated by feminist theorists. In this essay I will work toward a model of self-identity which can address some of the concerns of both *relational feminism*, which argues that the ideal of self-identity too often conceals a defense against connection with others, and *postmodern* and *post-structuralist feminism*, which argues that the concept of self-identity can be understood only in terms of the system of meaning which produces it: a system predicated on a logic of exclusion of non-identity or difference. My attempt to clarify a normative ideal of self-identity comes out of a conviction that we need to uphold a commitment to women's struggles for identity and autonomy in the context of feminist critiques of defensive atomistic individualism and critiques of the concept of the disembedded subject as the free and unfettered author of his destiny. We need to make a space for an understanding of self-identity and autonomy which *will* not clash with our conviction that individuals must be understood as embedded, embodied, localized, constituted and fragmented, as well as subject to forces beyond our control. We need to understand ourselves clearly as actors capable of learning, of changing, of making the world and ourselves, better.

So it is important that I begin by saying what a defensible ideal of self-identity is *not*. It is *not* some sort of essentialist ontology, not an idealist conception of an original pregiven authentic self. lt. is not an alienated individualism severed from connections and solidarities, severed from collective struggles, immune to systems of power and oppression. It is not an attempt to repress or deny the embodiment, fragmentation, dividedness, and multiplicity of human selves, or the constitution of subjects in and through language and power.

The concept of self-identity I defend can be defined as the capacity to experience oneself as an active and relatively coherent *participant* in a social world. Essential to self-identity, then, is 'the ability of a person to relate to him or herself and to be able to relate to others in a meaningful way, to act and react self-consciously' (cf. Forst 1992). This emphasis on a capacity for *meaningful* interaction with self and others takes us in two directions, for it introduces both reflexivity and intersubjectivity as essential components of self-identity. Reflexivity, for the meanings of my relationships to myself and to others come down to me: I am the one faced with the question of who I am and who I want to be. I am the one who must invest my existence with meaning for me: this meaning can be generated only through my participation in social meanings, which are intersubjectively constituted. The very concept of a self, of an I, of a me, is something which is constructed only through intersubjective interactions, which take place always in contexts of shared meanings. Similarly, my identity as this specific individual is constructed through my participation in communities, institutions, and systems of meaning, which organize my interactions with, and through which I interpret my interactions with, the world, my self, and others. My identity is produced through a complex process through which I am identified, and identify myself, in terms of intersubjective contexts of meaning.

The capacity, and the responsibility, to problematize and define one's own meaning (one's own identity) is both the burden and the privilege of modern subjects. As a subject who is no longer defined by a fixed position in a social system, I am (relatively) free (or, at the least, I aspire to a normative ideal of freedom) to determine, through my practices, who I am and who I am going to be. The flip side of this freedom is the burden of self-definition: every action, every decision becomes self-defining; every action, every position is open to question.[1] This freedom and this responsibility are absolutely inescapable in our daily lives. At the same time, along with the increasing need for self-definition goes an increasing production and differentiation of identity-attributes: of possible roles, attachments and affiliations, values, beliefs and commitments, needs and desires, styles and modes of expression. We are exposed to more and more frameworks for reflection on and demystification of the constitutive influences which shape our identities (such as family and relationship dynamics, unconscious processes, collective identities, economic, social, and linguistic systems, systems of power and oppression...).

Central to self-identity, then, is the capacity to sustain and in some sense reconcile multiple and often conflicting identities and to understand, criticize, and reconcile multiple and often conflicting interpretations of those identities, not to mention the capacity to live with and somehow reconcile all of the ambiguity and complexity of our lives that does *not* (and never will) readily lend itself to this identity-work. Ideally, these reconciliations are achieved not through the imposition of an identity which excludes or represses difference and non-identity (the concern of postmodernists), but through a capacity to reflexively and practically accept, live with, and make sense of differences and complexity. This capacity is based not on a denial of connections with others (the concern of relational theorists), but on a cognitive and affective acceptance of intersubjectivity and autonomy, and of the dependence on and independence from others, which underlies a capacity to recognize when my meaning differs from the meaning of others, and when my identity is bound up with the identity of a partial or general 'we'.

This is, of course, an enormously demanding project, the difficulty of which is increased as various identities are recognized as bound to systems of oppression, and with communities and institutions that define themselves through exclusions. This is acutely expressed by Gloria Anzaldúa, who writes of her ongoing attempts to make some sense out of the conflicts among her various identities as a Catholic-raised, lesbian Chicana (Mexican, Anglo American): 'I have so internalized the borderland conflict that sometimes I feel like one cancels out the other and we are zero, nothing; no one' (Anzaldúa 1987:63).

The experience of lack of self is the familiar dark side of a culture characterized by a growing pressure for self-identity under conditions of increasing fragmentation. But the other side of this pressure and this fragmentation is a freedom of conscious self-determination and a capacity for analysis: Anzaldúa describes her conscious choice to live her life as a lesbian and describes her struggle for self-analysis and self-making as a 'path of knowledge' which opens up a process of analysis and critique of social and cultural institutions governing race, class, gender, and sexuality.

Essential to an individual's capacity to problematize and define her own identity are cognitive and practical capacities for self-knowledge, self-realization, and self-direction,[2] which involve cognitive capacities for learning, for critique, and for organization, and practical capacities for expression, engagement, commitment, and flexibility. The development of self-identity requires the learning of social and linguistic norms, through which the expression or realization of one's specificity, and the development of a capacity for the critique of norms, becomes possible (I also want to say that it is through these practices of expression and critique that social and linguistic norms change and are kept open and diverse). The development of self-identity requires the cognitive capacity to reflect on who I am and what matters to me, and to organize diverse identities and identity-attributes into some sort of meaningful narrative or constellation. It also requires the practical, existential capacity to discover and define and *commit* to what matters to me, to my meaning, while remaining flexible and open to change. To some extent, all of this depends on an ability to resolve particular differences and conflicts into more general meanings.

This notion of self-identity as a capacity to *resolve* differences and conflicts has not been popular among feminist theorists. Iris Young, for example, argues that 'any individual subject is a play of differences that cannot be comprehended' and that the struggle for self-identity (and the struggle for reciprocal recognition with others) is necessarily based on a logic of identity which *necessarily* denies differences (Young 1990:310-11). For Young, identity and difference are mutually exclusive; thus, she argues for an ideal of 'unassimilated otherness' (1990:301). Similarly, Luce Irigaray, Diana Fuss, and Jessica Benjamin all argue that the attempt to resolve contradictions is an act of domination, and it is better to leave contradictions and paradoxes unresolved (on this see Weir 1995). All of these theorists make these arguments in the name of a model of the self as an open process of constant change.

But the struggle to resolve conflicts through an openness to difference is essential to the practice of change and the generation of new meaning. It is impossible to understand the developments in the self-understanding of feminists, and the feminist movement, without acknowledging the role played by individual and collective struggles to understand differences and make sense of and resolve conflicts. To take just one example, the 'Sex Wars' debates were provoked by some women's struggles to explore sexuality, pleasure, violence, and desire past the boundaries set by anti-porn feminism. At the individual level, the struggle of a particular woman to analyze, articulate, and make sense of the relationships between her sexual desires, fantasies, and practices and her feminist values requires a struggle to reconceptualize the relationship between her feminist values and her experiences of pleasure and desire. In the process, both the understanding of feminism and the understanding of desire – and, in turn, her own self-understanding – undergo change, a change that could not have happened if she had simply accepted paradox and had made no attempt to resolve it; if, that is, she had not taken either her desires or her commitment to feminist values seriously enough to attempt to resolve the apparent conflict between them. It is such individual and collective struggles to resolve conflicts which fueled the opening up of feminist discourses about pleasure and desire and radically changed the landscape of feminist theory and practice.

The struggle to make meaning through attempting to resolve apparent contradictions is essential to the ongoing constitution of self-identity. Since it is impossible to make meaning in abstraction from the practical activity of making meaning for and with other people, the development of self-identity is possible only through the development of a capacity for mutual understanding, within intersubjective relationships. But this means that we have to be able to conceptually abstract from the relationships themselves to the intersubjective *meanings* which mediate relationships.

To put this another way, the problem of the *identity of the self* is bound up with the problem of the identity of meaning, and with the problem of the identification with, or the relationship to, others. It seems to me that attempts by feminist theorists to formulate a positive conception of self-identity often founder because one or the other of these elements is left out. *Relational theories*, like Nancy Chodorow's, focus on the relationship between self-identity and identification with others, but leave out any consideration of identity of meaning. Because they lack any concept of mediation through identity of meaning in language, they see the identity of the self and identification with others as locked in eternal opposition or merged into one. On the other hand, *poststructuralist theories* tend to focus on the structural homology between the identity of the self and the identity of meaning in language, but leave out any conception of mediation through social relations with others. Thus, they see the identity of the self and the identity of meaning in language as united in a logic or structure of totalizing repressive identity. The effect is that each is unable to *abstract,* either from concrete relationships or from the system of language, to a concept of the individual as a participant in the intersubjective constitution of *meaning*.

It is crucially important that feminist theorists reconsider a common tendency to see abstraction as the enemy. For example, Judith Butler argues that we need to reject any conception of agency as a capacity for reflexive mediation, because such a conception falsely 'separates [the] subject from its cultural predicates', abstracts from the subject's color, sexuality, ethnicity, class, and the 'illimitable et cetera', and abstracts from the process of signification or the linguistic constitution of the subject. Furthermore, the postulation of a capacity for reflection upholds a false 'epistemological' conception of a subject who is separated from and opposed to its object/other (Butler 1990:143-44). This argument is surprisingly similar to the arguments of relational theorists like Evelyn Fox Keller (1985), Susan Bordo (1987), and Sandra Harding (1982), among others, who criticize a characteristically masculine emphasis on abstraction, which they associate with the separation of subject and object, the denial of connections to others, and the domination of the other/object. What is common to these otherwise disparate arguments is an association of abstraction and separation with domination or repression.

While there is much to be learned from feminist critiques of the abstraction of the individual from the intersubjective relationships and the contexts of power, language, and meaning that constitute us, there is also a danger here of sliding into absurdity. Once we get to the point where we reject any abstraction of the individual from contexts and any postulation of the individual's capacity for reflection on contexts, we effectively deny any capacity of agents to participate in, criticize and change those contexts. In rejecting abstraction, feminist theorists forget that the capacity to abstract from particular relationships, from linguistic systems and social norms, is essential to a capacity to *criticize* those relationships, systems, and norms. The challenge, then, is not to reject abstraction for embeddedness, but to theorize a capacity for abstraction for detachment for critique, which is not opposed to but continuous with, and in fact constitutive of, participation.

Toward a developmental theory of self-identity

For the early Frankfurt School theorists, the capacity for critique was the essential achievement of individuation. But in the melancholy story of the 'Dialectic of Enlightenment', the development of the individual's capacity for critique entails an internalization of authority which, paradoxically, obliterates all motives for critique, and inhibits any capacity for genuinely independent thought (Horkheimer & Adorno 1972). Jessica Benjamin argues that Adorno's problem was that he was unable to shake his liberal bourgeois faith in reason and the autonomous individual, abstracted from contexts and relationships, and thus was unable to imagine any process of self-development besides the internalization of dominating reason

(Benjamin 1977). Benjamin argues that the way to get out of the circle of internalizing domination for the development of reason is to reject both internalization and reason – to reject both internalization of social norms as the means, and autonomous rationality as the goal, of self-development. Benjamin's solution is to shift to a different model of self-development, focusing on spontaneous self-assertion and affective identification with particular others. But Benjamin's model of a spontaneous and embedded self provides the self with no capacity for abstraction from or critique of given contexts, and thus no capacity for participation in a social world. As a result, she is left advocating that we accept the paradox between spontaneous practices of self-assertion, on the one hand, and experiences of attunement with others, on the other (cf. Benjamin 1988; and Weir 1992). This is a variation on the old opposition between the individual and society, the paradox of social identity and self identity, identity with and difference from others, which is a false paradox.[3] Like Adorno, Jessica Benjamin is unable to *mediate* the paradox of the self because, like Adorno, she equates the development of independent and critical reason with the development of domination.

In what follows, I propose that Jürgen Habermas' model of the development of self-identity as the development of a capacity for critique will serve feminism better than models of the self which reject resolution and abstraction, and hence, participation and critique. I shall supplement Habermas' model with Julia Kristeva's model of the development of self-identity through practices of affective identification and expression. Both Habermas and Kristeva, I shall argue, theorize the identity of the self in relation to both the identity of meaning in language and the identification with, or relationship to, others. But where Habermas focuses on the interaction of identity of meaning in language with intersubjective recognition, which underlies the development of moral identity through an orientation to normative validity, Kristeva focuses on the interaction of identity of meaning in language with affective relations with others, which underlies the realization of a self through a capacity for expression.

Both Habermas and Kristeva propose models of individuation as a capacity for participation in a social world, and both presuppose that this capacity depends on a capacity for mutual understanding through the internalization of linguistic and social norms. Both develop theories of internalization which are very different from Adorno's, and from Jessica Benjamin's. For Habermas, what is internalized is not simply authority but an experience of mutuality and a capacity for critique. For Kristeva, internalization is not simply a response to threat (as it is, still, for Habermas), but a source of pleasure.

Habermas

At the center of Jürgen Habermas' account of the development of self-identity is the capacity to question and criticize conventions. This requires a capacity to conceptually abstract from given contexts through an appeal to principles. And this capacity is learned through the internalization of social and linguistic norms. For Habermas, the development of self-identity is predicated on the development of moral identity.

Habermas draws on the work of George Herbert Mead to articulate a theory of the development of self-identity through linguistically mediated interaction. For Mead, 'The fact that all selves are constituted by the social process [...] is not in the least incompatible with, or destructive of, the fact that every individual self has its own peculiar individuality' (Mead 1962:201 quoted by Habermas 1992:185). In fact, it is only through 'the social process' that a 'peculiar individuality' can be realized. From Mead, Habermas draws a description of how socialization, the learning and internalizing of linguistic and social norms, produces not simple conformity to those norms, but true individuation. I shall take up this description at the ontogenetic level – at the level of individual development.

The crux of the interpretation Habermas draws from Mead, and what takes it beyond Freud, and beyond the thesis of the Dialectic of Enlightenment, is the concept of the perspective of the 'generalized other': the idea that through linguistic interactions a human child develops an understanding of social norms not simply as expressions of arbitrary choice or self-interest, but as subject to demands for and tests of validity.[4] For Mead, the child's self-identity, in both its epistemic and its practical dimensions, develops through the mechanism of taking the perspective of another, who, in an interactive relationship, takes up a performative attitude toward the self.

In the first stages of taking the attitude of the other, the child understands the interaction with parents as a reciprocal satisfaction of interests expressed as imperatives. Once the child comes to recognize that the parents' expression of imperatives is connected with the parent's provision of care, the child responds to the threat of withdrawal of care by internalizing the parents' attitude toward herself (Habermas 1987:34).[5] At first, the internalized attitudes are still tied to the concrete roles of a particular self and other. The attitudes or roles become detached from specific persons, and the transition to the perspective of the generalized other begins, with the introduction of a third-person or objective perspective. Thus far, the description of development applies as much to Freud as to Mead.

> Freud and Mead realized that these patterns of behavior become detached from the context-bound intentions and speech acts of individual persons, and take *on* the external shape of social norms insofar as the sanctions connected with them are internalized through taking the attitude of the other, that is to say, to the degree that they are taken into the personality and thereby rendered independent of the sanctioning power of concrete reference persons (Habermas 1987:34).

At first, the objective or generalized norm of action is understood only in terms of an imperative which rests on choice – in this case, on the generalized choice, or arbitrary will, of the group. It is only with the transition to what Mead calls the perspective of the generalized other – and here we move beyond Freud – that the child comes to understand group norms not in terms of arbitrary will or choice and self-interest, but in terms of claims to validity: in terms of mutual obligations and expectations. The mechanism of internalization is essential to the development of this understanding.

> The authority of the 'generalized other' differs from authority based only on disposition over means of sanction, in that it rests on assent. When A regards the group sanctions as his own, as sanctions be directs at himself, he has to presuppose his assent to the norm whose violation he punishes in this way. Unlike socially generalized imperatives, institutions claim a validity that rests on intersubjective recognition, on the consent of those affected by it: 'Over against the protection of our lives or property, we assume the attitude of assent of all members in the community. We take the role of what may be called 'the generalized other' (Habermas 1987:38-39, quoting Mead 1964:284).

In other words, through internalizing the attitude of the generalized other, the child comes to recognize 'objective' social norms as her own. Thus, I come to recognize or constitute myself as a member or participant in the 'we'. This connection between the self and the 'we' is internalized, both in the sense of the development of understanding, and in the sense of the setting up of a motivational structure. In learning to orient her behavior to norms and take part in normatively regulated interactions, the child understands her self as a participant in a 'we', and comprehends the meaning of a valid norm – i.e., that it rests, ideally, on the assent of each and all, and as such is subject to criticism on the grounds that there are good reasons for my not assenting. The child makes a transition from a motivational structure based on interests and imperatives to a motivational structure based on an orientation to validity claims – on a recognition of shared expectations and obligations. Thus, internalization is the mechanism of both a comprehension of the meaning of social norms as, in principle, valid norms and an anchoring of those norms in a motivational structure.

It must be stressed that this account of the development of self-identity only works if we stipulate that the generalized other represents not an actual community consensus, but an ideal, a standard against which any norm must be measured. Contrary to what Habermas, and Mead, often seem to suggest, there is in modern societies no given social world of conventional norms that the child simply takes over and internalizes. Rather, a child internalizes many different and conflicting normative positions. In order to participate effectively in interactions with primary others, and with institutions, a child may take the attitude of her mother's appeal to an 'ethic of care', her father's appeal to an ethic of rights, her grandfather's appeal to an ethic of particular traditional conventions, and the ethic of strategic rationality in the pursuit of self-interest upheld by her favorite TV show. (More likely, each of her reference persons will represent a mixture of these attitudes and others). She will have to deal with differences between her mother who thinks homosexuality is sick and her aunt who is a lesbian and a gay rights activist, a black teacher who teaches the principles of universal equality and black pride and white friends who are racists. There is no actual given perspective of a unified conventional 'we' which is the generalized other. What is internalized is a capacity to appeal to principles, to standards of normative validity. The child is forced to individuate through taking positions with respect to given conflicts. Ideally, she learns to do so through abstracting from her particular loyalties to each of her different reference persons, to appeal to principles.[6]

The crucial point here is that for Habermas, Mead's concept of taking the attitude of the other, which Mead understands as calling forth a response in oneself that one also calls out in the other, cannot be understood on the model of a simple response to a stimulus, but must be understood through a model of linguistic interaction. The response, can be understood 'in the full dialogical sense as an "answer"'; hence, what is internalized is not simply assent, taking the attitude of the other demands 'internalizing yes/no responses to statements or imperatives' (Habermas 1987). Habermas takes this idea from Tugendhat, who notes that 'consent only has significance against the background of the possibility of refusal' (Tugendhat 1986:229).[7] What is internalized is a capacity for critique.

For Habermas, the capacity for critique grounded in linguistic communication underlies the development of both moral identity and more general personal identity. In analyzing the structure of role perspectives inherent in linguistic communication, Habermas follows Mead, who systematically connects 'the role-taking effective in socialization with the speech situations in which speakers and hearers enter into interpersonal situations as members of a social group' (Habermas 1987:58). One takes over a reflected sense of self or 'me' by adopting the others' perspective or expectations toward oneself. But the structure of linguistic interaction is such that the other, in recognizing you as a participant in interaction, expects you to take a position in response to her speech act. Thus as a participant in the interaction, one must accept the freedom and responsibility of taking a position in response to the other's speech act. It is this freedom – and this responsibility – demanded of participants In linguistically mediated social interaction, which is the source of individuation.

> The performative attitude that ego and alter adopt when they act communicatively with one another is bound up with the presupposition that the other can take a 'yes' or 'no' position on the offer contained in one's own speech act. Ego cannot relinquish this scope for freedom even when he is, so to speak, obeying social roles; for the linguistic structure of a relation between responsible actors is built into the internalized pattern of behavior itself (Habermas 1987 2:59).

The demand to 'take a position' is not restricted to questions of moral principle and the justification of norms; this is a demand found in any communicative interaction. In my response to another's speech act I am necessarily taking a position Thus, individuation is an ongoing process: the development of a sense of self-identity (of a 'me') takes place through a continual of reflection on and assimilation of the actual positions taken, in practice, in my responses to other's speech acts. The element of spontaneity and unpredictability is introduced by the 'I' which acts in response to the acts of others.

> Thus in the socialization process an 'I' emerges equiprimordially with the 'me', and the individuating effect of socialization processes results from this double structure. The model for the relation between the two agencies is the 'answer' of a participant in communication who takes a 'yes' or 'no' position. Which answer ego will give in any instance, what position he will take, cannot be known in advance – either by him or by anyone else (Habermas 1987:59).

For Habermas the development of self-identity is a response to the demands inherent in the structure of linguistic communication.

> The individuation effected by the linguistically mediated process of socialization is explained by the linguistic medium itself. It belongs to the logic of the use of the personal pronouns, and especially to the perspective of a speaker who orients himself to a second person, that this speaker cannot *in actu* rid himself of his irreplaceability, cannot take refuge in the anonymity of a third person, but must lay claim to recognition as an individuated being [...].
>
> Among the universal and unavoidable presuppositions of action oriented to reaching understanding is the presupposition that the speaker qua actor lays claim to recognition both as an autonomous will and as an individuated being (Habermas 1992:190-91)

In linguistic communication, the speaker is required to recognize and take responsibility for herself as a 'me', and to take positions in response to others as an 'I'. The demand made of participants in linguistically mediated interaction, that they accept the freedom and responsibility of taking an affirmative or negative position in response to an other's speech act, is what underlies the development of moral identity as a critical relation to social norms, and of personal identity as a critical relation to oneself.

Moral identity is based on the recognition 'that a norm deserves to be valid only insofar as [...] it takes into account the interests of everyone involved, and only insofar as it embodies the will that all could form in common, each in his own interest, as the will of the generalized other' (Habermas 1987:39). It is this orientation to the validity of a norm that provides the individual with the basis for critique: if anyone's interests are being excluded, then the norm is not valid. If anyone presents reasons for not consenting, then the validity of the norm is called into question. And this is what makes it possible for the individual to abstract from particular norms to universal principles, to move from simple conformity to or deviance from given norms to a capacity to relativize and criticize given norms in the name of universal principles, but to do so as a participant in a social world.

For Habermas, this capacity for critique which is built into linguistic interaction, and built into the internalization of norms, is essential to not only moral but more general personal identity.

> The identity of the ego can [...] be stabilized only through the abstract ability to satisfy the requirements of consistency, and thereby the conditions of recognition, in the face of incompatible role expectations and in passing through a succession of contradictory role systems. The ego-identity of the adult proves its worth in the ability to build up new identities from shattered or superseded identities, and to integrate them with old identities in such a way that the fabric of one's interactions is organized into the unity of a life history that is both unmistakable and accountable (Habermas 1987:98).

The self-identity of the adult depends on the ability to take over and be responsible for integrating all of the different, often conflicting, positions one takes, into a narrative that is meaningful to others and to oneself. This requires a cognitive ability to resolve conflicts among particular positions by abstracting to more complex meanings, and by reflecting on practices in a process of self-critique: by asking the questions, what kind of person am I, and is this the person I want to be? For Habermas, this cognitive process of self-evaluation calls for an 'appropriative form of understanding' (1993:5).

But if the capacity for critique is essential, it is not a sufficient condition of the development of a meaningful and recognizable self-identity. There also has to be an existential commitment to the meanings you produce through your practices, and through which you critically judge and guide your practices.

What Habermas' developmental model does not answer is how we come to be able to make that commitment to a recognizable, integrated, and meaningful self-identity and keep it relatively open, flexible, and non-defensive. This model is unable to account for varying levels of identity competence; to account for why many – probably most – of us fail to successfully develop coherent and meaningful self-identities and typically err either on the side of rigidity and defensiveness – a failure to question and criticize – or on the side of mushy indistinctness – a failure to abstract from particulars and resolve contradictions. Nor can this model account for why this failure often takes the form of a spirited resistance to identity, abstraction, resolution, and integration. To fill in this gap, I draw on the work of Julia Kristeva.

Kristeva

Kristeva's work is characterized by a profound ambivalence with regard to the nature of society, and hence of language and individuation. There are two different models in Kristeva's work of the development of identity through the internalization of linguistic and social norms. On one hand, Kristeva could be described as a Derridean poststructuralist with a stoic individualist twist. In this guise, Kristeva sees the 'sociosymbolic order' as a closed structure that is essentially repressive and essentially patriarchal. To this extent she agrees with Derrideans, but she differs from them insofar as she insists that the structures of language and individuation are essential for human social interaction and participation. Thus, the only solution is to stoically accept the closed, repressive, patriarchal order of language as the only means of participation in social interaction, while at the same time constantly subverting it. Self-identity is a constant oscillation between stoic acceptance and subversion of the Law:

> A constant alternation between time and its 'truth', identity and its loss, history and that which produces it: that which remains extra-phenomenal, outside the sign, beyond time. An impossible dialectic of two terms, a permanent alternation: never the one without the other (Kristeva 1977:8).

But there is another track in Kristeva's work: in many of her writings, Kristeva understands individuation in terms of a not-impossible dialectic between system and practice, as a constant process of investment in and internalization of a language system that is constantly transformed through individual and social practices. Kristeva's 'subject-in-process' is a subject who develops and changes through taking up positions, or identities, through an investment in a sociosymbolic order and thereby realizing and expressing her own heterogeneity (and in turn transforming language and society).

Against Derrida's invocation of a constant negativity in resistance to any identity, Kristeva argues that the refusal of identity renders negativity merely positive, leaving us in a space in which difference no longer exists. In its relentless subversion of identity, Derrida's 'trace' 'marks anteriority to every entity and thus to every position: [...] the trace dissolves every thesis – material, natural, social, substantial, and logical – in order to free itself from any dependence on the *Logos*' (Kristeva 1984:143). The effect of this resistance position, to any thesis, or identity is a theory which 'gives up on the subject, and must remain ignorant [of the subject's] functioning as social practice' (1984:142). For Kristeva, the subject constitutes itself only through positing, through taking positions or identities within a social world and a symbolic order — only by engaging in a world of shared or identical meanings, through which one can realize one's own meaning.

Like Habermas, Kristeva focuses on the need to take positions in everyday social interactions as central to the constitution of self-identity. Both Habermas and Kristeva argue that the capacity to take positions requires the development of a capacity to identify oneself with a social 'we', in a shared symbolic meaning-system. But whereas for Habermas the need to take a position means the need to relate to norms in a critical and questioning manner, for Kristeva taking a position tends to mean taking a position of identity within the symbolic order which will allow 'non-identity' or difference to emerge – to be realized or expressed – thereby producing a new position. Whereas for Habermas the pressure to individuate inheres in the freedom and responsibility to take an affirmative or negative position in response to others' speech acts, Kristeva analyzes the pressure to individuate in terms of the tension between unconscious drives and socio-linguistic systems, and analyzes the positing of identity as a condition for the expression or articulation of desires — and hence, the realization of a self and its meaning – in language. Kristeva provides no mechanism for moving from a conventional to a postconventional, critical, moral identity, because she does not recognize a connection between identity of meaning and intersubjective validity. What she does offer is an analysis of the constitution of identity in terms of the expression or articulation of a self, through the expression of bodily heterogeneity and of affects, in language which is meaningful to oneself and to others. She provides an account of the development of a practical self-identity – of an identity which is postconventional insofar as it is an ability to relate meaningfully to differences within oneself and between self and others. At her best, Kristeva understands the tension between drives and language — both, forces beyond the individual's control – not as barriers to, but, as Axel Honneth has put it, as 'enabling conditions' of the development of self-identity (Honneth 1992). For the development of individual identity, or individual meaning, is only possible through the expression or realization of one's specificity in language – in a system of shared meanings, through interaction with others.

Kristeva's psychoanalytic analysis of the development of identity in terms of expression, rather than repression, produces some surprising results: against Lacan and Freud, who tend to argue that learning symbolic and social systems entails the repression of aggressive and pleasure-seeking drives, Kristeva argues that the development of a capacity for signification, or linguistic competence, emerges out of a deployment or expression of those drives. In the Freudian-Lacanian scenario:

> The symbolic function is [...] dissociated from all pleasure, made to oppose it, and is set up set up as the paternal place, the place of the superego. According to this view, the only way to react against the consequences of repression imposed by the compulsion of the pleasure principle is to renounce pleasure through symbolization by setting up the sign through the absence of the object, which is expelled and forever lost.
> What this interpretation seems to rule out is the pleasure underlying the symbolic function (1984:149).

For Kristeva, the move into language and a social world – into linguistically mediated interaction – is not a fall, not a renunciation of pleasure. Rather, it is 'a separation which is not a lack but a discharge and which [...] arouses pleasure' (1984:151). The pleasure Kristeva describes here is associated with what she calls abjection: an aggressive drive (corresponding to Freud's anal drive) for expulsion, destruction, separation, which underlies the rejection of dependence on the power of others, the separation of self and other, and the distinction between subject and predicate in language. Abjection interacts with the (oral) drive for incorporation: a drive toward both having and being, possession of and identification with others, and investment in language. Kristeva describes the development of a capacity for signification – for linguistic competence and an orientation to meaning – in terms of the pleasures of abjection and incorporation (1982 and 1987). And it is these experiences of pleasure which, for Kristeva, motivate the internalization of symbolic and social norms.

Thus, whereas Habermas argues that norms are initially internalized only in response to a threat and initially represent only the arbitrary dictates of authority, Kristeva argues that the development of linguistic competence and the development of self-identity through the internalization of socio-symbolic norms is a pleasurable process.[8] Moreover, she argues that these processes represent *for the child* a deliverance from utter dependence, from helplessness in the face of authority, to a means of signification – a means of participation in a social world through an orientation to meaning.

While Kristeva often advocates the 'constant alternation' between identity and non-identity as the 'impossible dialectic' of the self, in many of her writings Kristeva upholds a normative ideal of an integrated self —

a complex self-identity based on a reflexive and affective recognition and acceptance of the difference and non-identity within the self. It is only through the cognitive recognition and affective acceptance of the complexity or internal differentiation of the other that the child comes to recognize and accept both the separateness of her self from others with whom she interacts, and the internal differentiation of her own self.

The developmental condition for this recognition and acceptance is the transition from prelinguistic or drive-based, to linguistically mediated interaction with others, and hence, the opening up of a social world. Central to this process is the internalization of social and linguistic norms. This internalization is mediated by experiences of pleasure, by affective relations, and by cognitive development.

According to Kristeva, the child moves from a relation to the primary caretaker based on satisfaction of needs to a relation based on a shared orientation to meaning. Too often, Kristeva describes this path of development in the terms of Lacanian psychoanalysis, as a transition from a relationship of immediacy or merging with the mother to an acceptance of the paternal Law of the symbolic order. Kristeva's twist to this story is that the investment in the phallic symbolic order is mediated by an identification with an idealized father and that the motivation for investment in the symbolic order is the recovery of the mother (the primary object) in language and meaning (see, for example, Kristeva 1989:43).

But Kristeva also tells the story in another way. In this other version, the child moves from a need-based relationship with the first caretaker (who is, typically, the mother) to a recognition that the mother's needs are not wholly satisfied by the child, that she has an other meaning in her life beyond the child. The child has to recognize, in some rudimentary way, that the mother is complex and internally differentiated. And the child is forced to recognize this through the mother's failure to satisfy all of her demands. In the process she learns that there is a realm of meaning that can satisfy desires, and she is able to identify with the mother's desire for and investment in that meaning. It is this identification with the mother's desire – with the mother's means of participation in a social world, with her investment in a shared social meaning – which mediates, ideally, the child's internalization of linguistic and social norms.[9]

The motivation for this internalization is not simply the threat of punishment but the promise of the gift of meaning – of a means for mediating relationships with primary others and for participating in a larger social world where desires can be satisfied.

It is this affective investment in social meaning which underlies the capacity to affectively accept one's own differentiation from others and the differentiation within oneself. It also underlies the capacity to develop an integrated sense of self, which will not dissolve into differences. One is able to realize one's self through expression of one's 'non-identity' in terms of shared meanings and this expression is mediated through affective investment in discourse with others.

Kristeva argues that the transference relationship – i.e., the relationship of identification with a loved other – is:

> a true process of self-organization. This means that once the accidents, aggressions, and errors of my discourse (of my life), have been inserted into the transference dynamic, they are no longer those failures of a finalistic linear process that anguished me before. To the contrary, in transference love, 'errors' are overcompensated; they produce the libidinal self-organization that has the effect of making me more complex and autonomous. Why? Because, as they are introduced by *means of discourse* into transference (into love...), the death drive, or the 'negative' in Freud's sense of the term, enters the service of symbolic apprenticeship, autonomization, and greater complexity of the individual (1987:14).

The failure to develop an integrated sense of self-identity, is characterized by Kristeva as the development of linguistic competence through the leaning of linguistic norms in the relative absence of any affective investment in those norms. One is able to address oneself to a universal other, but not to a particular other. Or, as Kristeva puts it, you get the 'kit of representation but without the caboodle of drive. The caboodle remained in the emptiness of maternal fusion and/or maternal absence' (1986:266). This happens when social and linguistic norms are experienced as primarily repressive and are only adopted in response to threat. And this happens in a social world in which too many given norms are oppressive – where, in particular, mothers, or primary caregivers, too often do not fully experience themselves as participants.

In this case, meaning comes to be understood only on the level of the universal and is non-particularized. To affectively invest in general or universal meanings one needs to be able to make meaning for another – for, in particular, a loved other. The use of language without an addressee of discourse – without someone who is spoken to – leaves it empty of signification for the speaker (1986:264). The strength of Kristeva's account, for feminism, is her insistence that the affective relationship cannot serve as an end in itself, as a means of producing individual or particular meanings. Rather, it serves as a means of investing in a world of shared meanings, of constituting and experiencing oneself as a participant in that world and of making those meanings constantly open to diversity and change.

The account of the development of self-identity that I presented here is, of course, far from complete. I show only that any understanding of the development of self-identity must take both of these constitutive elements into account: both the capacity to relate to norms in a critical way and the capacity to express – or realize one's own meaning through affective investment in discourse with others. Both of these capacities entail the internalization of social and linguistic norms, an internalization of shared or identical meanings through relationships of identification with others. Both provide a way to unlock the paradoxes of the self: of individual identity versus social identity, of drives versus language, autonomy versus relationship to others.

In closing, I call attention to some unsolved problems in Habermas' and Kristeva's theories, which I have been unable to deal with adequately here. Both Habermas and Kristeva tend to conflate the learning of social norms with the learning of linguistic norms: for Kristeva, the two are conceptually conflated in the concept of a sociosymbolic order; Habermas differentiates conceptually between them, but the differentiation is not always evident in his analysis. Perhaps that is why neither provides much of an understanding of the ways in which particular as opposed to general or universal collective identities and affiliations, influence and interact with the development self-identity. I tried to redress the latter omission to some extent in this essay; the former problem proves more resistant.

Notes

1 Here I want to point out that the line which Habermas draws between crucial existential choices and trivial preferences, dispositions and inclinations is in practice increasingly blurred. Even 'preferences in automobiles and sweaters' (Habermas 1993:4) are more and more subject to what Charles Taylor calls 'strong evaluations' (Taylor 1985:15f.).

2 This is a variation on Diana Meyers's categories of self-discovery, self-definition, and self-direction (Meyers 1989).

3 In fact, I tend to side with Ernst Tugendhat: there are no paradoxical phenomena, only inappropriate premises and inadequate categories (see Tugendhat 1986:3). Habermas invokes this same paradox in his early paper 'Moral Development and Ego Identity' (1979a:90).

4 Habermas differentiates among three types of validity claims: claims to truth, normative validity, and sincerity, which correspond respectively to objective, intersubjective, and subjective domains. (There is also a fourth claim to linguistic intelligibility.) Here we are focusing on the claim to normative validity or rightness. See Habermas 'What is Universal Pragmatics?' (1979b).

5 Habermas' claim, following Freud, that the internalization of social roles and norms is a response to anticipated threat is challenged by Kristeva.

6 Habermas argues that she appeals to an ideal 'unlimited communication community' characterized by symmetrical relations of unforced reciprocal recognition. (See Habermas, 1992:186-88).

It can also be said, however, that in one sense there is a substantive, empirical agreement among all members of modern societies, which is implied by Habermas' procedural model for the discursive determination of normative validity: at some level, all individuals socialized in modern societies share the ideal of the rights of all individuals to freedom and equal respect, and the concomitant obligation of all to uphold those rights for others. This universal ideal will be held, at some level, by each individual, coexisting with, and logically contradicting homophobic, racist, traditionalist and pure self-interest positions.

7 Habermas draws on Wittgenstein's analysis of the concept of a rule to argue that the connection between identical meanings and intersubjective validity is based on the capacity for critique (1987:15f.).

8 Kristeva's model is therefore more useful than Jessica Benjamin's, which relies on the substitution of identification with particular others for the internalization of social and linguistic norms and leaves us with no capacity for shared meaning. Kristeva argues that affective identification mediates and often subverts, but cannot replace internalization of norms.

9 I develop this interpretation *in* 'Identification with the Divided Mother: Kristeva's Ambivalence' (1993) and in *Feminist Theories of Identity* (Weir 1994).

References

Anzaldúa, G. (1987), *Borderlands/La Frontera*, Spinsters/Aunt Lute: San Francisco.

Benjamin, J. (1977), 'The End of Internalization: Adorno's Social Psychology', *Telos* 32, (Summer 1977).

— (1988), *The Bonds of Love: Psychoanalysis, Feminism, and the Problem of Domination*, Pantheon: New York.

Bordo, S. (1987), *The Flight to Objectivity: Essays on Cartesianism and Culture*, SUNY Press: Albany (NY).

Butler, J. (1990), *Gender Trouble*, Routledge: New York.

Forst, R. (1992), 'How (Not) to Speak about Identity: The Concept of Person in a Theory of Justice', *Philosophy and Social Criticism*, 18/3-4.

Habermas, J. (1979a), 'Moral Development and Ego Identity', *Communication and the Evolution of Society* [Trans. Th. McCarthy], Beacon Press: Boston.

— (1979b), 'What is Universal Pragmatics?', *Communication and the Evolution of Society* [Trans. Th. McCarthy], Beacon Press: Boston.

— (1987), *The Theory of Communicative Action*, Vol. 2 [Trans. Th. McCarthy], Beacon Press: Boston.

— (1992), 'Individuation through Socialization: On George Herbert Mead's Theory of Subjectivity', *Postmetaphysical Thinking*, [Trans. William M. Hohengarten], MIT Press: Cambridge (MA).

— (1993), 'On the Pragmatic, the Ethical, and the Moral Employments of Practical Reason', *Justification and Application: Remarks on Discourse Ethics* [Trans. C. Cronin], MIT Press: Cambridge (MA).

Harding, S. (1982), 'Is Gender a Variable in Conceptions of Rationality? A Survey of the Issues', *Dialectica* 32, 2/3.

Honneth, A. (1992), 'Decentered Autonomy: The Subject after the Fall', paper presented to the Society for Phenomenology and Existential Philosophy, Boston, October 1992.

Horkheimer, M. & Adorno, Th. (1972), *Dialectic of the Enlightenment*, Continuum: New York.

Keller, E.F. (1985), *Reflexions on Gender and Science*, Yale University Press: New Haven.

Kristeva, J. (1977), *About Chinese Women*, [Trans. Anita Barrows] , Manon Boyars: New York.

— (1982), *The Powers of Horror: An Essay on Abjection*, [Trans. L. Roudiez], Columbia University Press: New York.

— (1984), *Revolution in Poetic Language* [Trans. M. Waller], Columbia University Press: New York.

— (1986), 'Freud and Love: Treatment and Its Discontents', *The Kristeva Reader* [ed. Toril Moi], Columbia Univerity Press: New York.

— (1987), *Tales of Love*, [Trans. L Roudiez], Columbia University Press: New York.

— (1989), 'Life and Death of Speech', *Black Sun: Depression and Melancholia*, [Trans. L. Roudiez], Columbia University Press: New York.

Mead, G.H. (1962), *Mind, Self and Society* [ed. Ch. Morris], University of Chicago Press: Chicago.

— (1964), *Selected Writings* [ed. A. Reck], University of Chicago Press: Chicago.

Meyers, D. (1989), *Self, Society, and Personal Choice*, Columbia University Press: New York.

Taylor, Ch. (1985), 'What is Human Agency?', *Human Agency and Language*, Cambridge University Press, Cambridge.

Tugendhat, E. (1986), *Self-Consciousness and Self-Determination* [Trans. P. Stern], MIT Press: Cambridge (MA).

Weir, A. (1992), 'The Paradox of the Self: Jessica Benjamin's Intersubjective Theory', *Thesis Eleven* 32.

— (1995), *Sacrificial Logics: Feminist Theory and the Critique of Identity*, Routledge: New York.

— (1993), 'Identification with the Divided Mother: Kristeva's Ambivalence', in Oliver, K. [ed.] *Ethics, Politics and Difference in Julia Kristeva's Writing*,: Routledge: New York.

— (1994), *Feminist Theories of Identity*, Routledge: New York.

Young, I. (1990), 'The Ideal of Community and the Politics of Difference', in Nicholson, L. [ed.] *Feminism/Postmodernism*, Routledge: New York.

8 Subjectivity in process

Kristeva, discourse theory, and the trials of psychoanalysis

Marianna Papastephanou

> The history of the speaking being (spatially bound precisely because he speaks) is only spatial variation, never shattering the limits of the speaking/forming, but rather displacing it by means of a *praxis* or a *technè*. It is henceforth clear that meaning's closure can never be challenged by another *space*, but only by a different way of *speaking*: another enunciation, another 'literature' (Kristeva 1980b:281).

I shall argue that Kristeva's theory and a pragmatic philosophy of language[1] converge significantly on salient philosophical issues. Where they part company is in few but crucial assumptions. Some of them I regard as problematic and in particular responsible for weaknesses in Kristeva's arguments. This somewhat uneven treatment of the two sides does not aim at concealing the potential for reciprocal contributions to refining both psychoanalysis and discourse theory. Nor does it question the quality, import, novelty, and originality of Kristeva's insights. It is rather based on my misgivings about some socio-political and philosophical presuppositions of psychoanalysis in general that Kristeva's theory inherits from Freud and Lacan. This might not have been the case, if her theory of subjectivity had brought into play other developmental-psychological ideas which do not suffer from the same problems as psychoanalysis. Hence I begin with the common focal points; then I move on to the effect of them on the idea of subjectivity; and from there set out to unfold the argumentation which grounds my objections to psychoanalysis.

Convergences

The affinities involve their rehabilitation of the importance of context, history, and practice in language as against both traditional-philosophical and structuralist accounts; their treatment of hermeneutics; their intervention concerning Husserl's phenomenology; and their positive evaluation of Enlightenment ideals.[2] The constellation 'practice, language and history' forms an affirmative web on which Kristevan and Apelian-Habermasian projects on subjectivity, critique, pragmatics are woven. Consequently, the targets of their polemic are conversely associated with an absolutization of the constellation 'stability, formal logic, abstraction'. In brief, proponents of this absolutization reserve a privileged space in their philosophy for non-situated, monological, and ostensibly value-free postulates without acknowledging the interrelation of *praxis* and *theoria*.

Apel attacks formal logic for failing to account for history and practice. He writes: 'the logico-mathematical type of logos is, as analytic logos, minimally informative' (1993:46). When it becomes the predominant mode of reasoning, it leads to a bracketing of every categorial pre-understanding of the world, and consequently, to an abstraction from praxis, history, and language. The unmitigated penchant for formal logic eventually promotes what Heidegger termed 'de-worlding' [*Entweltlichung*], i.e., a departure from a contextual world-understanding and an over-preoccupation with the 'present-at-hand' (Apel 1991).[3] Kristeva also attacks formal-mathematical logic in her endeavor to rehabilitate context. She argues that linguistics stands at a crossroad: either to limit itself to exploring formalized systems of meaning by means of a mathematical logic and regarding meaning as deriving from the intentionality of an ego 'cut off from its body, its unconscious and also its history' (Kristeva 1986b:28); or to conceive of the I as a split subject, exposed to the conflict of the superego (social constraints, modes of production, family structures, etc.) with the id (Freudian drives).

Concomitant with the rehabilitation of the flux of lived experience, which positivism and scientism discarded, is that both sides reclaim a *procedural* production of subjectivities. Instead of a Husserlian search for the origin of the thetic [*Ursprungsphilosophie*], the thetic itself is proclaimed the motor of a process aimed towards meaning and identity. In Kristeva, the thetic is the threshold of language – the latter perpetually striving to harness psychosomatic modalities. 'Such a standpoint constitutes neither a reduction of the subject to the transcendental ego, nor a denial [...] of the thetic phase that establishes signification' (1986c:99).

In discourse theory,[4] articulate speech is the royal road to a never-ending process of individuation and socialization. The shift from the philosophy of consciousness to the philosophy of language guarantees that the subject remains immersed in its lifeworld without the ideals of its autonomy, individuality and uniqueness being jettisoned.

In the same vein, the commitment to the constellation 'practice, language, and history' opens new prospects for a redemptive hermeneutics. Kristeva critically combines marxian, Freudian, and early-Lacanian themes. Similarly, the proponents of a pragmatic philosophy of language draw on Marx, Freud, traditional hermeneutics Schleiermacher and Dilthey), and the *Verstehen-Erklären* controversy. Both sides converge in their understanding of psychoanalysis as critical reconstructive science or critical hermeneutics.

More specifically, like Kristeva, the early Habermas sees in Freudian psychoanalysis the redeeming critical force which unearths excommunicated meanings. Kristeva writes commenting on Freud's significance: 'the notion of "infantile sexuality" allows for the examination, not of he who does not speak (in-fans) but of what within the speaker is not yet spoken, or will always remain unsaid, unnamable within the gaps of speech' (Kristeva 1980b:272). Let us now compare this with the following Habermasian idea: '[...] the privatized portion of excommunicated language, along with the undesired motives of action, are silenced in the neurotic and made inaccessible to him. [...] Thus psychoanalytic hermeneutics, unlike the cultural sciences, aims not at the understanding of symbolic structures in general. Rather, the act of understanding to which it leads is self-reflection' (Habermas 1987:228). Although influenced by a psychoanalytic idiom different from the Lacanian, one which is more optimistic as to the efficacy of analysis, namely Alfred Lorenzer's interpretation of Freud, Habermas, like Kristeva, pinpoints the significance of under-current linguistic elements which pervade personal biographies or *Lebensgeschichten*. Both, Kristeva and Habermas, are not ambivalent about the critical-hermeneutic role of psychoanalysis. However, to the extent that discourse theory connects this role with reason and self-reflection, it promotes more explicitly and consistently than Kristeva's account the emancipatory cognitive interest which underlies psychoanalysis.

In her essay 'Psychoanalysis and the Polis' (19886d), Kristeva dismantles the binary opposition between theory and practice in a way reminiscent of Habermas' coupling of reason and human interests. Psychoanalysis is first and foremost a critical-reconstructive science, a hermeneutics both critical and subversive. Interpretation is regarded as change (Marx) as well as cure (Freud). Similarly, no hermeneutic science may pretend to be value-free, disinterested, severed from the lifeworld which engenders it. 'We must recognize that all contemporary political thought which does not deal with technocratic administration – although technocratic purity is perhaps only a dream – uses interpretation in Marx's and Freud's sense: as transformation and as cure' (Kristeva 1986d:305). On Apel's account, the emancipatory interest of knowledge reflected in individual life histories on the one hand, and social history on the other, points to psychoanalysis and critique of ideology respectively (Apel 1984:213-17).

The speaking subject

Once more, we encounter Kristeva's and the linguistic-pragmatic philosophers' determination to avoid the Scylla and Charybdis of a metaphysical subject and its liquidation. Whereas solipsism dooms *Verstehen* either to a perennial battle with, or a subordination to, an ostensibly impartial and non-situated nomological Science, the effacement of the subject annihilates all possibilities for hermeneutically unearthing hidden realities. Kristeva laments the fact that through Saussure's linguistic structuralism, 'the problem of truth in linguistic discourse became dissociated from any notion of the speaking subject' (Kristeva 1980c:24). She also gainsays the pertinence of some deconstructive approaches to Husserl, not due to a supposed lack of serious philosophizing on the part of deconstructionists, but due to their refusal (by discrediting the signified and with it the transcendental ego) of 'what constitutes one function of language though not the only one: to express meaning in a communicable sentence between speakers' (1980d:131, 280). At this juncture, to accommodate hermeneutics, critique, and psychoanalytic truth in her theory without sidestepping the post-Freudian and post-Hegelian legacy, Kristeva brings the idea of the subject to the Lacanian court. And the punishment is Sissyphian rather than capital.

Like Lacan's, Kristeva's subject is divided. It belongs to both the semiotic chora[5] and the symbolic device. What challenges the identity of the subject and renders it a subject-in-process is a split [*coupure*] caused by the tension between the conscious and the unconscious. For discourse theory the identity of the subject is always displaced and reshaped via the simultaneous development of two processes (the definitions of which are reformulations of Humboldt's insights): individuation and socialization through conversation. Where discourse theory meets Kristevan psychoanalysis on the issue of subjectivity is in the acknowledgment of a conflictual tension formative of subjectivity (in Habermas's terms: individuation versus socialization); where they diverge is on the acknowledgment on the part of discourse theory that to account for the conflictual tension should not lead us lose sight of a dialectics of reconciliation. Following Humboldt, Habermas considers language the *Erzeugung* which socializes but simultaneously individualizes the subject (Habermas 1984:74). The identity of the subject is always displaced by the different contexts and the different language games that inform it, but its capacity to reason and speak, its position in space and time, its social role and its biography configure it into an autonomous, irreplaceable and unique individual. For Kristeva, what engenders a split subject is the semiotic element, the repressed surplus of libidinal forces, in its encounter with order and signification; for Habermas, what engenders the identity of the subject while simultaneously delivering it over to a perennial reshaping is the communicative element, the mechanism of reaching understanding, 'which socializes and individuates in one act' (Habermas 1991:218). In both cases the subject is in process, a process in the Kristevan sense, signifying movement, but also a *legal proceeding* where the subject's identity is called into question.

Kristeva remains faithful to the earlier Lacanian insights about a split subject rather than Lacan's later subtle revision of it due to the structuralist influence – a choice also mirrored in her criticisms of Saussure for his effacement of the subject. The tension between a theory of subjectivity and a theory of the abolition of the subject is attenuated by Kristeva via a further development of the idea of a split subject. In her own words, 'a subject of enunciation takes shape within the gap opened up between signifier and signified that admits both structure and interplay within; and structural linguistics ignores such a subject. Moreover, because it left its place vacant, structural linguistics could not become a linguistics of speech or discourse; it lacked a grammar, for in order to move from sign to sentence the place of the subject had to be acknowledged and no longer kept vacant'.[6]

Divergences

At first sight, discourse theorists' aspirations display an affinity to those of Kristeva. However, an analysis in depth of the arguments which sustain both philosophies would reveal major disparities. These concern, among other things, the treatment of the idea of communication, some further elaborations on the posited ego, and the assessment of sociality.

In a vein reminiscent of Adorno and Lyotard on the bipole 'artistic experience versus representation', she always contrasts poetic language to communication, regarding the latter as pervaded by a logical systematicity and associated with contractuality, oppression and strategicality. It is precisely this indictment of communication that Apel and Habermas undo by propounding a distinction between communicative and strategic rationality and a transformation and redefinition of the Shibboleths of Modernity.

For discourse theory, Husserl's phenomenology failed convincingly to account for meaning and signification (precisely in its communicative dimension) due to its being embroiled in an inappropriate philosophical paradigm, the subject – object model of thought (see Habermas 1987:218). For Kristeva, Husserl's theory is considered adequate at precisely the point where Habermas considers it to have failed, i.e., language as communicating meaning. As Kristeva writes: 'to the extent that poetic language operates with and communicates meaning, it also shares particularities of the *signifying operations elucidated by Husserl...*', '*meaning and signification*, however, do not exhaust the poetic function'.(Kristeva 1980d:132, emphasis added). The question is: do they exhaust other linguistic functions, i.e., everyday communication? And if meaning and signification do so, is it in the Husserlian way that they do so? By delimiting the space, namely, the poetic function, which Husserlian theory fails to exhaust, Kristeva decisively attenuates her attack on Husserl. By conceding that the semiotic is always subordinate to the symbolic in all cases apart from madness, poetry and saintliness, she offers to an almost unaltered Husserlianism a whole range of amenable modes of being and acting. At the end, this is not helpful even to phenomenology itself, since its import and validity remain subsumed under some untenable solipsistic premises and cannot be transferred to a different paradigm in order to be redeemed. To further elaborate on this, I quote Kristeva once again:

> Therefore, the thetic predicative operation and its correlatives (signified object and transcendental ego), though *valid for the signifying economy* of poetic language, are only one of its *limits*: certainly constitutive, but not all-encompassing. While poetic language can indeed be studied through its meaning and signification (by revealing, depending on the method, either structures or process), such a study would, in the final analysis, amount to reducing it to the phenomenological perspective and, hence, failing to see what in the poetic function departs from the signified and the transcendental ego and makes of what is known as "literature" something other than

> knowledge: the very place where social code is destroyed and renewed, thus providing, as Artaud writes, "A release for the anguish of its time" by "animating, attracting, lowering onto its shoulders the wandering anger of a particular time for the discharge of its psychological evil-being" (1980d: 132, first emphasis added).

Thus, for Kristeva, a Husserlian explanation of language holds albeit only for a particular dimension of language, whereas for discourse theory the merits of Husserl's insights should be rescued from a paradigm which dooms them to a solipsistic framework and which reduces meaning, communication, and signification to closed and immutable structures.

Following in the steps of Freud and Lacan, whenever Kristeva confronts questions of normativity, sociality, and institutions, she merely extends psychoanalytic explanations hoping that the Law of the Father is a notion adequate to account for what is usually considered to be in the province of social science, and particularly after Weber, in need of being examined action-theoretically. My aim is by no means to deny that disciplines, theories, fields of research overlap; rather I object to a Hegelian-systematic tendency to consider a particular framework of thought all-encompassing, and even more so when this framework hardly involves conceptual tools pertinent to the alien subject-matter.

Having acknowledged some crucial affinities and disaffinities between Kristeva and discourse theory, I proceed with an assessment of their significance. I move on to my disagreements with critics and to my own criticisms.

One of the first to interpret Kristeva in relation to discourse theory was Iris M. Young. My disagreement with Young's otherwise interesting discussion of Kristeva and Habermas concerns the following point. According to Young, 'this [Kristeva's] understanding of language bursts open the unity of the subject which Habermas presupposes, as the sender and receiver and negotiator of meaning. The subject is in process, positioned by the slipping and moving levels of signification, which is always in excess of what is grasped or discursively understood' (Young 1986:394). True, the unconscious motives of action and the subtle power mechanisms operating within signification are not perfectly accommodated within the framework of discourse theory. This is a point that will preoccupy us later on regarding the distinction between strategic and communicative action. But this does not necessarily impose a unity on the subject. In other words, it is not only the specific Kristevan version of Lacan's theory of signification which bursts open the unity of the subject.

As we have seen, the Humboldtian standpoint also contributes to considering the subject as an open and porous structure.

As to whether Kristeva clearly rejects irrationalism, I would go along with Young in highlighting Kristeva's emphatic refusal 'to reverse the privileging of reason over emotion and body' (Young 1986:394). I contend, however, that to refuse to reverse the hierarchical relation of two poles is one thing, to leave the poles themselves untouched is quite another. Kristeva does both, and in so doing, she fails to offer the redefinition of reason that would truly allow for a retrieval of emotions as worthy of philosophical-political attention. Thus, I cannot endorse Young's contention that Kristeva's theory of language provides a more 'embodied' alternative to that proposed by Habermas, first and foremost, because I believe that a theory of language is inescapably complemented, implicitly or explicitly, with a theory of reason. What I will explore in the rest of this essay is precisely how this interdependence of implicit assumptions about reason, language, and social order unmasks some crucial problems confronting post-Lacanian psychoanalysis. However, before I move on to such an examination, I would like to mark my distance from other criticisms of Kristeva, which might appear similar to my own.

Unlike Young, who seems to be more sympathetic to Kristeva's views, Judith Butler charges Kristeva with essentialism and biologism (Butler 1992). Whereas these charges do not exactly emanate from a misrepresentation of Kristeva's work, they do not do it justice either, at least in the way they are put. Neither Freud nor Kristeva assume a corporeal reality to which we might have unmediated and direct access. As Kristeva writes:

> Instinctuality is simultaneously revealed as innate and hereditary, but, within the Freudian framework, it is already protected from substantialist interpretations. For although the child enters the world with polymorphous instinctual drives, these conflict with repression and the latter produces the several variants of libido fixation ("subjective structures"). It follows that neurosis – or the speaking subject – can never be dealt with at the level of drive, or through a child at zero degree of symbolism, but rather always through a narrative "texture", that is, a texture of language and phantasm' (Kristeva 1980b:275).

Another criticism directed by Butler against Kristeva refers to the supposed lack of critical potential of the latter's project, due to the presentation of the symbolic as an inescapable condition of subject formation. Therefore, any critique is doomed to fail to question patriarchy since the semiotic is and will always be submerged in the symbolic and no discourse is less patriarchal than the other to any significant extent (Butler 1992:163).[7] However, Butler seems to play down the dialectic between semiotic and symbolic processes which produces qualitatively different types of discourses. Kristeva defines the symbolic as follows: 'The symbolic (*le symbolique*), as opposed to the semiotic, is the inevitable attribute of meaning, sign, and the signifying object for the consciousness of Husserl's transcendental ego. Language as social practice necessarily presupposes these two dispositions, though combined in different ways to constitute *types of discourse*, types of signifying practices' (1980:134).[8]

I find Kelly Oliver's interpretation of Kristeva to the point when she states that the critical aspect of language in Kristeva's work can be rescued if we pay attention to a subtle distinction between *le symbolique* and *la dimension symbolique*.

> Whereas Lacan uses the symbolic to refer to the Symbolic order, Kristeva uses the symbolic in two senses – to refer not only to the Symbolic order but also to a specifically symbolic element within the Symbolic order that she opposes to the semiotic element. [...] So the semiotic is not strictly opposed to the Symbolic order. Rather, the semiotic is part of the Symbolic order. [...] The symbolic is the element within the Symbolic against which the semiotic works to produce the dialectical tension that keeps society going (Oliver 1993:101).

Kristeva does not identify the whole of Symbolic order with patriarchy. Thus, Butler's criticisms against Kristeva's reluctance to level emancipation and agency with a full-scale refusal of the Symbolic misfire.

Nevertheless, the Kristevan identification of signification, thesis, and order with the (patriarchal) symbolic is not without problems. It still incriminates discourse (apart from poetry) and sociality or norms; it still associates egoism, self-preservation, stability, and unity with the thetic threshold to civilization; and finally, it still embeds critique in a libidinal Other. Hence, although I would not fully endorse Butler's criticisms and furthermore find her Foucauldian perspective concerning norms[9] equally untenable, my reservations bear some similarity to hers and primarily concern Kristeva's reliance on certain psychoanalytic conjectures.

Freud's viciously circular account of the emergence of social order

While Lacan initially set out to divest psychoanalysis of its scientistic and biologistic accretions, his treatment of language as restriction of desire and normativization of life-within-society may be seen to have smuggled in certain elements of Freudian biologism by the back door. In the later Freud, institutions and norms are imposed on nature and generate and preserve social life; in Lacan, language serves this purpose. Lacan replaces social norms with language as that which marked the emergence of an ordered human reality. He writes: 'the Primordial Law is therefore that which in regulating marriage ties superimposes the *kingdom of culture on that of a nature* abandoned to the law of mating. The prohibition of incest is merely its subjective pivot, revealed by the modern tendency to reduce to the mother and the sister the objects forbidden to the subject's choice, although full license outside of these is not yet entirely open. This law, then, is revealed clearly enough as identical with an *order of language'* (Lacan 1970:66, emphasis added). This conception of a natural (non-normative) condition as the original one, that which has a temporal priority and in which desire has a genuineness lost in cultivated life is unmasked, in its Freudian version, as circular by Cornelius Castoriadis. If we take up the Freudian myth, in *Totem and Taboo*, we may briefly say that it is about the *group* of *exiled* brothers who *conspire* to kill the oppressive father and establish social order by introducing norms regulating action and, out of a sense of guilt for the parricide, allow only an annual ritualistic sacrifice of a totem symbolically to reiterate the moment of the murder of the father.

Following Castoriadis, one cannot but wonder whether the myth does anything more than summing up the now dated neo-Darwinian social theories of Freud's era and, in particular, whether it is informative as to the origin of societies at all. For it simply presupposes what it aims to prove, i.e., all that has to appear at the end of the myth as the inevitable conclusion of the premises. It is viciously circular because the superimposition of culture over nature is already tacitly presupposed.[10] After all, without a preexisting and dominant social order it would have been impossible for the brothers to have feelings of guilt. Even love for somebody (as opposed to paternal or maternal instincts), be it the father or a brother or a friend or so forth, which would generate a sense of responsibility to the other, and consequently guilt in case of failing to meet her/his expectations, could hardly be explained as a matter of a 'nature abandoned to the law of mating'. Those words pertaining to the myth that

I have highlighted above, (group, conspire, exiled), reveal precisely the circularity of the argument. A sense of a 'we' underlying a group-formation alludes to the existence of a society already differentiated enough to allow for explicitly conceptualizing otherness; forming an alliance to achieve a goal (the murder and the introduction of prohibitions) betrays the previous existence of a symbolic order both as social norms and articulate speech; finally, that the brothers were exiled before their return and parricide proves that exclusions, sanctions, and power relations which the Symbolic as Order supposedly generates, had already predated it.

Kristeva aligns herself with Lacan as to the prohibitive nature of language. She writes:

> Language as symbolic function constitutes itself at the cost of repressing instinctual drive and continuous relation to the mother. On the contrary, the unsettled and questionable subject of poetic language (for whom the word is never uniquely sign) maintains itself at the cost of reactivating this repressed instinctual, maternal element. If it is true that the prohibition of incest constitutes, at the same time, language as communicative mode and women as exchange objects in order for a society to be established, *poetic language would be* for its questionable subject-in-process the *equivalent of incest*: it is within the economy of signification itself that the questionable subject-in-process appropriates to itself this archaic, instinctual, and maternal territory; thus it simultaneously prevents the word from becoming mere sign and the mother from becoming an object like any other – forbidden (Kristeva 1980d:136).

Therefore, her account of language presupposes the shaky ground on which Freud and then Lacan based their conception of social order. Even her definition of the chora as a totality surreptitiously privileges unity over plurality in a Hegelian and Lacanian mode, i.e., by considering it prior to the identity-shaping thetic dimension and the latter a necessary evil imposed on it.

Lacan narrows the general assumption about the introduction of social order down to articulate speech and so more or less does the Kristevan version of the story, but such a linguistic turn does not question the plausibility of the Freudian myth itself as a hermeneutic device for analyzing the emergence of a society. Due to its circularity, the myth does not assist our understanding of society and speech and therefore it does not justify the supposed relevance of the tension between drives and civilization. Where the myth in all its versions fails is in its aspiration to understand the passage from nature to culture and from in-fancy to speech, by opposing an antecedent non-differentiated biological unity to a differential, identity-shaping, and order-imposing symbolic disposition.

The oppositions between biology and symbol, eros and thanatos, unity and manifoldness, silence and word, passivity and activity, as crystallized in post-Freudian psychoanalysis, are also problematic at an ontogenetic level of a developmental-psychological account of enculturation. Concerning Kristeva's endorsement of this account, it would suffice here to quote Nancy Fraser on Lacan: 'I will note only that Lacan himself was remarkably unconcerned with empirical confirmation and that recent research on the development of subjectivity in infants and young children does not support his views. It now appears that even at the earliest stages children are not passive, blank slates on which symbolic structures are inscribed but, rather, active participants in the interactions that construct their experience' (Fraser 1992:185, emphasis added).

The Lacanian understanding of the self places the subject in a special relation to its world and to truth. Lacan proposes three registers of human reality: the real, the symbolic, the imaginary. Reality is accounted for by Habermas in a similar constellation, i.e., 'objective, social, and subjective worlds', which would be made to correspond to the Lacanian view but only at the cost of obliterating the very many differences in the context which generated both theories.

On Lacan's account, speech is an act involving subjects and co-subjects (others) whereas language – and here one may detect the Lacanian indebtedness to structuralism – is a form determined by a system of differences in which the subject has no place. Whilst speech bestows identity, language blocks it. Alienation is situated in the register of language. But, since speech is not possible in the absence of articulation, order, and difference, the identity shaped by speech acts is always filtered by a static, inert, and formal system to which any true identity or reality is resistant. It is not accidental that the Lacan of 1953 recognized the subject whereas the Lacan of 1958 liquidated it. Thus, the imaginary register of reality differs remarkably from the notion of the subjective world as defined by Habermas regardless of the fact that the Habermasian subject is not the traditional Husserlian transcendental ego either. Moreover, the ontological and epistemological symmetry granted to the three worlds by discourse theory does not hold for the Lacanian registers of reality since the real, by resisting symbolization absolutely, and the ego, by being subordinate to the laws of language, bear very little metatheoretical significance.

Lacan's and Kristeva's assessment of the symbolic is affirmative to the extent that it stresses its being necessary, ineluctable, and ubiquitous. But that does not make the assessment positive. For, despite speech's inescapability and identity-forming role, language suppresses rather than redeems the libidinal forces, truncates via conceptualization rather than depicts reality, and to use Heideggerian terms, conceals rather than reveals Being. Phallocentricity, tyranny, and rigidity are endemic rather than contingent attributes of social order.

What is wrong about this phallicization of social or linguistic order, among other things, is that it loses sight of the fact that socialization and articulate speech as such may also involve a potential for collective agency and emancipation. Whereas Kristeva, unlike Lacan, who more blatantly equates the symbolic wholesale with strategicality and teleological reason, seeks to emend his account of language by introducing a semiotic disposition, her move misses the point from the moment that the semiotic's association with a prelinguistic, maternal origin becomes manifest. This reduction of the semiotic to a pre-reflexive source makes it impossible for the semiotic to attain some sort of axiological priority over the symbolic. However, such a priority is necessary if one aspires to couple the semiotic with an emancipatory interest and a critical force. It is for this too that a parallel between the Habermasian distinction of communicative and strategic rationality and Kristeva's distinction of the semiotic and the symbolic dispositions cannot be directly drawn. Moreover, by holding the semiotic always subordinate to the symbolic excepting only art, holiness, and psychosis where the semiotic tremor is more likely to be felt, Kristeva tacitly propounds an asymmetry between everyday human encounter and artistic experience and, like Adorno, proposes the latter as the locus of mimesis, thus opening her theory to serious implications such as elitism or artistic exclusivity.

Kristeva assumes an asymmetrical relation between the subjective on the one hand, and the objective and social world on the other. Although she does not consider the Symbolic as absolutely dominated by the symbolic, but argues that the symbolic and the semiotic are inseparable in their function, she does not establish a priority of the semiotic over the symbolic (perhaps rightly so, since the emotivist character of her notion of the semiotic would lead on to serious predicaments) – one that would render critique more effective just as can the priority of communicative over strategic. Since poetry and psychosis are the main dimensions where the semiotic sways, empathy and mutual understanding is reduced to a private episode of individual biographies; intersubjectivity and communication become divested of any ethical significance. Kristeva's ethics cannot be other than particularistic and as such unable to account for collective agency. Even at an I/Thou level her ethics cannot get rid of the Hegelian master-slave narrative (to which Lacan's theory of subjectivity is, via A. Kojeve, heavily indebted).[11] For reciprocity, responsibility to the Other, and equality are relegated to the sphere of contractuality and social preservation. Similarly, care, love, and empathy are ousted from the community and the public sphere, either to be assigned to the familiar (m)other or to become entirely eroticized. It is not accidental that *Einfühlung*, which in everyday German signifies 'empathy', in the Freudian terminology amounts to 'amatory identification'.

The attribution of a somewhat negative character to what is for Lacan the cause of differentiation and remoteness from an original unity may lead further to granting unity a priority over plurality since differentiation is coupled with alienation. This offers further proof that Lacan remained a Hegelian in regarding the pluralities of symbolic subjects and objects as alienated manifestations of an original One. In my view, the idea of a non-differentiated unity of nature from which the subject emerges (or the Hegelian Spirit begins its self-alienating adventure) underlies the idea of the mirror stage, when the latter is assumed to provide the child with a rudimentary identity as a being separated from others but also to trigger an alienation, a rift s/he will perpetually strive to undo without ever succeeding. Moreover, it underlies the Kristevan interpretation of the Freudian notion of castration: she defines it as 'the imaginary construction of a radical operation which constitutes the symbolic field and all beings inscribed therein. This operation constitutes signs and syntax; that is, language, as a *separation* from a presumed state of nature, of pleasure fused with nature so that the introduction of an articulated network of differences, which refers to objects henceforth and only in this way separated from a subject, may constitute meaning' (Kristeva 1986e:198).

Kristeva and reason

In the light of the previously explored difficulties which render Kristeva's arguments less than persuasive, I return to the critical comparison between discourse theory and her psychoanalytically inspired work. Only this time reason will become the focal point. For as I have already noted, what I consider one of the major weaknesses of Kristeva's argument, and perhaps predictably so, if we consider her somewhat uncritical endorsement of Freud's and Lacan's coupling of order with the oedipal stage, is that her critique of reason is not complemented with a new formulation.

Frequently, poststructuralist detractors of discourse theory lose sight of the fact that moderate criticisms are often more effective than blanket critique. Thus, they oversimplify Habermas's commitment to the unfinished project of Enlightenment, mistaking him for an advocate of Occidental logocentrism. However, Habermas avoids this charge precisely by being critical without being completely dismissive. He writes: 'A different [from the Nietzschean critique of reason – M.P.], less dramatic, but step-by-step testable critique of the Western emphasis on logos starts from an attack on the abstractions surrounding logos itself, as free of language, as universalist and as disembodied. It conceives of intersubjective understanding as the telos inscribed into communication in ordinary language, and of the logocentrism of Western thought, heightened by the philosophy of consciousness, as a systematic foreshortening and distortion of a potential always already operative in the communicative practice of everyday life, but only selectively exploited' (Habermas 1987:311).

To take up again a point which I mentioned only in passing before, I agree with Iris M. Young that Kristeva 'is quite clear in rejecting an irrationalist conception that would hold that all utterances are equally sensible and simply reduces any speech to play' and that she does not reverse the privileging of reason over feelings (Young 1986:394). What is not clear is whether Kristeva's theory can accommodate a non-Husserlian account of rationality. Because she does not offer an alternative theory of reason, due to the psychoanalytic framework within which she develops her critique of Occidental rationalism; and because, on the other hand, she does not resort to aestheticizations or liquidation of the subject, due to a subtly polemical engagement with other poststructuralist idioms, Kristeva oscillates between an affirmative stance toward phenomenology that leaves Husserl's assumptions about a teleological reason untouched (as we have already seen with the above quotations about the necessity of the thetic) and a dismissive critique of reason wholesale, as we will see later on.

She recognizes the necessity of reason, but because she remains within the phenomenological framework of a subject-object philosophy, she fails to redefine it as something other than purposive rationality. She often seems to level what she calls 'transcendental rationality', which signifies the mechanism steering the process of enculturation, with what sounds more like strategic or purposive rationality. It would suffice to consider for instance the following remark: 'through the permanent contradiction between these two dispositions (semiotic/symbolic), of which the internal setting off of the sign (signifier/signified) is merely a witness, poetic language, in its most disruptive form (unreadable for meaning, dangerous for the subject), shows the constraints of a civilization dominated by transcendental rationality' (Kristeva 1980d:139-140). Unlike Habermas, she does not provide a new conception of rationality of a positive communicative character. Thus, to teleological reason she contrasts mythico-magical otherness or the mystical beyond (disapprovingly) or the unsettling vibrations of a repressed instinctuality (approvingly). As she writes: 'If the metaphysical solidarity of "meaning", "origin", and "forming" is thus posited as the limit of any attempt at clarification (and also therefore of linguistics), and perhaps also of all analysis (and perhaps of psychoanalysis), it still seems clear that any spatial representation provided for within a universal language is necessarily subject to teleological reason, contrary to what "romantic minds" might maintain, attracted as they are to the "mythico-magical"' (Kristeva 1980b:280). When she opposes the poetic language in its most subversive modes to transcendental reason she commits herself to a coupling of art with the emancipatory ideal, thus availing her theory to some of the merits and demerits such a move entailed for Adorno.

Kristeva confronts the same problem with the first generation Frankfurt School: how to defend a non-self-defeating reason, or in other words, how reason can criticize itself without this critique being automatically complicit. As she argues: 'But if semiotics thus openly recognizes its inability to apprehend the heterogeneity of the signifying process other than by reducing it to a systematicity, does it thereby declare its own intellectual bankruptcy?' (Kristeva 1986b:30). The very idea of an immanent critique of reason becomes paradoxical if the target of the critique is simultaneously its vehicle. If reason is only teleological, systematic, and formal, it can be attacked as such only from the standpoint of a 'wholly other'. Not by accident, for Kristeva as for Adorno, mimesis cuts the Gordian knot. In Kristeva's words:

> Mimesis is, precisely, the construction of an object, not according to truth but to verisimilitude, to the extent that the object is posited as such (hence separate, noted but not denoted); it is, however, internally dependent on a subject of enunciation who is unlike the transcendental ego in that he does not suppress the semiotic chora but instead raises the chora to the status of a signifier, which may or may not obey the norms of grammatical locution. Such is the connoted mimetic object.

And further on,

> In imitating the constitution of the symbolic as meaning, poetic mimesis is led to dissolve not only the denotative function but also the specifically thetic function of positing the subject. In this respect modern poetic language goes further than any classical mimesis [...] because it attacks not only denotation (the positing of the object) but meaning (the positing of the enunciating subject) as well (Kristeva 1986c:109).

Inter- and/or Intra- *subjectivity?*

The import of the Humboldtian insight about individuation and socialization as (trans)formative processes of subjectivity can be rescued via a retrieval and reformulation of a theory of rationality. This is needed within psychoanalysis as much as discourse theory needs to readdress questions pertaining to the subjective world and the aesthetic sphere, raised by post-Freudian and post-Piagetian psychology. To account adequately for inter-subjectivity, psychoanalysis would have to undergo a radical questioning of those particular assumptions which treat sociality, order, the symbolic, communication, and even intersubjectivity itself as burdened with the negative task of suppressing feelings, desires, and pleasure. It is also dubious whether prohibition is the primordial task of culture, if we acknowledge that a positive task is also performed linguistically, namely, that culture channels emotions and gives them voice thus always displacing the ego's identity. It is only through language and culture that the I can be shaped and as such encounter otherness. And this can be maintained without any recourse to the metaphysical notion of an initial closure of the subject which is supposedly undone via enculturation but rather by rejecting all metaphysical tenets about an ostensibly (in)formative pre-reflective/pre-linguistic consciousness.

On the other hand, whilst the distinction between communicative and strategic action and the corresponding rationalities is very important from a socio-theoretical point of view for rehabilitating speakers' mutual understanding, empathy, and ideal role-taking, as well as for associating power with language, it does not sufficiently take account of the subconscious side of strategicality as it manifests itself not only in silencing certain meanings but also in privileging some particular hermeneutic material over other.

In agreement with Andrea Nye, Nancy Fraser points out that Kristeva's theory addresses almost exclusively questions about intrasubjective tensions thus forfeiting the ability to account for intersubjective phenomena such as affiliation and struggle (Fraser 1992:189). This charge, if reversed, may also apply to discourse theory. However, that intrasubjectivity (Kristeva) and intersubjectivity (discourse theorists) appear as complementary should not prescribe in advance a complementarity or compatibility of their corresponding implicit assumptions. When, in her otherwise illuminating essay 'Toward a Model of Self-Identity: Habermas and Kristeva', Allison Weir seems to promote the idea of such a compatibility, she overlooks the discrepancy of the implicit assumptions of both sides. The incrimination of the thetic dimension and of communication is incompatible with the socio-theoretical and philosophical presuppositions surrounding the Frankfurtian distinction between strategic and communicative action. I would rather suggest an encounter and a constructive exchange between two projects which share more philosophical legacies than they explicitly acknowledge and which differ in respect of subtle but none the less important philosophical points.

Notes

1 I use this term, interchangeably with the term 'discourse theory', to refer to the philosophy which revolves around Habermas's conception of communication and the concomitant reformulation of reason, language, and (Kantian) ethics. I borrow the term from Wellmer (1993), but I somewhat enlarge it. A broadly defined pragmatic philosophy of language includes names like that of Karl-Otto Apel, Albrecht Wellmer, Axel Honneth, Thomas A. McCarthy, and Hauke Brunkhorst.

2 As to this latter point, because it would demand to take up Kristeva's later work, and since the present essay focuses rather on her earlier views, I shall limit myself to a reference to Christopher Norris (1994:79-92), thus avoiding a direct preoccupation with a comparative study of this issue.

3 Apel, 'Wittgenstein and Heidegger: Language Games and Life Forms', [Engl. translation, typescript in my possession], 345-352.

4 For Habermasian criticisms of Husserl's transcendentalism and his subject-object paradigm of thought, see Habermas (1987:170-175).

5 For concise accounts of Kristevan terminology (chora, signifiance, phenotext/genotext, heretic ethics etc.) see Leon Roudiez's introduction in Kristeva (1980) and Elizabeth Grosz (1989)

6 Kristeva (1980:127). My interpretation of Kristeva's theory as a redefinition instead of denial of subjectivity is on a par with Susan Hekman's analysis, although, unlike Hekman, I am not convinced that Kristeva actually has the conceptual tools for 'describing a subject that is constituted by discourse but is by no means passive'(Hekman 1991:56). Also contra Hekman, I fully sympathize with Kristeva's universalism as expressed by the idea that 'there is a universal foundation that informs the constitution of the subject in all discourses' (Hekman 1991:57); I have

misgivings as to whether this foundation is the dialectic of *the semiotic and the symbolic*.

7 In 'The Body Politics of Julia Kristeva' (1992:170), Butler writes: 'By relegating the source of subversion to a site outside of culture itself, Kristeva appears to foreclose the possibility of subversion as an effective or realizable cultural practice'.

8 In Kristeva's, 'Revolution in Poetic Language', one reads that the semiotic and the symbolic are two modalities 'inseparable within the *signifying process* that constitutes language, and the dialectic between them determines the type of discourse (narrative,metalanguage, theory, poetry, etc.) involved', (1986:92).

9 Concerning Foucault's treatment of norms it would suffice here to quote David Ingram: 'Either Foucault conceives of norms as systemic functions of a disciplinary power that confronts the agent as an external fate to which s/he must passively submit, or he conceives them as coercive effects of unregulated wars between strategic actors seeking their own subjective advantage. In neither case are they conceived as obligations whose peculiar force derives from their *presumed* satisfaction of genuine social needs' (1994:236).

10 For a very illuminating and thoroughly critical analysis of this myth, see Castoriadis (1993:33f.).

11 On Kojeve's influence on Lacan, see Peter Dews (1987).

References

Apel, K.-O. (1984), *Understanding and Explanation: A Transcendental-Pragmatic Perspective* [Trans. G. Warnke], MIT Press, Cambridge (MA).

— (1991), 'Wittgenstein and Heidegger: Language Games and Life Forms', [Engl. translation], typescript in my possession.

— (1993), 'Challenge of a Totalizing Critique of Reason and the Program of a Philosophical Theory of Rationality Types', in Freundlieb, D. & Hudson, W. (eds.), *Reason and its Other: Rationality in Modern German Philosophy and Culture*, Berg: Oxford.

Butler, J. (1992), 'The Body Politics of Julia Kristeva', in Fraser, N. & Bartky, S.L. (eds.), *Revaluing French Feminism: Critical Essays on Difference, Agency, & Culture*, Indiana University Press: Bloomington.

Castoriadis, C. (1993), 'I Simvoli tis Psychoanalisis stin Katanoisi tis Genesis tis Koinonias' [The Contribution of Psychoanalysis to the Understanding of the Emergence of Society], *Anthropologia, Politiki, Philosophia*, Ypsilon: Athens.

Dews, P. (1987), *Logics of Disintegration*, Verso: London.

Fraser, N. (1992), 'The Uses and Abuses of French Discourse Theories for Feminist Politics', in Fraser, N. & Bartky, S.L. (eds.), *Revaluing French Feminism: Critical Essays on Difference, Agency, & Culture*, Indiana University Press: Bloomington.

Grosz, E. (1989), *Sexual Subversions: Three French Feminists*, Allen & Unwin: Sydney.

Habermas, J. (1984), 'Moral Development and Ego Identity', in *Communication and the Evolution of Society* [Trans. Th McCarthy], Polity: Cambridge.

— (1987a), *The Philosophical Discourse of Modernity* [Trans. F. Lawrence], MIT Press: Cambridge (MA).

— (1987b), *Knowledge and Human Interests*, [Trans. J. Shapiro], Polity Press: Cambridge.

— (1991), 'A Reply', in Honneth, A. & Joas, H. (eds.) *Communicative Action*, MIT Press: Cambridge (MA).

Hekman, S. (1991), 'Reconstituting the Subject: Feminism, Modernism, and Postmodernism', *Hypatia* 6/2 (Summer 1991), 44-63.

Ingram, D. (1994), 'Foucault and Habermas on the Subject of Reason', in Gutting, G. (ed.), *The Cambridge Companion to Foucault*, Cambridge University Press, Cambridge.

Kristeva, J. (1980a), *Desire and Language: A Semiotic Approach to Literature and Art* [Ed. L. Roudiez], Blackwell: Oxford.

— (190b), 'Place Names', in *Desire and Language: A Semiotic Approach to Literature and Art* [Ed. L. Roudiez].

— (1980c) , 'The Ethics of Linguistics', *Desire and Language: A Semiotic Approach to Literature and Art* [Ed. L. Roudiez].

— (1980d), 'From One Identity to an Other', *Desire and Language: A Semiotic Approach to Literature and Art* [Ed. L. Roudiez], Blackwell: Oxford.

— (1986a), *The Kristeva Reader* [Ed. T. Moi], Blackwell: Oxford.

— (1986b), 'The System of the Speaking Subject', *The Kristeva Reader* [Ed. T. Moi].

— (1986c), 'Revolution in Poetic Language', *The Kristeva Reader* [Ed. T. Moi].

— (1986d), 'Psychoanalysis and the Polis', *The Kristeva Reader* [Ed. T. Moi].

— (1986e), 'Women's Time', *The Kristeva Reader* [Ed. T. Moi].

Lacan, J. (1970), *Ecrits: A Selection*, Routledge: London.

Norris, Ch. (1994), 'Scepticism and Enlightenment: Kristeva *contra* Post-structuralism', *Truth and the Ethics of Criticism*, Manchester University Press: Manchester.

Oliver, K. (1993), 'Julia Kristeva's Feminist Revolutions' *Hypatia* 8/3, Summer 1993, 94-114.

Wellmer, A. (1993) 'The Institution of a Common World and the Problem of Truth', in Freundlieb, D. & Hudson, W. (eds.), *Reason and its Other: Rationality in Modern German Philosophy and Culture*, Berg: Oxford.

Young, I. (1986), 'Impartiality and the Civic Public: Some Implications of Feminist Critiques of Moral and Political theory', *Praxis International* 5, 381-401.

Liberation, globalization and the Latin American context

9 Discourse and liberation: the claims and contexts of two types of universalistic ethics

Hans Schelkshorn

Preliminary remarks

The discourse theory of ethics developed jointly by Jürgen Habermas and Karl-Otto Apel and the liberation ethics of Enrique Dussel have come to attain representative status for the respective political contexts out of which they arise. The passionate discussions they have provoked confirm their significant position. Discourse ethics continues the European tradition of universal morality at a purified level; it integrates critically the two waves of Enlightenment European history has crossed. On the other side, the Latin American 'philosophy of liberation' marks the temporary climax of a development towards a genuine Latin American thinking. The first impulses of this development lie in the independence movements of Latin American colonies in the 19th century. In the following, however, I will refer only to Dussel's conception (above all to his five volumes on ethics of liberation: 1973 1-2, 1977, 1989 4-5), which is one among the many different lines of 'philosophy of liberation' (see Cerutti-Guldberg 1983, which is the most comprehensive but not impartial description of the first phase of 'liberation philosophy' in Latin America) because it lends itself very well for a critical comparison with discourse ethics.

I will not try to develop a systematic comparison between discourse and liberation ethics, which I have done elsewhere (Schelkshorn 1992, 1997).[1] This essay should be understood as a contribution to a dialogue which has been going on between Apel and Enrique Dussel (the first encounter is documented in Fornet-Betancourt 1989). I intend to compare their two moral theories in such a way that the strong and the weak points of each ethics become manifested in light of the other. I also have to indicate an important limitation of this essay: Dussel's 'philosophy of liberation' and the 'transcendental pragmatics' of Apel claim to have reformulated the Aristotelian project of a 'first philosophy'. This question, and the concomitant problem of an 'ultimate foundation' (*Letztbegründung*) of ethics, I will leave out of consideration.

Context and provocations

A moral theory responds to specific problems, for instance, the ecological question, which lead Hans Jonas to develop a new foundation of ethics; or when moral claims themselves become questionable, as was the case with Freud's unmasking of the claims of conscience. It is therefore advisable to first look at the specific contexts of discourse ethics and liberation ethics.

Discourse ethics as an ethics in the context of science and technology

At the beginning of his important article 'Das Apriori der Kommunikationsgemeinschaft und die Grundlagen der Ethik' (1980:255f.), Apel outlines the 'paradoxes of the problem situation' that moral theory faces today. On the one hand, the global expansion of modern science and technology has generated moral problems of planetary extension. Today, therefore, we need a macro-ethics more than ever. On the other hand, the identification of rationality with value-free science dissolves the fundamentals of ethics within general validity. Just like religion migrates into the realm of private subjectivity, unable to obtain its own rationality in face of the dominion of scientific reason, so has ethics. Orthodox marxism attempted to bridge over the gap between subjective action and objective science, but the price was a deterministic concept of history, thus fulfilling the totalitarian tendency of positivistic reason. According to Apel, the philosophies of Western societies have reproduced that duality in the division of labor between analytical and hermeneutic philosophy, thus resulting in the privatization of morality. Politics, similarly, falls within the competence of instrumental rationality, which in turn is based on conventions that can only be 'grounded' through irrational decisions. A rational discussion of aims is no longer possible.

Apel therefore develops his discourse in a situation where the general validity of morality threatens to collapse in the tongs of analytic philosophy and hermeneutics. The moral skepticism which represents the common sense of the two main streams of philosophy in the twentieth century has become the central provocation for discourse ethics. This is the reason why his strategy for discourse ethics aims at a *fundamentum inconcussum* by reflection on the conditions of doubt, continuing Descartes' ideas on the level of linguistic pragmatics. The surprising point of this strategy is that the moral principle of universalization doubted by moral skepticism is already affirmed in the act of doubting as a form of argumentation. Argumentation is impossible without the moral presuppositions of renouncing violence and accepting equal rights. With the strategy of the performative *elenchus*, Apel tries to make visible the secret moral pillars in the illuminated dome of value-free science and the colorful greenhouse of hermeneutics.

Liberation ethics in the context of dependence and underdevelopment

In the early seventies, almost at the same time as Apel developed his new theoretical path, Dussel developed in Argentina the 'ethics of liberation'. Dussel reflects the same planetary process that Apel has defined as the expansion of science and technology, but from a political and economic perspective. Colonialism and the neocolonial dependence of Latin America, and the whole Third World in general, is the central provocation to Dussel's moral theory. At the theoretical level, he is faced with the critique of the Western model of development by the 'theory of dependence'. Despite the general rumor going around today that there is a crisis in or even an end to *dependencia* theory, it seems to me that the enduring merit of *dependencia* theory is that it broke the charm of *desarrollismo* [developmentalism], and definitively put on the agenda the question of an independent and genuine path of development for the peoples of the Third World. This question could not remain on the borders of social sciences, but became a philosophical theme as well. Salazar Bondy has pointed out precisely the specific epistemological provocation of the theory of dependence. He diagnosed Latin American eurocentrism as a reflection of its political and economic dependence (Bondy 1968:113f). According to Bondy, the imitative thinking of Latin American philosophy is at the same time victim and perpetrator of oppression. In as much as philosophy is alienated from its own culture and reality by eurocentric imitation, it stabilizes and deepens the cultural alienation of oppressed people. Philosophy discovers itself as an ideological moment in a global system of domination. The 'philosophy of liberation' is an effort to escape this involvement in a credible way.

Against this background Dussel himself has felt the need to develop a new foundation for philosophy. He has fulfilled this task in two steps: first, by a radical critique of the universalistic claims of European rationality; second, by searching for a critical standpoint which is unquestionable by ideology critique. Although we cannot completely escape the ambiguity of history in the perspective of the ethics of liberation, solidarity with the poor allows the most critical position with regard to the structures of oppression and ideological justification of the 'real communication community'. The standpoint from where the vicious circle of alienated and at the same time alienating thinking can be partly overcome, is the life of the oppressed, who are excluded by the system. The ethics of liberation tries to escape its involvement in cultural imperialism through its preferential option for the poor. That means that the process of liberation of Third World peoples becomes the central theme of the philosophical discourse. Latin American philosophy seeks its authenticity by understanding itself as a critical and solidaristic reflection on the every day struggle for liberation of the oppressed in the periphery.

Justice through practical discourse and responsibility as liberation: two central intuitions of discourse ethics and the ethics of liberation

The basic principle of discourse ethics is related to the rational adjudication between conflicting interests and claims. 'Rational' means that only the strength of the better arguments should decide the conflict. According to W. Kuhlmann the basic constellation is:

> the conflict of interests and claims between subjects of reason of approximately equal strength and competence and of equal rights (Kuhlmann 1987:99, my translation)

Discourse ethics reconstructs and grounds the moral intuition of universal justice with reference to a consciousness of the fallibilistic status of scientific theories and the experience of cultural relativism. Material questions, therefore, can be answered only preliminarily; their validity is justified by the consensus of the concerned – the community of investigators within the scientific discourse, the affected and concerned in a conflict situation within practical discourses. In this way discourse ethics helps to expose and conceptualize an essential aspect of the factual moral consciousness of Western societies.

The ethics of liberation departs from a different standard situation, namely, the situation of domination, of the denied discourse, and of the instrumentalization and exploitation of human beings. The original situation is the encounter with the poor, the provocation of the oppressed. Discourse ethics assigns this moral experience to the ethics of sympathy and compassion, associating it with irrationality and even an instinctive reflex (see Apel 1984:49-69; 1986:25). According to my interpretation, the ethics of liberation reconstructs the intuitions of the traditional ethics of compassion and love on the actual level of consciousness. The traditional forms of compassion are corrected radically, e.g. the reduction of compassion to private relations, to the practice of alms, to paternal care, or to partiality without the correcting idea of justice. The most important elements of the transformation of the ethics of care are as follows:

1 A metaphysics of otherness: any man/woman is not only an example of universal humankind (difference of a prior unity), but is, due to his/her liberty, a being of radical heterogeneity and *distinction* (in opposition to simple difference); correcting the personalistic tradition of philosophy, Dussel removes the category of the 'Other' from its private idyll – the Other is not only the private friend but also the other gender, the other generation, the other social class, the other nation, the other culture. The strongest moral claim lies on the other outside of the social totality – orphans without families, the poor outside the welfare state, the old outside the society based on efficiency, the strangers outside their native country.

2 A theory of understanding: the only way to understand the exteriority of the other is through the experience of encounter, proximity (Dussel 1985:§ 4.3).

3 A theory of the praxis of liberation: the cry of the oppressed demands justice; the sense of liberation is differentiated from Heel's master and slave dialectic, and from a specific sense of emancipation which neglects the economic dimension of oppression. The paradigm for an authentic liberation is the *exodus* in the bible; the central elements are:

a) the point of departure is domination as the negation of the constitutive and historical exteriority of the other, the instrumentalization of his/her face; domination is the denial of the relation 'face-to-face', the totalization of the I or We.

b) exodus as the outbreak from the system of domination; the process of self-finding which means the detachment of introjected power and the affirmation and reconstruction of one's own identity.

c) the construction of a new order where the oppressed could live as an original and different person in equality with others.

The ethics of liberation transforms the intuitions of the ethics of compassion into an ethics of commiseration (Dussel 1985:§ 2.6.8.2) on the level of modern political consciousness. The demand of the poor are responded to through an analysis of the structural causes of poverty, and, departing from this analysis, the construction of a more just order of society. In our day, the intuitions of the ethics of compassion can be reformulated only as a political ethics, as an ethics of commiseration without any paternalization. The encounter with the poor has to be transformed into the solidaristic commitment with the poor on their way toward liberation. It depends on the historical situation whether liberation is a reform of the system or becomes a revolution. Thus the ethics of liberation corrects and integrates the legitimate aims of a revolutionary morality without either a deterministic or an utopian theory of history. Liberation is a historical process without the guide rope of dialectical laws of history.

Critical coordination of discourse ethics and the ethics of liberation

A point of convergence: the absoluteness of ethics amidst the plurality of cultural lifeworlds

At this point in our consideration we can make a first comparison between discourse ethics and the ethics of liberation: Faced with the universal relativism of contemporary philosophy, Apel searches for an irrefutable base where the absoluteness and universality of theoretical and practical reason can be grounded. Dussel's problem is more complex: on the one hand, his appropriation of Heidegger and Ricoeur allows him to break with the totalitarian universality of European reason, and to find a legitimate way to an autochthonous cultural lifeworld; on the other hand he does not want to sacrifice the absoluteness of ethics to hermeneutic *culturalismo* lest the critique of the exploitation should loose the ground under its feet. Therefore Dussel and Apel have the same problem with hermeneutic philosophy: both want to ground the absoluteness of ethics in a way that the plurality of the lifeworlds is not oppressed by a totalitarian universalistic thinking. Apel finds the solution in a transformation and renewal of transcendental reflection. The hermeneutic description of cultural lifeworlds presupposes a transcendental anticipation of an ideal communication community that preserves philosophy from a free fall into total relativism. Dussel avoids relativism by recourse to Levinas: the unconditionality of moral claims which is grounded in the liberty and the exteriority of the Other, which can be oppressed but never completely controlled. Even if the Other is killed, he/she keeps his/her secret for ever. The demands of the Other, of the poor, transforms the attitude of phenomenological description. The phenomenological concept of 'experience' which is quite different from scientific objectification, includes an understanding where the horizon of the interpreter is widened by phenomena, but the 'epiphany', or irruption of the poor, provokes the phenomenological description to a moral decision, to a solidaristic attitude of the interpreter with the poor. This is – if I have understood rightly – the sense of Dussel's phrase 'from phenomenology to liberation' (Dussel 1985:§ 2.6.8.2).

Against this background, it becomes obvious why Apel's strategy cannot immediately solve Dussel's problems, and vice versa. While Apel finds himself in a theoretical universe which is cleaned of every ethical element, Dussel responds to a situation where philosophical discourse finds itself already implicated in the ideological justification and legitimation of oppression, and participation in the cultural alienation of his own people. In spite of these differences Apel and Dussel have a common aim. Both want to develop ethics as macro-ethics – Apel because of the planetary expansion of modern science and technology, Dussel because of the global dimension of the North-South conflict. Both try to ground a planetary ethics beyond ethnocentrism. Both, discourse ethics and the ethics of liberation, intend to preserve the absoluteness of ethics in such a way that the cultural forms of the good life are not destroyed. How these common intentions can be realized show their respective corrections to Kant's categorical imperative.

The search for successful universality: corrections to the categorical imperative

Discourse ethics and the ethics of liberation share the thesis which has acquired an almost common sense character in actual philosophy, namely that Kant's formulation of the categorical imperative cannot serve moral universality as he intended. The complete reversibility of standpoints, of 'universal role taking', which Kant demanded, remains imprisoned in the net of a given lifeworld, if it is merely monologically realized *in foro interno* by an individual. It is therefore possible that members of different lifeworlds may universalize different norms without subjective compulsion.

Discourse ethics responds to this problem through its demand for practical discourses, where all concerned should solve consensually their conflicting claims and interests. Moral theory restricts itself to the reconstruction of the 'moral point of view'; the viewpoint of impartiality outlined only by rules of discourse formation, rules which constitute the indispensable conditions of argumentation in order to enable a fair solution of conflicts. The tree of philosophical ethics, after the purgatory of science and hermeneutics, has lost almost all its leaves of substantial morality. All that remains is the structure of a procedural principle as guarantee for a just solution of conflicts. But the profit of this extreme formalism is that moral theory can integrate the fallibilism of science and the cultural relativism of hermeneutics without giving up the absoluteness of ethics. Discourse ethics restricts the field of moral questions to the narrow area of conflicts between various forms of 'good life' which are not touched in their substance. Delegating controversial questions to practical discourses of the concerned and affected, discourse ethics avoids the trap of any universalistic morality, namely the universalization of particular norms. This should also be a debatable conception of planetary ethics for philosophies of the Third World.

But how does the ethics of liberation solve the problem of successful universalization? In his critique of Kant (1973b:75-118; 1973 2:67-69), Dussel refers to the historical and cultural relativity of human subjectivity which marks the limits of every concrete universalization. Therefore, every universalization is factually limited; but delimitation implies exclusion. Because the mere 'idea' of unlimited universality can not overcome the factual limitation of concrete universalization, Dussel tries to open the factual totality of society from the perspective of the excluded person(s) (in the sense of concrete negation). The demands of the oppressed, of those 'beyond' the system, break the veil of the pretended universality of a concrete society. The irruption of the poor unmasks the factual consensus in its ideological character. The 'monological' universalization (of an individual, a group, a class, a people, a culture, etc.) is broken concretely by the liberating praxis of the oppressed.

In the perspective of the ethics of liberation, the process towards successful universality is not a process of approximation to an ideal, like a developing, evolving and unfolding of a communication community; it is rather an 'ana-dialectical' process of the praxis of liberation. The oppressed Other erupts into the system and opens it to a more extensive totality where there will be new poor who will through new liberation movements fight again against the limits of the new existing Totality. The 'vehicle' on the way to successful universality is not only practical discourse, but also the liberating praxis of the oppressed.

The problem of monological discourses and the ana-logical understanding of the Other

Discourse ethics and the ethics of liberation share the intention to overcome monological universalization through real interactions. With regard to discourse ethics, however, W. Lütterfelds has shown the possibility of monological understanding even within practical discourses (1986:90f.). The understanding of argumentation of others is dependent on one's own horizon of understanding, in which something can count as 'reason'. Thus, the reasons proposed by the other person remain still my own reasons, and therefore discourse ethics would continue monological universalization despite the demand for practical discourses. Lütterfelds draws the conclusion that the 'egological base' (Lütterfelds 1986:103) of real argumentation cannot be eliminated. But he ends with the thesis that a theory of discourse which takes into account the contradiction between monological and universal reason, is 'still missing' (1986:103). Apel has answered that the recourse to the 'egological base' of argumentation is 'unnecessary' because it was never left. However, he has not answered the unsolved problem of real argumentation pointed out by Lütterfelds: how can alien argumentation break out of the horizon of understanding in such a way that the idea of consensus does not become a mere idea which conceals dissent as already liquefied? Habermas has outlined that consensus depends on 'empathetic sensitivity by each person to everyone else' (Habermas 1990:202). But the problem remains unaffected and unexplained, if the question of how to think of non-monological empathy is not cleared up. My thesis is that Dussel's theory of an analogical understanding of the Other (Dussel 1974:181-193; 1973 2:52-59) could complement discourse ethics on this point.

The material core of practical discourses are interests and needs, which should be examined with respect to their universability. Although 'normative obligations do not extend beyond the boundaries of a concrete lifeworld' (Habermas 1989-1990:48), the reasons given by those who are involved and affected in order to advance their claims, are rooted in their particular lifeworlds, their concrete backgrounds of plausibility. Whether the idea of consensus becomes a chimera or not, depends entirely on the possibility of understanding the claims of the Other from his own lifeworld. Dussel's theory of knowledge is precisely related to this problem. The point of departure is the constitutive heterogeneity of the Other in her lifeworld; the 'irruption of the Other', the immediate encounter of 'face-to-face' inaugurates the process of understanding. The constitutive moral act, even prior to verbal understanding, is to open oneself to the other; that means, to break out of one's own horizon, to break out of the plausibility of one's own lifeworld (de-totalization). Because the plausibility of verbal information and exchanges is rooted in its own history and lifeworld, it is not possible to understand the Other completely. The world of the Other can never become my own. Therefore, personal understanding depends on the revelation of the Other; it demands an involvement with the lifeworld of the Other. The 'egological base' is not left at any time because I can understand something only by relating it to my own horizon; but this horizon is broadened, expanded more and more through the encounter with the Other. The Otherness of the Other emerges with the continuing decentralization of the I or We; the exteriority of the Other which could not be 'comprehended' within the framework of the initial pre-understanding, now appears without lifting the veil of its mystery.

It seems that discourse ethics and the ethics of liberation describe the same thing from different sides; therefore they stress different aspects. Apel's point of departure is the situation of argumentation. He shows that in this situation the Otherness of the Other is already accepted. Argumentation implies and presupposes respect for the Other. Dussel's point of departure is the situation of domination, of the refusal of respect for the Other. Therefore the acceptance of the Other, of the oppressed, the detotalization of the I or We, moves into the center of moral theory. Argumentation appears only as a consequence of this original moral act. The theory follows the way from domination over interpellation and respect for the Other, to the understanding of her appellation and argumentation.

But Dussel's thesis of the constitutive exteriority of the Other does not intend to glorify 'dissent' as Lyotard has done. On the contrary, according to Dussel the quality of factual consensus depends on the commitment to enter the lifeworld of the Other and to begin to understand the Otherness of the Other.[2] This cannot be substituted by the cognitivistic account of justice in the sense of weighing claims without respect for persons. There is no justice without a deep understanding of the Otherness of the Other, of her history, her life-, her horizon of plausibility for her claims.

'Solidarity' and the problem of partiality

Up to now discourse ethics has defended the principle of justice as the integral core of moral theory on two fronts: on the one side, against Jonas' ethics of responsibility (see Apel 1988:179-216; 1987:89-116), and on the other side, in the context of the Kohlberg-Gilligan-controversy (see Habermas 1990:171f. and 1989-1990; Apel 1988:137f., 452f.). Whereas W. Kuhlmann (1987:114f.) concedes a 'surplus' in Jonas' concept of responsibility which cannot be fulfilled by an ethics of justice, Apel and Habermas try to strictly deduce responsibility and solidarity from the discourse-ethical principle of justice. Discourse partners in practical discourses do not only commit themselves to the moral principles of argumentation, like the equality of the dialogue partners, their right to fair say etc., they also commit themselves to 'co-responsibility' in the sense of a 'solidaristic responsibility for the settlement of problems' (Apel 1992:140f.; 1988:451). Habermas accentuates this co-responsibility as the other side of justice in the sense of the 'maintenance of the integrity of this form of life' (Habermas 1989-1990:47), in which dialogue partners must be interested to the same extent that they must also be interested in the freedom to respond to raised validity claims. Here I neglect the question whether the intentions of Gilligan and Jonas are integrated by discourse ethics in this way. From the perspective of liberation ethics, this question has to be suspended.

Apel's notion of 'co-responsibility', and Habermas' concept of 'solidarity' presupposes that we must only protect and extend the already existing social ties of the real community of argumentation in light of ideal universality (the aspect of emancipation). The ethics of liberation develops its concept of responsibility in a situation where the social tie is torn, where human communication is interrupted. Indeed, in this situation the universal idea of justice is also present, and insofar, we have to concede to Habermas: 'Without these idealizing presuppositions, no one, no matter how repressive the social structure under which she lives, can act with an orientation to reaching understanding' (Habermas 1989-1990:48). But the praxis of solidarity and the function of actions oriented to understanding changes in the context of domination: solidarity turns into partiality for the oppressed. Partiality means that the legitimacy of claims is anticipated because it cannot be vindicated (redeemed) consensually in a situation of domination. Processes of understanding therefore need the oppressed's consciousness of their own situation, through which the internalized role of servant is transformed, challenged and fought against, and through which a new identity is established. These processes can be described better through the different aspects of the reproduction of the lifeworld, as they have been outlined by Habermas (cultural tradition, social integration, socialization) (Habermas 1987:140f.); but with the important difference that in this context we must speak not solely of the 'reproduction', but also of the 'reconstitution' of the lifeworld of the 'oppressed' (Habermas 1987:143, schema 22).[3] The oppressed begin to identify with themselves, they begin to discover their own history (tradition), which was unknown to the dominant public until now. They free themselves from the societal norms that justified their oppression (coordination of actions), they begin to live in the moral norms of their own tradition, in communities of resistance, thus building up new identities. A practical discourse such as Apel demands, presupposes the exodus of the oppressed, the exodus from their role as servants; if the identity of one of the partners of dialogue is broken by oppression, discourse itself turns into its opposite.

The partial anticipation of universality, however, has to be vindicated at a given time. This problem was not dealt with sufficiently by Dussel. Successful liberation leads to a new totality based on justice. In this situation the claims of the former oppressed have to be redeemed too in a practical discourse of all concerned in order to avoid the dialectic between the dominator and the dominated. The ethics of liberation has not develop suitable categories for this problem. On this point the contribution of discourse ethics is extremely worthy. The limits of liberation ethics become immediately obvious if the evidence of domination is not strong enough. In that case the option for partiality (i.e. 'the preferential option for the poor') must be open to a rational discourse of all concerned. Whoever insists here on the evidence of domination, places himself in the field of dogmaticism. What looks like cynicism in front of the suffering of the people in the Third World becomes more relevant with regard to terrorist organizations like the RAF in West Germany. Dogmatism is the latent danger of partiality,[4] cynicism the danger of an ethics which demands practical discourses without consideration of the political and economic conditions that would make their implementation possible.

The labor theory of value versus the procedural principle of justice: the problem of 'material' justice

Liberation ethics has complemented the principle of partiality with a theory of economic justice, thus also reformulating Marx's labor theory of value (for Dussel's interpretation of Marx see Dussel 1983, 1985, 1988, 1990). Dussel is aware that this would be commented in Europe as an understandable but anachronistic fascination of the Third World with Marxism (1989). Despite many controversies within critical theory, there is a consensus among many philosophers, including Habermas, that alienation cannot be described primarily in terms of economic categories. Delegating even principles of a just distribution to practical discourses (Habermas 1990), the proceduralism of discourse ethics implies a critique of the marxist labor theory of value. Habermas (1987:338f.; 1982:223f.) raises two main objections to the labor theory of value which represent a certain consensus in Western Europe: Marx did not distinguish sufficiently between class-specific institutionalization and the positive structural differentiation in capitalism. Marx, therefore, does not possess criteria to differentiate between the rationalization and reification of post-traditional lifeworlds. The theory of value presupposes (1) a pre-modern romantic form of economy; (2) a productivistic approach, because it interprets alienation below the level of interaction.

I think that these objections are only partially correct with regard to Dussel's theory of value, especially if we neglect the question concerning a philological interpretation of Marx. According to Dussel, any production stands in the context of interaction. Its *telos* is the reproduction of human life, which is always a life in community. In its abstract sense economy is a practical-productive relationship; that means that there is a relationship between persons mediated by a product of labor. The theory of value is not a complete phenomenology of the relationship between humans and nature. It accentuates only those aspects that should be relevant for economic justice. Therefore the product is defined only under the perspective of the self-objectification in human work; the 'value' of a product is measured by the quantity of the 'objectified life'. The two axes of the theory of value are the following: *First*, the difference between the value of the product and the value of the working person – the 'origin of all values' – who must not be degraded to a mere value. *Second*, a theory of a just exchange within the criteria of the quantity of objectified life. An unjust exchange must not be considered as an unfortunate circulation of material objects, but as a loss of 'life'.

Maybe the crucial question concerns the function that this theory can obtain. In Dussel's ethics of liberation the labor theory of value seems to be a fourth formulation of the categorical imperative in economic terms. The imperative 'treat the other not only instrumentally but respect him/her as a person' can be translated into the terms of the labor theory of value: 'treat the other not only as value but respect him/her as the "origin of values"'. Respect for the other has to stand the test of just exchange.

Thus the labor theory of value is the criterion of all economic systems. Its validity cannot be limited to a pre-modern form of production (cf. Honneth 1980:185-233). Liberation ethics receives the theory of value because of two main reasons: it is related to the most serious problems of the Third World, its economic exploitation; and second, the labor theory of value allows liberation ethics to connect itself with the experience of the poor who must offer their working power for the cheapest salaries. Although they work very hard, separated from their families and their village, the poor are not able to reproduce their material and social life. Thus the theory of value fits very well with the preferential option for the poor. The labor theory of value has not only the function of a moral criterion, but also suggests a model for a new economic system, which meets Habermas' objections. As historical experience shows, we cannot deduce an economic system from the theory of value, we can only – perhaps – diagnose economic injustice. But economical systems are not unlimitedly available. The revolts of the peasants at the end of the Middle Ages failed because the oppressed were missing a practical and effective alternative to the dominant economic system. The economic crisis was not primarily the effect of a moral failure, its roots lay in the whole feudal system. Therefore the conflict could not be solved by the reconstitution of the 'old right' (see Bauer & Matis 1988:58). This is not a plead for an amoral system theory. But it seems to me that criteria other than those of the labor theory of value are legitimate in the discussion about economic systems, for instance the teleological criteria of efficiency, or Rawls' principle of fairness. It is understandable that Dussel is afraid to disguise the real misery with these abstractive theories. Liberation ethics has rightly criticized the system theoretical viewpoint of the economic sciences. But the moral impulse of liberation ethics threatens to vaporize without practical alternatives. Today we cannot deny a disillusionment with the history of the alternatives. On the other hand the revival of the neoliberal *desarrollismo* shows how the social sciences move in a circle. No strategy has achieved more than punctual successes, which cover the universal helplessness like shop windows. But the poor cannot afford this theoretical skepticism while struggling for their survival. It is the indisputable merit of liberation ethics to have asserted the justified claims of the poor on the level of an ethical reflection.

Apel's complementarity principle and the ethics of liberation

Both moral theories obviously presuppose a specific historical situation to which their categories are related. Discourse ethics is aware of this fact. The procedural principle depends on a 'form of life that *meets it half-way*' (Habermas 1990:208) – not in regard to its validity, but to its realization. Apel himself speaks of a 'limit' of discourse ethics (1980:278). At this point we can observe bridges between these two moral theories.

When faced with 'the facts of misery', 'moral questions are open'. As Habermas says, 'Wherever this is the case, wherever existing conditions make a mockery of the demands of universalist morality, moral issues turn into issues of political ethics' (Habermas 1990:209). Apel admits that 'as members of an oppressed class or race, they possess *a priori* a moral privilege vis-à-vis the *socially privileged*, a right to bring about equality even prior to acknowledging the rules that only have to be accepted once real equality exists' (Apel 1980:179). Habermas notes that 'the issue of revolutionary morality (which incidentally has never been satisfactorily discussed by Marxists, Eastern or Western) is fortunately not an urgent one in our type of society' (1990:209). But Apel diagnoses that also the real lifeworlds of constitutional states are still shot through with power interests. Therefore the application of discourse ethics is still a serious problem even within democratic social structures. This is why Apel introduces the complementarity principle (part B) into discourse ethics that would mediate between strategic and consensual action. On the other hand, liberation ethics does not reduce its realm of validity to the situations of obvious oppression, because every society has its oppressed, its poor. At this point Apel and Dussel treat the same sort of problems side by side but with different instruments. Apel works with types of rationality; the strategic rationality of action – excluded in part A of discourse ethics – it now receives an important role under the rule of the procedural principles of argumentation: to serve life and to establish institutions for practical discourses.

Dussel's theoretical instruments are rooted in a personalistic philosophy. They reconstruct the historical 'logic' of human relationships. Every social totality, from the intimacy between man and woman, up through the totalities of peoples and states, builds up a horizon which excludes and oppresses the Other. Therefore, solidarity has to transcend the real regnant social totality, and reach out to those who are outside. The 'ana-dialectic' describes the historical logic of totalization and detotalization, of domination and liberation, of subsumption and irruption of the Other. It is obvious that both theoretical instruments are not contradictory; they are close to one another and could complement each other. The praxis of liberation also has to decide continuously between mere strategic and consensual action, and real practical discourse is always limited in regard to time and to members who can really participate, etc.; that means, every factual discourse is limited. It is almost unavoidable that factual discourses imply consensus at the cost of third parties. Negating the factual consensus by the concrete negation of the poor, preferential solidarity corrects the idea of a mere linear and evolutionary realization of the ideal communication community. At this point liberation ethics converges with an objection of Albrecht Wellmer against discourse ethics. Exclusions of, for instance, women, foreigners, blacks, gays, and others are rooted in collective patterns of interpretation which can hardly be corrected with reasons, 'but with the *pressure* of a struggle for recognition and under the *influence* of new experiences' (Wellmer 1991:198). The liberating action of the excluded provokes the experiences which are the basis of a consensual elimination of inequality.

The utopian horizon

Discourse ethics and liberation ethics try to reconstruct the anticipations which are included in moral intuitions. They agree completely that the vanishing point of moral practice does not prescribe a historical project, but only the horizon in which all projects can be criticized. This is the conclusion reached by the critique of utopia in the last decades. Transcendental anticipation just breaks the totalitarian dynamics of utopia by overcoming the absoluteness of any historical project. Although Apel and Dussel agree about the function of counterfactual anticipations as 'regulative ideas', they differ about the contents of moral anticipations. Discourse ethics describes the ideal communication community through the idea of complete understanding. Dussel has objected that Apel reduces the ideal community to a community of language, in opposition to a community of bodies (Dussel 1989:78-84).

In my opinion this does not mark the crucial difference,[5] because in fact, discourse ethics treats the dimension of the human body in the context of the question of ideology. According to Apel, complete understanding implicates the linguistification of the unconscious or 'natural' elements of communication. This demands a temporary objectification of the Other; but any objectification must be integrated into a dialogue that is oriented to mutual understanding. Therefore the ideal communication community includes as the 'transcendental presupposition of every critique of ideology' the 'postulate of a non-distorted and in basically unlimited verbalization of extra-linguistic communicative competence', and that means the 'overcoming of what is merely "natural"' (Apel 1980:224). This postulate seems to exceed even the critique that Wellmer formulated against the scientistic tendency of the ideal communication community. Wellmer speaks of the idea 'of a definitive language', 'the original dream of logical empiricism', of 'complete transparency' (Wellmer 1991:174f.). Human liberty threatens to disappear in the 'permanent daylight' (Nietzsche) of reason. In front of this idea Dussel asserts the exteriority of human liberty as the abysmal source of human vivacity which cannot be absorbed by the light of transparency. Therefore the specific ethical anticipation is the 'proximity' between human persons; the proximity with timeless synchrony, full with the richness of freedom, so that the Other remains with respect to the one, the regnant totality, an eschatological exteriority. The proximity of persons, not the crystalline clearness of arguments, mobilizes moral praxis.

Consensus cannot be the adequate moral anticipation. In contrast to theoretical discourse, consensus is only an element within moral practice that seeks to restore distorted relationship and communication. Therefore, the adequate ethical anticipation has to be reconstructed from the other side of the practical discourse, from the side of solidarity as Habermas says. The anticipation of solidarity is not the consensual clearness of arguments but the proximity between humans. Whether in the face-to-face of the child-mother relationship in nursing, or the sex-to-sex of the man-woman relationship in love, or the shoulder-to-shoulder of colleagues in an assembly where the fate of a country is decided, or the word-hearing of the teacher-pupil relationship in the apprenticeship of living, proximity is the word that best expresses the essence of persons, their first (archeological) and last (eschatological) fullness (Dussel 1985:2.1.4.3).

Challenges, successes and the self-understanding of discourse ethics and the ethics of liberation

If one were to place the two moral theories into the original context of the other, their strengths and weakness would become immediately obvious. The ethics of liberation seems to be insecure in front of theoretical skepticism. The evidence of the option for the poor – that needs no arguments in the context of real misery – loses a bit of its plausibility in a theoretical room where claims are only proven on whether they can be doubted or not. On the other hand, the strict transcendental reflections of discourse ethics threaten to ignore the pressing questions that arise in the context of misery and oppression, though the foundation seems to be unassailable in the secured rooms of academic discussions. Obviously discourse and liberation ethics are developed in regard to different standards of foundation by which they want to be measured. Dussel tries to expose and ground the original ethical practice in front of the relationships of domination in all lifeworlds and cultures: the proximity of a face-to-face. Apel searches for a situation that is unavoidable for the moral skeptic: the situation of argumentation with its unavoidable moral presuppositions.

Without discussing here the question of an 'ultimate foundation' of ethics, we can relate these two types of theoretical grounding of morality. Insofar as the ethics of liberation competes with other moral theories, it works in an argumentative situation where it cannot avoid the presuppositions that discourse ethics has already outlined. Therefore in regard to the foundation of the philosophical theory it seems to me that the transcendental reflection of Apel reaches deeper than liberation ethics. However, liberation ethics is not defeated with this, because moral theory could be restricted to the small field of unquestionable sentences. Responsibility is not identical with this principle of justice, as Wolfgang Kuhlmann has shown (1987:114f.). The limits of discourse ethics become evident where claims cannot be asserted. Kuhlmann speaks of groups 'whose membership is denied because of their competence: sick persons, Negroes, Jews etc.'. He speaks of the problems of the embryos, the question of abortion and our relationship to nature (1987:115). These dimensions of responsibility do not necessarily mean the supererogatory practice of love; they belong to fundamental moral intuitions which every society needs in order to preserve humanity. Surely, it is possible to construct bridges to these problems by discourse ethics too, but even Kuhlmann concedes that they are more or less unsteady (Kuhlmann 1987:115). Liberation ethics tries to reconstruct precisely this responsibility from the experience of the exteriority of the Other who suffers silently oppression, the exteriority of the unborn, they who have no voice, or even the exteriority of 'dumb' nature.[6]

Thus we come to the question of the theoretical extension of discourse and liberation ethics. The thesis I tried to present and defend here was that the ethics of liberation reconstructs a certain aspect of an ethics of responsibility and solidarity, integrating from this perspective the intuitions of justice. On the other side, discourse ethics grounds responsibility and solidarity as the other side of justice. Neither one can be reduced to the other as I tried to show with some examples. A last word on the self-understanding of these moral theories. According to its theoretical position, discourse ethics delegates questions of ethical contents to their discussions within their respective lifeworlds. It restricts itself to the justification, and to reminding us, of the moral 'point of view'. Material positions have to be regarded only as contributions in an open discourse. This modesty of philosophical moral theory is correct in view of the fact that moral judgments depend more and more on the data that science may provide. But this modesty may be only a virtue in a situation where institutions for practical discourses already are established.

The material implications of discourse ethics are immediately obvious under totalitarian conditions (Honneth 1986:183-194). In such a situation, the deduction of the procedural principle loses its function of being a mere contribution, and unavoidably receives a prophetical character, for instance in statements against censorship, against judgments without a fair trial, etc. Here is a bridge to understanding a little bit better the often breathtaking categorical resoluteness of liberation ethics. Pressed by the daily death of the poor in the Third World, the academic modesty of discourse ethics becomes questionable for liberation ethics. The adequate form to do philosophy is as prophetical philosophy, as the reduplicated 'cry' of the poor (Dussel 1974:195). Dussel's 'philosophy of liberation' intends, just as Apel also attempts, to 'inspire the practical action of human beings by means of a dialogical constitution of sense' (Apel 1973 1:220), with the difference that now it is inspired through the liberating action of the oppressed. The Philosophy of liberation understands itself as an 'analectic pedagogy of liberation' (Dussel 1974:194), not as a paternalistic avant-garde, not as a revolutionary idea that has to take root in the masses, but as a critical assistance, in solidarity, of the poor on their way toward liberation:

To think of everything in the light of the provocative word of the people - the poor, the castrated woman, the child, the culturally dominated youth, the aged person discarded by the consumer society – shouldering infinite responsibility and in the presence of the Infinite; that is philosophy of liberation (Dussel 1985:5.9.5.1).

(Translated from the German by Eduardo Mendieta)

Notes

1 In *Diskurs und Befreiung. Studien zur philosophischen Ethik von Karl-Otto Apel und Enrique Dussel* (1997), I develop this approach in the perspective of an intercultural ethics as basis for a critical theory oriented towards global questions.

2 Apel and Habermas have developed very similar theories of understanding with regard to the foundations of the human and social sciences, albeit not in the context of moral theory. See Apel (1984) and Habermas (1984).

3 See Habermas (1987:143, schema 22), where he lists the phenomena that arise when the lifeworld comes into crisis. These observations correspond in many aspects to Dussel's description of the lifeworld of the poor.

4 This is the cause of the strained relation between the ethics of liberation and the scientific discussion on the development of the Third World. That the philosophy of liberation departs from a situation of domination is but a correction and further development of the theory of dependence, and in no way its abandoning, as has been the case in Europe. It is obvious that this situation builds limits for the dialogue between both moral theories.

5 Dussel's critique is correct with regard to the themes of the factual application of the discourse ethics, where the global economic problems are not treated sufficiently.

6 See Habermas essay 'Morality and Ethical Life', (1990:210-211): 'It is just as difficult to answer the basic objection of ecological ethics: How does discourse ethics, which is limited to subjects capable of speech and action, respond to the fact that mute creatures are also vulnerable? Compassion for tortured animals and the pain caused by the destruction of biotopes are surely manifestations of moral intuitions that cannot be fully satisfied by the collective narcissism of what in the final analysis is an anthropocentric way of looking at things'.

References

Apel, K.-O. (1973), *Transformation der Philosophie*, Vols. 1-2, Suhrkamp: Frankfurt.

Apel, K.-O. (1980), *Towards a Transformation of Philosophy* [Trans. G. Adey & D. Frisby], Routledge & Kegan Paul: London.

— (1984), 'Die Situation des Menschen als Herausforderung an die praktische Vernunft', *Funkkolleg Praktische Philosophie/Ethik: Dialoge*, Vol. 1, Suhrkamp: Frankfurt.

— (1984), *Understanding and Explanation: A Transcendental Pragmatic Perspective* [Trans. G. Warnke], MIT Press: Cambridge (MA).

— (1986), 'Grenzen der Diskursethik? Versuch einer Zwischenbilanz', *Zeitschrift für philosophische Forschung* 40/1, 3-31.

— (1988), *Diskurs und Verantwortung. Das Problem des Übergangs zur postkonventionellen Moral*, Suhrkamp: Frankfurt.

— (1992), 'Normatively Grounding "Critical Theory" through Recourse to the Lifeworld? A Transcendental-Pragmatic Attempt to Think with Habermas against Habermas', in Honneth, A., McCarthy, Th., et al. (eds.), *Philosophical Interventions in the Unfinished Project of Enlightenment*, [Trans. W. Rehg], MIT Press: Cambridge (MA).

— (1997), *Ethics and The Theory of Rationality: Selected Essays*, Vol. 2 [Ed. E. Mendieta], Humanities Press: Atlantic Highlands.

Bauer, L. & Matis, H. (1988), *Geburt der Neuzeit. Vom Feudalsystem zur Marktgesellschaft*, Fischer: München.

Cerutti-Guldberg, H. (1983), *Filosofía de la liberación latinoamericana* (Fondo de Cultura Económica: Mexico (DF).

Dussel, E. (1973a) *Para una ética de la liberación latinoamericana*, Vols. 1-2, Siglo XXI: Buenos Aires.

— (1973b), *Para una destrucción de la historia de la ética*, Ser y Tiempo: Mendoza.

— (1974), *Método para una Filosofía de la liberación*, Sigueme: Salamanca.

— (1977), *Para una ética de la liberación latinoamericana*, Vol. 3, EDICOL: México (DF).

— (1979), *Para una ética de la liberación latinoamericana*, Vols. 4, USTED: Bogotá.

— (1980), *Para una ética de la liberación latinoamericana*, Vol. 5, USTED: Bogotá.

— (1983), *Filosofía de la producción*, Nueva América: Bogotá.

— (1985), *Philosophy of Liberation*, Orbis Books: Maryknoll.

— (1985b), *La producción teórica de Marx. Un comentario a los 'Grundrisse'*, Siglo XXI: Mexico (DF).

— (1988), *Hacia un Marx desconocido. Un comentario de los Manuscritos del 61-63*, Siglo XXI: Mexico (DF).

— (1989), 'Die "Lebensgemeinschaft" und die "Interpellation des Armen"', in Fornet-Betancourt, R. (Hrsg.), *Ethik und Befreiung*, Augustinus-Buchhandlung: Aachen.

— (1990), *El último Marx (1863-82) y la liberación latinoamericana*, Siglo XXI: Mexico (DF).

Fornet-Betancourt, R. [Hrsg.] (1990), *Ethik und Befreiung. Dokumentation der Tagung: Philosophie der Befreiung: Begründungen von Ethik in Deutschland und Lateinamerika*, Augustinus-Buchhandlung, Aachen.

Habermas, H. (1982), 'A Reply to My Critics', in Thompson, J.B. & Held, D. (eds.), *Habermas: Critical Debates*, MacMillan: London.

— (1984), *Theory of Communicative Action*, Vol. 1 [Trans. Th. McCarthy], Beacon Press: Boston.

— (1987), *Theory of Communicative Action*, Vol. 2 [Trans. Th. McCarthy], Beacon Press: Boston.

— (1989-1990), 'Justice and Solidarity: On the Discussion Concerning "Stage 6"', *The Philosophical Forum*, Vol. XXI, 1/2, Fall-Winter, 1989-1990.

— (1990), *Moral Consciousness and Communicative Action* [Trans. Ch. Lenhardt & S. Weber Nicholsen], MIT Press, Cambridge (MA).

Honneth, A. (1980), 'Arbeit und instrumentelles Handeln', in Honneth, A. & Jaeggi, U. (Hrsg.), *Arbeit, Handlung, Normativität. Theorien des historischen Materialismus*, Suhrkamp: Frankfurt.

— (1986), 'Diskursethik und implizites Gerechtigkeitsprinzip. Eine Diskussionsbemerkung', in Kuhlmann, W. (Hrsg.), *Moralität und Sittlichkeit. Das Problem Hegels und die Diskursethik*, Suhrkamp: Frankfurt.

Kuhlmann, W. (1987), 'Prinzip Verantwortung versus Diskursethik', *Archivio di filosofía* 55, 89-116.

Lütterfelds, W. (1986), 'Die monologische Struktur des kategorischen Imperativs und Fichtes Korrektur der Diskursethik', *Zeitschrift für philosophische Forschung* 40.

Salazar Bondy, A. (1968), *Existe una filosofía en nuestra América?*, Siglo XXI, México.

Schelkshorn, H. (1992), *Ethik und Befreiung. Eine Einführung in der Philosophie Enrique Dussels*, Herder: Freiburg.

— (1997), *Diskurs und Befreiung. Studien zur philosophischen Ethik von Karl-Otto Apel und Enrique Dussel*, Rodopi: Amsterdam.

Wellmer, A. (1991), *The Persistence of Modernity: Essays on Aesthetics, Ethics, and Postmodernism* [Trans. D. Midgley], MIT Press: Cambridge (MA).

10 Modernity and postmodernity as challenges to discourse ethics

An ethics of global co-responsibility for an age of suspect foundationalism and rhetorical relativism

Eduardo Mendieta

If one understands by postmodernity the critique of the monological and autarkic self, the onto-metaphysics of history, and the hegemony of instrumental reason, then Karl-Otto Apel's thinking could be labeled with this jarring shibboleth.[1] This pronouncement will certainly cause dissonance as Karl-Otto Apel, along with Jürgen Habermas, is the founding father of discourse ethics, a theory of morality that seems to stand in complete opposition to anything one might associate with the postmodern. Apel has since the late sixties stubbornly pursued the question of the possibility of ethics and morality in an age of science in which the subject was reduced to epistemology and all rationality was a function of either deduction, induction or abductive thinking. In the early 1960s Apel's main contenders were the positivists and the critical rationalists (Apel 1973). In his view, scientism, the unchallengeable belief in the supremacy of scientific rationality that nevertheless abdicated before the need to provide justifications for moral norms, epitomized the paradoxical situation of modernity. On the one hand, the success of *homo faber* had lead to the blind trust in the ability of instrumental reason to decide on all practical questions. On the other hand, the more science permeated and controlled social life, the fewer questions about responsibility for the consequences of our actions became capable of being adjudicated. The more the consequences of modernization made ethics an imperative, the less it became either foreseeable or even possible (Poole 1991). Indeed, more substantively, there is an unequivocal sense in which the subject as an epistemic machine undercuts the very notion of agency, that is, the construing of subjectivity as knowing states of affairs eviscerates the possibility of moral accountability that is based on the notion of a self that sees itself as being capable of initiating acts that can transform and be transformed by others' intervention. Agency is the expression of the natality of the human being, as Arendt would put it (1981 1:11f.). This is part of the reason why postmodernity is so intricately associated with the pyrrhic victory of science that simultaneously forebodes the obsolescence of the subject (Eagleton 1996:69f.; Laclau 1996:20f.). For with the purported triumph of science, all human concerns and problems have become mere problems of management and technical implementation. Not too far behind this ideological belief, so well unmasked by Habermas in his 'Technology and Science as "Ideology"' (Habermas 1970), trails the notion of the 'end of history', as Arnold Gehlen so pointedly demonstrated (Gehlen 1975).

Today, however, no one is deluded about the utopia promised by science as technology and bureaucracy as modernization. Auschwitz, Hiroshima and the Gulags have rendered both suspect. Still, the question of the difficulty and necessity of an ethics for our modern societies remains a pressing issue. Today, however, Apel's contenders are no longer the technocrats and ideologists of scientism. They have become the very critics of scientism and the denouncers of totalitarian reason. These, however, like their predecessors, continue to pronounce an ethics appropriate for our post-scientific age at best an impossibility and at worst undesirable. The critique of scientism has turned into the total and totalizing critique of reason. Ethics and moral theory, as integral moments of modernity, have been equally thrown out with the bath water of rationality, even if the return to the ethical is one of the integral moments of postmodernity. It would seem as though the postmoderns thought that ethics was only possible as a rejection of rationality. For once we turn to the 'rational' justification of moral points of view or the rationalization of the 'lifeworld', they fear we are on the brink of the totalitarian leveling of differences and the suppression of the individual as unique and irreducible. The impulses and intentions are noble, but the means and tools seem inadequate and inappropriate to the task.[2]

In this essay I will attempt to show how Karl-Otto Apel's discourse ethics may be seen as a moral theory that not only discerned and anticipated the critique of modernity by postmoderns, but also formulated an alternative that navigates between the Scylla of relativism and the Charybdis of foundationalism. As such, Apel's architectonics of discourse ethics presents itself as a postmodern ethics; that is, an ethics that supersedes the epistemic notion of the self, the speculative metaphysics of history, and the ideology of scientism. To this extent, Apel's ethics must also be seen as a postmetaphysical ethics; that is, one that presupposes neither a substantive (onto-theo-teleological) notion of reason nor a philosophy of consciousness notion of subjectivity – subjects as epistemic machines plagued by Cartesian anxiety, in Bernstein's wonderful phrase (1988:16). In fact, the alternatives between foundationalism and relativism are revealed by Apel's approach to be rhetorical devices that occlude rather than disclose the challenges presented by the modernity/postmodernity dyad. For, once we have made the 'linguistic turn', we have to begin from both the recognition that all language games represent and embody a facticity *a priori*, that is, we are always products of contingent historical traditions, and on the other hand, we must still talk to each other across time and cultural sedimentations in terms of a *lingua franca* that does violence to neither dialogue partner.

This common language needed for intra and intercultural dialogue is one that can only be elaborated in terms of insight into the conditions of possibility of dialogue *überhaupt*. This remits us to the question of the validity of rules of dialogue, or what Apel has referred to as the question of the justification of validity (*Geltungsrechtfertigung*). Here, in the question of the possibility of dialogue in general, we encounter an anchor, or point of reference, that is not a foundation for it has not been arrived at by means of deduction, induction or abduction, which would have entangled us in the Münchhausen trilemma (Albert 1985:16-21; Apel 1987:250-290; Kuhlmann 1985:51-104). Instead, we find a point of reference that is disclosed by self-reflection. Indeed, Apel affirms that foundations are a foreclosure of reason's self-reflexivity. It is clear that Apel offers neither a foundation nor does he want to hold in abeyance by all means necessary the threat of relativism. Foundations are assailable, as Apel is willing to agree with Albert, and relativism is integral to the hermeneutical enlightenment of our period (Apel 1987b). Yet unconditional normativity and the rejection of historicism *zweiten Grades* (historicism raised to the second power) are not only possible, but necessary (Gadamer 1985:479). Only with reference to both is ethics made possible for a postmodern epoch.

Furthermore, I will attempt to show how Apel's version of discourse ethics is able to meet another fundamental challenge of the postmodern condition, namely the postcolonial or transmodernity challenge. This challenge, best articulated by Enrique Dussel, refers to the critique of the eurocentrism and ethnocentrism that still contaminates most Western thinking. I take not only this challenge, but also Apel's meeting it head on, to be particularly important and paradigmatic for what stands under the heading 'the crisis of modernity and the dawn of the postcolonial condition'. For, if the catastrophes of the short century of which Eric Hobsbawn speaks threw Western culture into a crisis of identity, the challenge of the 'Third World' and the 'Other' present an even more profound challenge of legitimacy (Hobsbawn, 1995). As Westerners we stand in need of not only vindicating ourselves before ourselves, but most importantly before the masses of humanity who have been both adversely and positively impacted by the Westernization of the world. The validity of the normative contents of modernity are only as good as they can meet the litmus test of the uncircumventable critique and skepticism of the 'Other' of Western culture. While others remained deceptively humble and onerously silent before this challenge, Apel has earnestly and consequently met the challenge.

In order to show how Karl-Otto Apel's work can be seen as a post-metaphysical and postmodern ethics, I will compare and contrast his thinking to the work of two other major thinkers that departing from very similar premises have arrived at very different conclusions. I will first look at Jean-François Lyotard's 'pagan politics' and complementary 'ethics of dissent'. I will then turn to the dialogue that Apel has had with Dussel's 'liberation ethics' over the last seven years. These comparisons and contrasts will be guided by the rubrics of self, community and language. These are no arbitrary categories (Wyschogrod 1992). They all stand at the center of each of these thinkers' formulations. Furthermore, they also overlap with the concerns expressed by the postmodern critique(s). In other words, the end of the subject refers to the challenge of the development of viable notions of selfhood or agency that can overcome the aporias of the Cartesian and Kantian subject. The end of history refers to the challenge of the non-metaphysical construing and formulation of notions of community that supersede the dead ends of teleologically, functionally or structurally determined forms of social-communal organization. Central to these questions is the legitimacy and legitimation of social power. In an unequivocal sense, the gravitational point of reference for all of these three philosophers is the question of the source, appropriation and distribution of social power. This, obviously, is the question of the political and of justice. Finally, the demystification and critique of instrumental reason, which has turned into the total and totalizing critique of reason, refers to the linguistification of all human cognitive and communicative processes. Indeed, the critique of reason can only be pursued as the critique of language. Yet, language itself can only be seen as contingent and historical and, as such, it does not seem to offer itself as a likely warrant for claims to universality. This, at least, is the claim that Lyotard makes, who goes so far as to claim that there is not 'language' per se, but only language games, particular genres, phrase regimes and traditions of saying and communicating in particular contexts that do not have universal binding power.

Apel's transcendental semiotics and discourse ethics

Apel's work can be described as the synthesis of three of the most important philosophical currents of twentieth century philosophy. As a student of Rothacker in the 1940s and early 1950s, he was deeply influenced by phenomenology, hermeneutics and the then influential movement of philosophical anthropology (Gehlen, Plessner). Later on, propelled by a systematic interest in the development of modern philosophies of language, he expanded his horizons by rigorously studying the work of Wittgenstein and ordinary language philosophy (Austin and Searle), as well as its more syntactically and semantically oriented variants (Analytic Philosophy, Russell, Quine, and others). This same systematic interest lead him to American pragmatism, in particular Charles Sanders Peirce's inaugural version and later reformulation under the name of pragmaticism (Apel, 1995; Mendieta, 1994). Apel's overarching philosophical endeavor has been to succinctly develop a methodologically relevant transcendental philosophy that does not fall behind the gains of either the scientific revolutions or nineteenth century hermeneutical enlightenment.[3]

For Apel, while each philosophical current, be it hermeneutics, analytic philosophy or pragmatism, may have pointed out abstractive fallacies in modern philosophy or elaborated quasi-transcendental conditions of possibility of meaning or understanding, be it in terms of some sort of semantic competence or pre-understanding that can be defined ontologically, each current by itself has failed to dialectically articulate the *quaestio facti* with the *quaestio iuris*. Whereas the former refers to the *Sinnkonstitution*, the constitution of meaning, the former refers to *Geltungsrechtfertigung*, the redemption of validity claims. In other words, while each one of these philosophical movements may be seen as a reformulation of the Kantian project, albeit now in terms of language, each one has failed to address itself directly to Kant's *Critique of Pure Reason* not just in terms of a description of what is, of how truth happens, but also, and most importantly, in terms of the conditions of normative intersubjective validity and possibility of progress of both the natural and human sciences (Apel 1973 1:35-36). Apel's project, thus, is the reformulation of both Aristotle's and Kant's quest after a *prima philosophia*. In Apel's case however, and in accordance with the linguistic turn of contemporary philosophy, this first philosophy can only be articulated as the dialectical tension between an apriorily given real communication community and an always already counterfactually presupposed ideal communication community. It is in this tension where Apel discovers the foundations of a normative macro-ethics that can be relevant to our globalized planet (Apel 1996; Kuhlmann & Böhler 1982; Dorschel et. al. 1993). The fundamental insight of this semiotic-pragmatic articulation of normative ethics implies a linguistic transformation of Kant's categorical imperative which is clearly captured in Apel's formulation:

> Who argues – and this means, one who, for example, seriously formulates the question of the basic ethical norm in a dialogue or also in a solitary self-understanding qua internalized dialogue – can be lead to recognize or to be convinced through self-reflection that, necessarily, inasmuch *as arguer*, he or she has already recognized a *basic ethical norm*. This basic norm can be made explicit in the following manner: The arguer has already given evidence *in actu*, and with that has recognized that Reason is *practical*, that is *responsible for human action*. In other words, that *the ethical validity claims* of Reason, as well as its *truth claims*, can and must be satisfied through *arguments*. This means that the *ideal rules of argumentation* in a communication community, in principle unlimited, of persons who recognize each other reciprocally as equals, represent *normative conditions of possibility of decision on ethical validity claims [ethischen Geltungsansprüchen] through the formation of consensus*, and that therefore, *with respect to all the ethically relevant questions of practical life, it is possible, in a discourse* which respects the rules of argumentation of a an ideal communication community, to *arrive*, in principle, at a *consensus*, and, therefore, that one *ought to aspire* in practice to bring about this consensus (Apel 1980:264-265).

Apel's interest in rehabilitating and transforming transcendental philosophy, now as a transcendental semiotics, has been motivated by, first, the aporetic division of labor between, on the one hand, the *Western system of complementarity* between value neutral scientism and decisionist subjectivism, and, on the other hand, the *Eastern system of integration* between praxis and theory, history and nature. This aporetic situation between late liberalism and scientific socialism is for him a clear indication that we need to develop a typological theory of rationality that navigates between the abstractive fallacy of scienticism and technocracy, and retrograde anti-Enlightenment rhetorical humanism (Apel 1973 1:65). The point of this challenge is to do justice to the process of Western rationalization (Weber) without falling into the extremes of either the mere acceptance and overvalorization of nomological, value neutral, instrumental rationality or the wholesale rejection of *ratio* as mere functionalization, instrumentalization or reification. The second main motive has been the accompanying *homo faber*'s overtaking of the limits of institutions and instincts, or, in other words, the growing disparity between our capacity to destroy and our ability to control our destructive potential through rational and normed means. In other words, Apel's central preoccupation has been: how can we develop a planetary macro-ethic in a situation where all kinds of normative claims have been deflated and rendered obsolete by either scientism or subjectivism.

It is against this context that we must understand how Apel, availing himself of all the conceptual tools bequeathed to him by the different philosophical traditions his philosophical system has absorbed, has been able to point to the limits of the modern concepts of self, society and the transcendental and/or normative. In terms of his critique of the monological, egological and autarkic concept of the self, Apel has pointed out, departing from Heidegger, Peirce and Wittgenstein, that subjectivity is a derivative mode of intersubjectivity. Our capacity to think of our selves as an 'I' or a 'Me' is predicated on the acquisition of symbolic or linguistic competencies that allow us to assume those roles. One of the major faults of modern philosophy, according to Apel, was to fall into the fallacy of methodological solipsism – as we already noted above. This is at least how he reads both Descartes and Kant. If the former abstracts the subject from the very context of its conditions of possibility, the latter hypostasizes these conditions of possibility into a monistic transcendental hypersubject. Departing from Wittgenstein's insight that 'one alone cannot follow a rule', and Heidegger's elaboration of our pre-understanding of the world, Apel arrives at a notion of intersubjectivity that is linguistically constituted, which is always spatially and temporally embedded. Apel speaks not just of the linguistic preconditions of self-understanding but also of a *Leibapriori*, a corporeal *a priori* that refers to our way of being in the world not solely or merely as epistemic machines (Apel 1958; 1963).

Societies, on the other hand, are not merely substantiations of a particular people's pathos or ethos. Societies, as historical instantiations of the normed conditions of intersubjectivity, anticipate, if always partially, the conditions of an ideal communication community (Apel 1973 2). In other words, in one way or another, already existing societies can constitute themselves only in so far as they already prefigure the conditions of an ideal communication community. In this way, societies are always capable of being self-critical and of calling for their own transformation from the stand point of those ideals they already presuppose and anticipate. Inasmuch, societies possess a normative dimension that points to a utopia, but one which is neither teleological nor substantive. Apel's motto, thus, could be utopia *sans* teleology (Apel, 1990a).

Justice as paralogy: Lyotard

Lyotard defines the postmodern as 'incredulity toward metanarratives', (Lyotard 1984:xxiv) one of them being the 'subject', one of the great heroes of modernity. Indeed, the '*self* does not amount to much' (1984:15). It counts as a 'nodal point'. It is, if anything, a *locus* in language; a place where communications intersect and interject. The subject is an interjection in language, a switch between addressee and addressor. Language makes possible the self, not the converse. In fact, Lyotard's work can be seen as progressively attempting to divest itself of any vestiges of a transcendental subject; as disentangling itself from the ruin of 'subject-systems' (be they liberal, marxist, capitalist, christian or the speculative; cf. *Diacritics* 1984:17-18). If in the *Postmodern Condition* Lyotard spoke of language games, in *The Differend* he has opted for 'phrase regimes' (Lyotard 1988:xii). Phrases, and genres, are present before any 'intention'. Language games, on the other hand, suggests a functional view of language: already existing subjects who 'use' language like a tool box. This, however, is misleading. A subject finds, constructs itself only because of the place that is granted to it by language, more precisely, by the poetics and pragmatics of phrase regimes. Indeed, the territory of language makes possible a geography of the self (Haber 1994:15). The self, if one can speak in these terms, is a positionality, a locality made possible by the phrase regimes that constitute social practices. Social practices, in fact, are phrase regimes. The confrontation, interaction, conflict, transition between 'phrase regimes' leaves behind the trace of that which we call the subject. The self is the detritus of the clash of genres. As such, the self is at best an abstraction, at worst an illusion.

To attempt to fix the subject, or the self, is to attempt to unify something that is thoroughly heterogeneous. It is in this sense that the vanishing of the subject in language is to be seen as part of the postmodern condition: the fundamental disbelief that something like an autonomous, self-regulating, self-positing subject could ever be attained or desired. This vanishing, however, as a critique of the metanarrative of a pristine, already existing subject or self to be saved or rescued from either society or the irrational, is seen as a freeing of the possibility of agency. From this perspective, Lyotard seems to give primacy to agency over selfhood and subjectivity. The latter are derivative and deficient modes of the possibility to be, to situate oneself within a social practice in accordance with the taking positions within phrase regimes. An agent is someone who judges in order to act without letting its 'course be inflected by a purposiveness which would legitimate it'

(Lyotard 1984a:18). In fact, for Lyotard reflexivity itself is the capacity to synthesize (in the Kantian sense) facts without determining laws; that is, to synthesize givens without criteria (Lyotard 1986:13). 'Reflection requires that you watch out for occurrences, that you don't already know what's happenning' (1986:xv).

Radical heterogeneity makes possible for empowered agency. To attempt to freeze the subject is to attempt to provide rules for the subject's positionalities within language. It is, in other words, to attempt to do violence to the very indeterminacy, irreducibility and heterogeneity of language. Like there is no language, as a formal system of syntactical-semantical rules, there is no 'subject' (Lyotard 1988:xii). The challenge, contrariwise, is to maintain the open-ended character of phrase regimes and genres that ensure the open horizon of agencies. What is of utmost importance is to maintain the hybridity of language games; their capacity to call forth unexpected, unruled 'moves'. The lifeblood of language games and phrase regimes is displacement, solecism and paralogy. If there are rules, these 'allow and encourage the greatest flexibility of utterance' (Lyotard 1984:17).

What is true of language is also true of selves and the communities to which they belong, if only temporarily, as players in the social practices that constitute them. The 'we' of a community is also always an illusion. It is the expression of an ideological move. The pronouncement of any 'we' always conceals the heterogeneity between a 'we' that is normative and a we that is a prescriptive; one is the addressor, the other the addressee. As either addressee or addressor, this purported 'we' is always radically heterogeneous. Who counts as a member of the we that can prescribe to others and to itself, and once addressed, who counts as a member of that unity called forth to a normative attitude, discloses the internal rift of a supposedly homogeneous 'we'. The 'we' of any normative claims always seems to shipwreck on the reefs of an ideal and a real 'we' (Lyotard 1988:99). The 'we' of any normative claims, in fact, is condemned to remain particular, even as it is torn asunder by the tension humanity 'must experience in its vocation for emancipation, a tension between the particularity, randomness, and opacity of the present and the universality, self-determination, and transparency of the future promised by emancipation' (Lyotard 1992:26). Most importantly, the attempt to fuse these two 'wes' leads to the terrorism of homogenization, to the elimination of radical difference.

Terror arises precisely when nothing has been emancipated enough, when not everything has fallen in line with the universal will expressed in consensus. The resistant particular, then, is seen as a resistance to the will to consensus to liberation. Here justice is obliterated in the name of emancipation, an ideal one, and consensus, as the asymptote of discussion and deliberation (Lyotard 1992:54). Justice, in fact, is not well served by the attempt to ground it on consensus, on truth. For Lyotard, neither truth nor consensus do justice to the heterogeneity of 'phrase regimes'. To attempt to converge on consensus, on a 'we' that is in agreement, is to attempt to prescribe in advance how displacements within language regimes ought to proceed and be negotiated. And this negotiation is the substance of justice, of ethics. Truth and consensus, in fact, cancel the need and possibility of justice. It is heterogeneity that makes consensus possible (Lyotard 1988:55). The goal of discussion is not consensus but dissent. Likewise, justice is coming to terms with the unrepresentable, the radically incommensurate, that which is silent or has been silenced, but needs to be put into language or be given a voice. Conversely, injustice is the threat to the right to speak or to be silent (Lyotard 1988:11). Even silence is an utterance that can be taken as a judgment. Justice is the question of the representation of the unpresentable, of the impossibility of evading conflict and heeding to divergent claims bereft of a universal genre – a *lingua franca* – that would allow for their meditation (1988:xii). Justice 'is to bear witness to the unpresentable' (Lyotard 1984:82).

> Justice here does not consist merely in the observance of the rules; as in all the games, it consists in working at the limits of what the rules permit, in order to invent new moves, perhaps new rules and therefore new games (Lyotard & Thébaud 1985:100).

We bear witness to the inassimilable by respecting the heterogeneity of language that, rather than converge, seeks to diverge, to transgress the very boundaries of its limits so as to discover and invent new moves or new phrase regimes. For language itself does not have any finality, not only because language as such does not exist (as a totality it is unrepresentable), but also because language is radically indeterminate, dependent on responses and countermoves which it cannot and does not prescribe (1988:xii, 59, 159). The task, in fact, once we recognize that consensus has become outmoded and suspect, is to 'arrive at an idea and practice of justice that is not linked to that of consensus'. This task begins to be addressed with the recognition of both the heterogeneity of genres and their circumscribed character, that is, their spatial and temporal finitude and locality (Lyotard, 1984:66). The principle of this justice would not be homology, but paralogy;

and dissent would be its highest value (Lyotard, 1984:xxv). It is this practice of justice that Lyotard calls 'pagan politics' (Lyotard and Thébaud 1985).

Enrique Dussel's liberation philosophy

While Apel's context was post-World War II ravaged Europe, one poised before the dual abysses of decisionistic subjectivism and value neutral scientism, Dussel's context was an underdeveloped, anthropologically, economically and politically stunted, colonized and exploited Latin America. And while Dussel also descends, like Apel, from the lineage of Heideggerian existential hermeneutics, his goal has been less an attempt to rescue or synthesize this philosophical tradition with other North Atlantic philosophies, and more to explode and unmask its complicity with the economic and political hegemony of the North over the South. At the same time, Dussel has had to confront other Latin American attempts to overcome a type of philosophical inauthenticity brought on by still effective traditions of colonialism and neocolonialism through the formulation of philosophical categories that would disclose the state of philosophical inauthenticity as the other side, the reverse, of that which presents itself as the norm, the normal and the authentic. In other words, while many Latin American philosophers up to then had attempted to resolutely extricate Latin America from the state of so called existential inauthenticity via the disclosure of the phenomenological, symbolic, existential elements of an autochthonous culture, that nevertheless continued to be thought of in terms of categories formulated by European philosophers, Dussel set out to de-construct, to question the very validity or reach of these same categories. For Dussel, then, the project has been one of developing a destruction or deconstruction not just of the Western ontological tradition, which begins with Heraclitus and concludes with Heidegger's own attempt to think beyond the metaphysics of presence, but also of the metaphysics that see the unmodernity of Latin America and, for that matter, all the peripheries of Europe as merely deficient modes of Europe's *ontos* and *logos*. In this sense, Dussel's philosophical endeavor has been to think beyond the ontology of a warring totality (as is implied by Heraclitus, Clausewitz and Nietzsche) that has as its dialectical dyads Ariel and Caliban (Rodó 1988; Retamar 1989). To supersede the ontology of the totality, the totality whose existence is predicated on the negation of the negative, the Other, as such, calls for the formulation of a meta-physics, an analectical metaphysics, an apophantic meta-physics, a metaphysics of alterity.[4]

Dussel, following Levinas, makes a strict distinction between ontology and metaphysics, that is, between that which is self-referential and predicates its existence on the negation of the negation, a totalized totality, and that which points to the other as Other, not the different but distinct. The dialectic, as a method of analysis, refers to the internal unfolding of the same. The dialectic, as understood from Plato through Marx, refers to the self-projection, self-duplication into the different, that is nothing but the negative image of the same, of the one. Against this, Dussel develops the analectical method. This method demonstrates how the totality is exploded not from within but from without. Just as the voice of God irrupts into the silence of the desert to reveal to the prophet the slavery of his people, the other as other, in its phenomenological manifestation, reveals itself in the face-to-face, challenging us, appealing to us to rupture our own horizons of comprehension. From phenomenology to Liberation is the name of the process of constituted intersubjectivity and trans-historicality. This analectical metaphysics mobilizes the always frozen totalities of self, society and transcendent. The *novum*, novelty, transformation moves from the periphery to the center, to use bell hooks' image. The epiphany of the other, as Other, disrupts the serenity of self-sameness. Strictly speaking, in Dussel's view, to come to rest on self-identity is to close ourselves to the challenge of our own intrinsic otherness, and the otherness of the other that interpellates from beyond the horizon of our own complacent world. In an analogous manner to Apel, then, Dussel has also criticized modern philosophy's egological focus. For Dussel, the ruling metaphor of modern philosophy has been the *ego cogito*, which is but the epistemological analogue of a more primordial figure, the *ego conquiro* that manifested itself in the persons of Pizarro and Cortés. The centeredness of the *cogito* duplicates the spatiality of world domination brought on through the development of the world system inaugurated in 1492. Societies, similarly, constituted themselves as self-same totalities. Europe became Europe as it differentiated itself vis-à-vis the other of the Indian, the Amerindian, the African and the Asian. The discovery, or invention, of America led to the discovery of history, but only of Europe's own history. Everything else was either pre-history or non-history (Hegel).[5] Insofar as the history of Europe has unfolded, propelled by an imperial or warring ontology, the normative has been but a shadow of its own self-sameness. In Dussel's analysis, Hegel's dialectic clearly illustrates this totalization of the totality, this inability to hear the pronouncement of the other, or to live in the proximity of the other as other (Dussel 1974).

Like Apel, and also for many of the same reasons, Dussel's central preoccupation has been: how can we develop a planetary macro-ethic in a context where three quarters of the world lives in the most extreme form of poverty, while the remaining quarter pillages and wastes more than its share of planetary wealth? Although this globalized situation can be analyzed in terms of an apophantic metaphysics, or an analectics, Dussel's grounding of a planetary ethics, in contrast to Apel and Habermas, reaches back to a more fundamental level of the transcendental conditions of possibility. In his analysis, and here is where he rehabilitates Marx, understanding and mutual agreement are only possible through the sustenance and preservation of LIFE, the primordial practical relationship (Dussel 1988). Thus following, but departing from Apel's and Habermas' transcendental or formal pragmatics, Dussel developed a 'transcendental economics', which is the grounding part of his liberation ethics (Dussel 1996; 1993). The fundamental insight of this ethical theory is that:

> Who *works* can be lead to recognize or be convinced through self-reflection that, inasmuch as *producer*, he or she has already necessarily recognized an *ethical norm*. This ethical norm can be made explicit in the following manner: who *works* has already attested *in actu*, and with that has recognized, that reason is practical, that is, responsible for human action; In other words, that the claims to *justice*, can be and ought to be satisfied through *acts-of-work*, which are not only technically adequate, but also practically *just* (Dussel 1996:58).

It is with this insight that we can substantively analyze the globalized, unequal consumption of planetary wealth. The present state of affairs, in Dussel's analysis, is attained through the development of a world-system that established itself with the discovery of Amerindia. 1492 is the birth-date of modernity, and its underside, the occluded Other. Modernity is the name of a planetary system of center-periphery, North-South, in which the modernity of one calls for the unmodernity of its other. Modernity, thus, is already in effect in those lands called pre-modern, or in the process of modernization, but as its other face or its underside. The boundaries of modern philosophy, as delineated from the other side of our horizon of understanding – the exteriority of the exploited Other – point to not just the conceptual exhaustion of foundational concepts but also their complicity in the preservation of a temporal and spatial symbolics of domination, i.e. the historically and institutionally established violation of the fundamental principle of an always already presupposed transcendental economics. It is in this sense that the myth of modernity is a sacrificial myth (Dussel 1993; 1996). In Dussel's view, the end of the Cartesian subject, or the Hegelian dialectic, calls not for the completion of the project of Modernity but for its radical re-construction. The limits of European philosophy are the very limits of its onedimensional view of modernity.

Beyond Lyotard's impasse

Given the above delineated reconstructions, I would like to list the challenges to Apel from the postmodern and neo-pragmatist camps.[6] I offer this list not as evidence of some particular strategy of argumentation, but as a series of conclusions that seem to stand out for me vis-à-vis my understanding of Apel:

1 Language is not formalizable into a system, and as such it is too amorphous and heterogeneous to serve as a foundation for anything. Furthermore, such foundations, were they to be had, are an unnecessary and even hazardous ballast.

2 Justice is threatened when we attempt to subordinate it to truth and we do this precisely when we try to explain prescriptives in terms of descriptives.

3 Persons are positionalities and potentialities empowered and made possible by language regimes that do not and cannot prescribe what the contents of these places ought to be.

4 There are no a priori rules that can ensure the viability of justice and ethics. These in fact arise when such rules are not given. Furthermore, there is no way to distinguish between ethics and prudence in the way that either Plato or Kant intended. Ethics stands in a continuum with other practices of discrimination and selection that do not presuppose some particular and unique *sub specie aeternitatis* standpoint. The Hegelian distinction, endorsed by both Apel and Habermas between *Moralität* and *Sittlichkeit*, is a dangerous and indefensible remnant from the metaphysical languages.

5 Ethics and political justice, therefore, can no more presuppose a particular type of subject than they can assume a particular type of argumentation that is warranted by either rationality or language.

6 There is no non-iterating difference between grounding *überhaupt* and that which is justifiable according to our communal practices. To that extent, we ought to give up projects that seek to ground democratic practices in some aspect of reason or language.

These conclusions seem to be entailed by the following assumptions:

A Language is irreducible to its denotative, referential function and in fact its world-disclosing function seems to have priority over the world-coping function of language which is expressed in its referential-semantical dimension. Furthermore, language's world-disclosing aspects seem to parallel the heterogeneity that dissent and paralogy presuppose, where the later are the conditions of justice.

B Self and agency are contingent historical configurations that cannot be explained or reduced to language, albeit there seems to be an elective affinity between the irreducibility of language and the undecideability of selfhood.

C Community itself is contingency par excellence. It is the realm of historicity *sui generis.*

D Political justice and ethical responsibility require no more than thick descriptions as they are only understandable in terms of historical narratives and not in terms of the growth of rationality or the instantiation of the normative. The goal is heterology and paralogy because these not only parallel language's openness but also allow for justice's and ethics' horizons of claims to widen.

I think that all of these assumptions can be boiled down to the following dual proposition: since there is no way in which the world-disclosing function of language can be coordinated or reduced to its world-coping function, then all we have is the second order historicity of language. Or, in other words, creativity is irreducible to truth; or, poetry is unaccountable. And conversely, since the world-disclosing function of language in fact explains its world-coping function, all we have is that truth has become Nietzsche's 'mobile army of metaphors'. Science is no more a matter of metaphors and metonymies than solidarity is a question of redescription and literalization of metaphorical ways of speaking. An ancillary proposition, which also entails the above list of consequences, is that the constitution of meaning, the whole question of the disclosure and articulation of meaning, supersedes the criteria of validity or the question of the justification of the standards under which something is accepted as either possessing meaning or being senseless. To this extent, all we have is historicism of a second level, as Gadamer puts it: 'It is, as it were, a second-degree historicism which not only opposes the historical relativity of all knowledge to the absolute claim of truth, but works out its ground, namely the historicalness of the knowing subject, and hence can no longer see historical relativity as a limitation of the truth' (Gadamer 1985:479-80). In Lyotard's case we need to replace 'knowing subject' and 'truth' for speaking agent and custom or linguistic practice. Here, however, is illustrated in a clear fashion how Lyotard *does* presuppose a notion of language, and how from it there follow certain beliefs about selves, communities, ethics, justice and political paganism. With this basic but unthematized assumption, a basic characteristic of his philosophical proposals is betrayed, namely that he withdraws from other positions that which he himself presupposes, namely the elaboration of a philosophy of language which is consequent to other dimensions of human activity and interaction. This betrayal, however, remains concealed by Lyotard's disavowal of the philosophical relevance of his assumptions with respect to his claims about justice and ethics, which in turn result in a series of grave and dangerous aporias.[7]

I would like to reiterate this conclusion. Lyotard presupposes a particular notion of language, one which stems from Wittgenstein, Heidegger and structuralist semiotics. This notion of language, furthermore, allows him to make certain claims about selves, communities and political organizations while eliding how these in turn derived from a particular construing of language as seen in the light of the pragmatic-linguistic-semiotic turn. In this elision, he withdraws from criticism his own assumptions. The question then becomes: is there a way in which one can begin with the same type of conceptualization of language, acknowledge this as a point of departure, and nevertheless not end up with the same conclusions? In my view, and reconstruction, Apel and Dussel offer answers to this question. I would like to turn to them at this moment.

Comparison and contrast with Dussel's liberation ethics

As we saw above, while for Apel the central problem has been to discover the normative foundations of a planetary macro-ethic so as to break through the blockade of scientism and subjectivism, for Dussel the central problem has been the ontological erasure of the other not just phenomenologically, historically, but also and primarily existentially, i.e. through their economic exploitation. If Apel's quest for a planetary macro-ethics led him to postulate the need for the growth in a planetary public sphere in which many international organizations may adjudicate on world problems, Dussel's similar quest has led him to discover the structural roots of the growing rift between First and Third World. If Apel's quest after the normative in the age of science and egoism led him to discover Kant and his children (Peirce, Wittgenstein and Heidegger), Dussel's quest after the root causes for the present state of planetary poverty led him to discover a Marx of ethics and metaphysics (Marx in the underground current of negative metaphysics, and negative theology, in Schelling, Rosenzweig and Levinas).

The limits of modern philosophy (modernity) have been clearly delineated by both Apel and Dussel, but from opposite sides of the boundary. If Apel has pointed out the limits of philosophy's concepts of self, society and the transcendental in terms of his semiotic, pragmatic and hermeneutical critique, Dussel has pointed out the limits of European philosophy in terms of his critique to its still in effect imperial ontology (where the Gulf War and the anti-immigration policies of fortress America and Europe are just the most recent reaffirmations of the *ego conquiro*), its self-referential dialectics, and above all its deep rooted eurocentrism. To be able to think of the type of ethics that we need in a *globalized* planet, in Apel's analysis, we need to abandon the Cartesian-Kantian models of the self, Hobbesian-Lockean conceptions of society and Hegelian-Kantian illustrations of the transcendental. In Dussel's analysis, on the other hand, we need to abandon the ontology of the self-sameness, the totalization of totalities that close upon themselves synchronically and diachronically, and we need to opt for an analectical or apophantic metaphysics.

The complementarity of discourse ethics and liberation ethics

The prior succinct description of Apel's and Dussel's philosophical projects allows us now to see in which ways they complement each other, perhaps thus offering an alternative to Lyotard's criticism of modernity on the grounds of a linguistic turn of philosophy.

1 Apel's discussion of linguistically constituted intersubjectivity allows us to discover how the process of self-identity can and ought to be normed. The voice of the other is not always the voice of reason, or the just, or

even the good. Otherness as such is not normative. It is our relationship to the voice, the face of the other which is normative. In the silence and desolation of the dessert, how can we tell whether the voice we hear is that of God or the Devil (Ricoeur 1992:329ff). Furthermore, Apel's critique of solipsism, and turn towards intersubjectivity, is really a turn away from subjectivity as something we have, possess or are. Instead, it is a move towards a notion of subjectivity as a field of action, a capacity or competency.[8] In Dussel's case, the privileging of the Other as the voice of the new, the source of negativity, disrupts the overall phenomenological tilt towards action and agency. Ought we not to consider the over emphasis on the Other as just the negative version of overemphasis on the I as the self-same?

2 Apel's discussion of the dialectical tension between the ideal and the real communication community allows us to negotiate a middle path between the extremes of Lockean and Hobbesian economic and political atomism, and neo-Aristotelian and neo-Hegelian substantivism. Most importantly, Apel's philosophical grounding of democracy allows us to develop a critical method that does not need to surrender to untenable historical teleologies or cynical technocracy. Dussel, on the other hand, by assuming the extreme vocabulary of metaphysics, can provide little in terms of concrete critiques to existing social conflicts. In terms of a metaphysical language, such conflicts become but stagings of great cosmic battles between the ruling ethos and oppressed others (Apel 1996).

3 Dussel's demystification of the myth of modernity challenges Apel and everyone else who assumes it as a project to reconsider not just the descriptive but also normative characteristics of modernity as a concept with a colonial, neocolonial and global history. Indeed, Dussel calls for a narrative of modernity that unveils the more determining factors of the development of a world-system. Dussel's critique of Modernity recontextualizes its temporal and spatial dimensions. modernity does not move from Europe and the United States to the South. Nor is modernity what comes after the elimination of religious irrationalism and political immaturity. Modernity is the spatialization and temporalization of a world-system of domination whose center is the heart of Europe, and whose time is that of eternal progress.

4 Dussel's discussion of the relations North-South and Center-Periphery has made concrete and explicit why we not only can but need to develop a

planetary macro-ethics. Indeed, while Apel's original concerns were the nuclear annihilation threat and the ecological crisis, he has, through his debate with Dussel, come to accept that the more fundamental problem is that of global poverty and the structural systems that have created and continued to maintain the unequal distribution and consumption of planetary wealth, which are behind that very same growing poverty of most of the planet.

Here, where both Apel's transcendental semiotics and Dussel's philosophy of liberation intersect, is revealed one of the most pressing limits of contemporary ethical theory in particular, and Euro-North American philosophy in general, namely the difficulty, possibility and pressing need to articulate the question of a *globalized planet*. Our fundamental concepts, as well as the horizons within which they are deployed, must reach horizontally and vertically, as well as synchronously and diachronically. 'Situating the Self', as Behanbib has eloquently argued, requires that we expand our views on what can and must be part of the narrative of modernity. This requires that we adopt a postcolonial perspective that supersedes not only eurocentrism but an equally fallacious romanticization of the Other. Apel understood this demand nominally inasmuch as he called for a planetary macro-ethics. Dussel has provided the experiential and historical evidence of this challenge inasmuch as he has clarified that the possibility of any ethical theory is internally entwined with what we take modernity to have been, to be and to promise.

Notes

1 On Apel's relationship to postmodernism see Apel's interview with Florian Rötzer in F. Rötzer (1987:69). On this particular reading of postmodernity, see Seyla Benhabib (1984).

2 I depart from the hermeneutically generous position that postmodernity is not simple nihilism, or anti-rationalism. In fact, I am of the opinion that postmodernity is an eminently 'ethical' movement; that is, I believe that its questioning and criticism is motivated by deeply felt convictions about the moral bankruptcy of our philosophical traditions and the need to face up to the new moral challenges brought on by globalization and the encounter with the 'Other'. On an ethical reading of postmodernity, see Martin Jay, 'The Morals of Genealogy: Or is There a Poststructuralist Ethics?' (Jay 1992:38-48; Critchley 1992; Bernstein 1991; Heller 1990). See also Axel Honneth (1995). Honneth's reading is an interesting one, even if inaccurate and ungenerous hermeneutically. Compare his more recent work on the theme 'The other of justice: Habermas and the ethical challenge of postmodernism' in Stephen White (1995). Cf. Bauman

(1994), and Drucilla Cornell (1992). Cornell's work is of particular importance because it takes up themes in the critical theory of the Frankfurt School and relates them to the insights of 'deconstruction', while analyzing issues of democracy and law (jurisprudence).

3 For an overview of Apel's thought, see my introduction to Apel (1994) and Fred Dallmayr (1987). The best treatment of Apel's philosophy exist, interestingly, neither in English nor in German, but in Spanish: Adela Cortina, who has translated Apel for the last two decades into Spanish, has written extensively on Apel and discourse ethics. See Cortina (1985, 1986, 1992).

4 These are some of the works referred to in this article: Enrique Dussel (1972; 1973; 1973a; 1980; 1983; 1983a; 1985).

5 See Leopoldo Zea (1970; 1978; 1988).

6 Although I refer primarily to Lyotard, I also take it that Richard Rorty formulates similar challenges to Apel's transcendental pragmatics.

7 Richard Bernstein writes: 'an uncritical celebration and valorization of plurality, differences, and otherness harbors its own dangers. What is too frequently obscure is the need to make critical discriminations and judgments. Not all forms of otherness and difference are to be celebrated. For example, there is something disingenuous in Lyotard's and Rorty's reiterated celebration of contingency and a plurality of forms of life. They presumably oppose all forms of universality and are suspicious of the reconciliation of differences. Yet they both advocate a type of plurality and contingency in which there is *universal* non-violent play. The type of 'reconciliation' they advocate is one in which we learn to live in peace with incommensurable vocabularies and forms of life. But they never thematize this legitimate *universal* regulative idea' (Bernstein, 1991:313).

8 Cf. Stephen Toulmin (1979) and Charles Taylor (1987). The best discourse ethical discussion on the shift from egologically oriented philosophy, or philosophy of consciousness to dialogical, communicative, performative view of intersubjectivity, in my view, is Dietrich Böhler (1985).

References

Albert, H. (1985), *Treatise on Critical Reason*, Princeton University Press: Princeton.

Apel, K.-O. (1958), 'Technognomie: eine erkenntnisanthropologische Kategorie' in Funke, G. [Hrsg.] *Konkrete Vernunft* [Festschrift für E. Rothacker], Bouvier: Bonn.

— (1963), 'Das Leibapriori der Erkenntnis: Eine Betrachtung im Anschluß an Leibnizens Monadenlehre' in *Archiv für Philosophie*, 12, 152-172.

— (1973), *Transformation der Philosophie*, 2 Vols., Suhrkamp: Frankfurt.

— (1984), *Understanding and Explanation: A Transcendental-Pragmatic Perspective* [Trans. G. Warnke], MIT Press: Cambridge (MA).

Apel, K.-O. (1986), 'Rekonstruktion der Vernunft durch Transformation der Transzendentalphilosophie (Interview mit Raúl Fornet-Betancourt und Klaus Hedwig)', *Concordia* 10.

— (1980), 'Notwendigkeit, Schwierigkeit und Möglichkeit einer philosophischen Begründung der Ethik im Zeitalter der Wissenschaft', in Kanellopoulos, P. (Hrsg.), *Festschrift für K. Tsatsos*, Athens.

— (1987a), 'The Problem of Philosophical Foundations in Light of a Transcendental Pragmatics of Language' in Baynes *et. al.* [eds.] (1987).

— (1987b), 'Fallibilismus, Konsenstheorie der Wahrheit und Letztbegründung' in Forum für Philosophie Bad Homburg (Hrsg.), *Philosophie und Begründung*, Suhrkamp: Frankfurt.

— (1988), *Diskurs und Verantwortung: Das Problem des Übergangs zur postkonventionellen Moral*. Frankfurt: Suhrkamp.

— (1990a), 'Is the Ethics of the Ideal Communication Community a Utopia?" On the Relationship between Ethics, Utopia, and the Critique of Utopia' in Benhabib and Dallmayr (eds.), *The Communicative Ethics Controversy*, MIT Press, Cambridge (MA).

— (1990b), 'Universal principles and particular decisions and forms of life: A problem of ethics that is both post-Kantian and Post-Wittgensteinian' in Gaita (ed.), *Value and Understanding: Essays for Peter Winch*, Routledge: London.

— (1993), 'Das Anliegen des anglo-amerikanischen "Kommunitarismus" in der Sicht der Diskursethik: Worin liegen die "kommunitären" Bedingungen der Möglichkeit einer post-konventionellen Identität der Vernunftperson?' in Brumlik und Brunkhorst (Hrsg.), *Gemeinschaft und Gerechtigkeit*, Fischer: Frankfurt.

— (1994), *Towards a Transcendental Semiotics. Selected Essays. Volume One* [Ed. E. Mendieta], Humanities Press: Atlantic Highlands (NJ).

— (1995), *Charles S. Peirce: From Pragmatism to Pragmaticism* [Ed. E. Mendieta], Humanities Press: Atlantic Highlands (NJ).

— (1996a), *Ethics and The Theory of Rationality: Selected Essays. Volume Two* [Ed. E. Mendieta], Humanities Press: Atlantic Highlands (NJ).

— (1996b), '"Discourse Ethics" before the challenge of "liberation philosophy"' in *Philosophy and Social Criticism*, 22, 2:1-25.

Arend, H. (1981), *The Life of The Mind*. One-volume edition, Harcourt Brace Jovanovich: New York.

Bauman, Z. (1994), *Postmodern Ethics*, Blackwell: Oxford.

Baynes, K., Bohman, J. McCarthy, T. eds. (1987). *After Philosophy: End or Transformation?*, MIT Press: Cambridge (MA).

Benhabib, S. (1984), 'Epistemologies of Postmodernism: A Rejoinder to Jean-François Lyotard', *New German Critique* 33, 103-126.

Benhabib, S. & Dallmayr, F. [eds.] (1990), *The Communicative Ethics Controversy*, MIT Press: Cambridge (MA).

Bernstein, R. (1991), *The New Constellation: The Ethical-Political Horizon of Modernity/Postmodernity*, MIT Press: Cambridge (MA).

— (1988), *Beyond Objectivism and Relativism: Science, Hermeneutics, and Praxis*, University of Pennsylvania Press: Philadelphia.

Böhler, D. (1985), *Rekonstruktive Pragmatik. Von der Bewußtseinphilosophie zur Kommunikationsreflexion: Neubegründung der praktischen Wissenschaften und Philosophie*, Suhrkamp: Frankfurt.
Camps, V., Guaridglia, O., Salmerón, F. [eds.] (1992), *Concepciones de la ética*, Editoral Trotta: Madrid.
Cornell, D. (1992), *The Philosophy of the Limit*, Routledge: New York.
Cortina, A. (1985), *Razón Communicativa y Responsabilidad Solidaria*, Sígueme: Salamanca.
— (1986), *Etica Mínima: Introducción a la Filosofía práctica*, Tecnos: Madrid.
— (1992), 'Ética communicativa' in Campas, V., Guardigliga, O., Salmerón, F., (eds.), *Concepciones de la ética*, Editoral Trotta: Madrid.
Critchley, S. (1992), *The Ethics of Deconstruction: Derrida & Levinas*, Blackwell: Oxford.
Dallery, A., Scott, C., Roberts, P. H. [eds.] (1992), *Ethics and Danger: Essays on Heidegger and Continental Thought*, SUNY Press: Albany.
Dallmayr, F. (1987), *Critical Encounters: Between Philosophy and Politics*, University of Notre Dame: Notre Dame.
Diacritics: A review of Contemporary Criticism (1984), 14/3.
Dorschel, A. et. al. [Hrsg.] (1993), *Transzendentalpragmatik*, Suhrkamp: Frankfurt.
Dussel, E. (1972). *Para una de-strucción de la historia de la ética,* Ser y tiempo: Mendoza.
— (1973), *Para una ética de la liberación latinoamericana.* 3 Vols., Siglo XXI: Buenos Aires.
— (1973a), *Hacia una Filosofía de la Liberación,* Bonum: Buenos Aires.
— (1974), *Método para una Filosofía de la Liberación. Superación analéctica de la dialéctica hegeliana,* Sígueme: Salamanca.
— (1980), *Filosofía ética latinoamericana*, Vol. 5, USTED: Bogotá.
— (1983a), *Praxis latinomaericana y Filosofía de la Liberación*, Nueva América: Bogotá.
— (1983b), *Filosofía de la producción*, Nueva América: Bogotá.
— (1985), *Philosophy of Liberation*, Orbis Books: Maryknoll.
— (1988), *Ethics and Community*, Orbis Books: Maryknoll.
— (1993). *1492: El Encubrimiento del Otro. Hacia el origen del mito de la modernidad*, Nueva Utopía: Madrid.
— (1996), *The Underside of Modernity: Apel, Ricoeur, Taylor, Rorty and the Philosophy of Liberation* [Trans. E. Mendieta], Humanities Press: Atlantic Highlands (NJ).
— (1997), 'The Architectonic of the ethics of liberation: On material ethics and formal moralities', *Philosophy and Social Criticism*. Vol. 23/3, 1-35.
Eagleton, T. (1996), *The Illusions of Postmodernism*, Blackwell Publishers: Cambridge (MA).
Forum für Philosophie Bad Homburg [Hrsg.] (1987), *Philosophie und Begründung*, Suhrkamp: Frankfurt.
Gadamer, H.-G. (1985), *Truth and Method*, Crossroad: New York.
Gehlen, A. (1975), *Einblicke*, Vittorio Klostermann: Frankfurt.

Haber, H. F. (1994). *Beyond Postmodern Politics: Lyotard, Rorty, Foucault*, Routledge: New York.

Habermas, J. (1970), 'Technology and Science as "Ideology"' in *Toward A Rational Society: Student Protest, Science, and Politics*, Beacon Press: Boston.

Heller, A. (1990), *Can Modernity Survive?*, University of California Press: Berkeley.

Hobsbawn, E. (1995), *The Age of Extremes*, Pantheon: New York.

Honneth, A. (1995), 'The other of justice: Habermas and the ethical challenge of postmodernism' in White (ed.), *The Cambridge Companion to Habermas*, Cambridge University Press.

— (1995b), *The Fragmented World of the Social: Essays in Social and Political Philosophy*, SUNY Press: New York.

Jay, M. (1992). 'The Morals of Genealogy: Or is There a Poststructuralist Ethics?', *Force Fields: Between Intellectual History and Cultural Critique*, Routledge: New York.

Kuhlmann, W. 'Solipsism in Kant's practical philosophy and the Discourse Ethics', *Graduate Journal of Philosophy*, Vol. 13/2, 159-179.

— (1985). *Reflexive Letztbegründung: Untersuchungen zur Transzendentalpragmatik*, Alber: Freiburg.

Kuhlmann, W. & Böhler, D. [Hrsg.] (1982). *Kommunikation und Reflexion: Zur Diskussion der Transzendentalpragmatik. Antworten auf Karl-Otto Apel*, Suhrkamp: Frankfurt..

Laclau, E. (1996). *Emancipation(s)*, Verso: London.

Lyotard, J.-F. (1984), *The Postmodern Condition: A Report on Knowledge*, University of Minnesota Press: Minneapolis.

— (1986), 'Grundlagenkrise', *Neue Hefte für Philosophie* 26, 1-33.

— (1988), *The Differend: Phrases in Dispute*, University of Minnesota Press: Minneapolis.

— (1992), *The Postmodern Explained: Correspondence 1982-1985*, University of Minnesota Press: Minneapolis.

Lyotard, J.-F. & Thébaud, J. (1985), *Just Gaming*, University of Minnesota Press: Minneapolis.

Mendieta, E. (1994), 'George Herbert Mead: Linguistically constituted Intersubjectivity and Ethics', *Transactions of the Charles Sanders Peirce Society*, XXX/4, 961-1002.

Poole, R. (1991), *Morality and Modernity*, Routledge: New York.

Retamar, R. F. (1989), *Caliban and Other Essays*, University of Minnesota Press: Minneapolis.

Ricoeur, P. (1992), *Oneself as Another*, University of Chicago Press: Chicago.

Rodó, J. E. (1988), *Ariel*, University of Texas Press: Austin.

Rötzer, F. [Hrsg.] (1987), *Denken, das an der Zeit ist*, Suhrkamp: Frankfurt.

Taylor, C. (1987) 'Overcoming Epistemology' in Kenneth Baynes, et. al (eds.), *After Philosohy: End or Transformation?*, MIT Press, Cambridge (MA).

Toulmin, S. (1979), 'The Inwardness of Mental Life' in *Critical Inquiry*, 1-16.

Wyschogrod, E. (1992), 'Does Continental Ethics Have A Future?', in Dallery, R. et. al. (eds.) *Ethics and Danger. Essays on Heidegger and Continental Thought*, SUNY Press, Albany.

Zea, L. (1970 [1957]), *America en la Historia*, Editorial Revista de Occidente: Madrid.

— (1978), *Filosofia de la Historia Americana*, Fondo de Cultura Economica: Mexico (DF).

— (1988), *Discurso desde la Marginación y la Barbarie*, Editorial Anthropos: Barcelona.

Index